Bob Reese

guy hubbard

Indiana University

art for elementary classrooms

Prentice-Hall, Inc., Englewood Cliffs, New Jersey 07632

Library of Congress Cataloging in Publication Data

Hubbard, Guy. (date)
   Art for elementary classrooms.

   Includes bibliographies and index.
    1. Art—Study and teaching (Elementary)—
United States. 2. Perceptual learning.
I. Title.
N362.H79   372.5'044   81-2486
ISBN 0-13-047274-3   AACR2

Printed in the United States of America

10 9 8 7 6 5 4 3 2 1

Editorial/production supervision by Barbara Alexander
Interior and cover design by Maureen Olsen
Art production by Gail Cocker
Manufacturing buyer: Harry P. Baisley

Prentice-Hall International, Inc., *London*

Prentice-Hall of Australia Pty. Limited, *Sydney*

Prentice-Hall of Canada, Ltd., *Toronto*

Prentice-Hall of India Private Limited, *New Delhi*

Prentice-Hall of Japan, Inc., *Tokyo*

Prentice-Hall of Southeast Asia Pte. Ltd., *Singapore*

Whitehall Books Limited, *Wellington, New Zealand*

To my late colleague and friend, Mary Rouse

Art is one of those things which, like air or soil,
is everywhere around us, but which we rarely stop to consider.

HERBERT READ

contents

part
One

preparing yourself in art

3

sculpture making
and other three-dimensional art

4

using pictures and objects for teaching

part
Two

prism: a guide to preparing art lessons

collection of color plates

LIST OF ILLUSTRATIONS

Children's Art Throughout the Book

College Student Art (Elementary Education Majors)

Illustrations by Laura Hansen
Photographs by Brian Lillie

preface
the book at a glance

This book has one purpose; to help prepare future classroom teachers to be responsible for the art education of elementary school children.

The reader is expected to be a person who is looking forward with pleasure to teaching children, but whose talent and experience in art is modest and perhaps even thought to be non-existent. As a result of such a background, feelings of inadequacy often arise regarding the teaching of art, which if not overcome can lead to children being deprived of a unique and valuable part of their education. This is all the more serious when one considers that next to a parent, the most influential person in an elementary school age child's life is likely to be the classroom teacher.

The college preparation of teachers in art education normally includes one and sometimes two courses in the study of art and its application to elementary classrooms. This book incorporates both of these functions, because future teachers typically have so little opportunity to prepare themselves to teach their own art that no occasion should be allowed to pass without emphasizing the close connection between learning and teaching.

The organization of the book is designed so that the entire task is outlined in the first chapter. Parts One, Two, and Three then elaborate on this opening statement. Part One introduces the reader to the basic knowledge and practice of two- and three-dimensional art that a classroom teacher needs when working with elementary school children. The art materials to be used are those commonly found in schools. Part One concludes with a chapter that explains how to use visual information of all kinds effectively in teaching art—including the student art work that has already been produced.

Part Two introduces a unifying concept entitled PRISM that is used throughout the book. Like a crystal prism, this analytical tool functions as a checklist for ensuring that all the parts of art lessons are fully represented. These five chapters deal with the decisions that must be made whenever a teacher prepares art instruction. Art teaching must have some underlying *purposes* (P). The children who are to do the learning will show various levels of *readiness* (R) that must be allowed for. A teacher must decide just what *instructional objectives* (I) are appropriate in view of decisions made at the preceding two stages. Since some *strategies for teaching* (S) are more effective than others, then all the possible opportunities need to be studied. Finally, a teacher is expected to *measure* the art achievements (M) of children.

Part Two also contains a collection of full-color reproductions of both children's art, with captions that identify the level and medium of each art work so that they may be referred to when teaching particular art concepts, and American art works. These are referred to throughout the book for their specific instructional value and use. The reason for the emphasis on American art is that the art of our own country is regularly neglected in favor of an international perspective. However, if people are to be well educated in art, the art of their own nation should be established first, and the elementary school is the best place for that to occur. The full-color reproductions are at the beginning of Chapter 5, and there is an additional section of black and white reproductions at the end of Chapter 9. In sum, Part Two introduces the pieces of an educational jigsaw puzzle which, when assembled properly, result in good art teaching.

Part Three, *Your Art Teaching Data Bank*, contains a variety of resource materials. Appendix A includes a series of twenty lessons that could be used by a new teacher as the beginnings of an art program. Appendix B includes a collection of instructional objectives (I) and strategies for teaching (S) from which students can construct their own art lessons.

Future classroom teachers do not know as much as they would like about art teaching when they go to their first jobs, but with the help of the material in this book, they will at least be able to establish an art program. They will also discover that art teaching can be an enjoyable task, in which the art of teaching art is more important to them than expertise as artists.

acknowledgments

For some of the unusual features of this book I am indebted to the knowledge and insight of several people whose careers are intimately involved with elementary education. Edrice Baker and Betty Rosentrater were chief among a group of classroom teachers who graciously gave their time to evaluate the manuscript and made valuable suggestions.

My thanks also to the many teachers and supervisors in different parts of the country who kindly provided examples of children's art to illustrate the text. My special thanks to my illustrator, Laura Hansen, for her beautiful drawings. I am very grateful to Barry E. Moore, curator of the International

Collection of Child Art at Illinois State University, who gave his time and expertise unstintingly when he opened the collection to serve my needs.

An equally important group of college instructors with close elementary school associations and considerable experience teaching elementary majors made significant contributions to the manuscript. Their suggestions carry the authority that complements that of teachers in the field. Principal among these critics were Carmen Armstrong, Blanche Rubin, Enid Zimmerman, Gene Mittler, and Gilbert Clark.

Since the final judge of any textbook is the person who must learn from it, elementary education majors were asked to respond to various draft materials. Gayle Brown made the most thorough assessment of all, and I am much in her debt.

My thanks also go to Lee Hutchinson, who repeatedly deciphered illegible handwriting and transformed it into an attractive, typewritten manuscript.

GUY HUBBARD

Bloomington, Indiana

1

an overview of
elementary school art

Art is included in school curriculums because serious-minded people believe that the education of children is incomplete without it. The task of achieving this goal calls for teachers to communicate the subject matter of art for the benefit of as many children as possible. A classroom teacher should be reasonably well prepared in art but not to the point of having to become an expert in art or an artist. The talents that need to be developed have to do with knowing what a particular group of children are able and willing to learn and possessing the skill to help them achieve it.

One way of putting art teaching—and any kind of teaching—into perspective is to imagine yourself as an author or playwright who decides to communicate a special message to people and invents a story or play to make it happen. The same person—you—then arranges for the children in your class to act out the story or play. This is like being the director of a movie or a stage play, but since you are part of this performance you are also an actor in your own production. Lastly, you are a critic. You decide whether the message of the story or play was as good as you had hoped. At the end, the only thing that counts is that the children in your class learned what you thought was right for them to learn. If they learned more that was worthwhile than you had in mind to begin with, then you have reason to be very pleased. If they learned less, then you need to think of ways of overcoming the problem. Success in such an effort is as much a work of art as the creation by any author, director, composer, or painter; and pride in this fact is your first step toward competence.

This chapter introduces the entire book by helping you understand what a single art lesson is like, how to put art lessons together into sequences, and how to plan an art program for a full year of school. Lessons are the building blocks of teaching and learning in school, so the first step is to understand what an art lesson is and how to design one.

THE ORGANIZATION OF AN ART LESSON

Five questions need to be answered every time an art lesson is prepared. These questions correspond with the concepts developed in depth in Part Two, namely: *P*, the underlying *purposes* for a given lesson; *R*, the *readiness* of a group of children to learn a particular kind of art; *I*, statements naming the *instructional objectives* for that lesson; *S*, the choice of *strategy for teaching* the objectives; and *M*, the way of *measuring* the success of the lesson. The following sample lesson illustrates the responses to each of the questions making up the acronym PRISM, which you will find to be a useful checklist as you prepare art lessons.

lesson 1

PEOPLE ARE THE SAME...BUT DIFFERENT

Purpose (The reasons for believing that children should learn the objectives in this lesson):
Children need to realize that although people are the same, some of the most interesting things about them are the ways in which they all look different.

Readiness (The reason for believing that a class of children can do this lesson successfully):
At the intermediate level children are usually able to observe differences and details in what they see and to put them into their art work.

Instructional objectives* (Some or all of these things are what a class should be able to do):

_____ * This sample lesson identifies objectives by the simple, three-part organization (Seeing, Knowing, Doing) introduced in Chapter 7. The lessons in Appendix A use the expanded organization, also introduced in Chapter 7.

A Seeing:
1. Point to the class pictures that show the most details and differences in them.
2 . Describe all the details and differences in the people shown in their own pictures.

B Knowing: Artists study all the differences in people they see so they can make their art more interesting.

C Doing: Draw and paint a picture with at least three people in it. The people are to fill most of the picture. They are to be your choice of thin, fat, tall, and short.

Strategies for teaching (The things you can do to help children learn the above objectives):

Preparations: Have each of the children in the class (or a selected group) stand in front of the class and be described. The different characteristics—all to be descriptive and *not* judgmental—may be listed on the board.

Delivery: (This is the least that needs to be done to teach the lesson): Have the class read their copy of the text silently. Help them read the text if they are poor readers. Ask them to suggest interesting pictures they might make. Have them describe what they see in the pictures. Distribute the art materials.

Motivational Support: Take a class to a supermarket or shopping center, and have them list in detail the kinds of people they see.

Subject Correlation:

Science: Classifying plants, animals, and minerals, and noting the differences within a classification.

Literature: The attention that writers give to the characters in their stories. Charles Dickens was a master of this kind of description.

Measuring achievement (Ways of finding out whether children have learned the objectives):

A Seeing:
1. Have the children—individually or as a group—select the class pictures that show the most details and differences.
2. Each is to tell you, or write down, all the details and differences shown in the people observed.

B. Knowing: Answer the question about why artists study the differences in people.

C. Doing: Check that they draw and color a picture of different-looking people in an environment. Artistic quality is *not* to be judged—only that they have made a picture in the way requested.

lesson 1

PEOPLE ARE THE SAME...BUT DIFFERENT

How To Do This Lesson

Read This:

In nature many things appear to be the same, but people all look different. People's bodies are short, tall, thin or fat. People are light skinned, dark skinned, and in-between. Hair comes in many different colors and types—straight, wavy, curly, etc. Have you ever touched someone's hair that was different from yours? People also wear their hair in all kinds of hair styles. Eyes, too, come in different colors and shapes, and so do noses, mouths, and ears.

Take a good look at all these differences. Artists study them in order to make their art more interesting. Now you are going to make a picture that has different people in it. Your picture should also show other things—maybe trees, grass, and rocks, or maybe houses, city buildings, clouds, or animals. But the people are the most important part. Make each person look different from the others in all the ways that happen in real life.

IN THIS LESSON YOU WILL:

1. Draw and paint a picture with three, four, or five people big enough to fill the paper.
2. Learn that artists study the differences in people so they can make their art better.
3. Describe all the things you did to the people in your picture to make them all look different.

Art materials you may use for this lesson:

Paper—white and colored
Pencils and erasers
Crayons or felt pens
Paints, brushes, mixing trays, water cans
Paper towels for cleanup

Look at these pictures:

[The class is then shown pictures illustrating different types of people. The following artists' works in this book could be used: Blackbear Bosin, *Prairie Fire* (see Figure B); Ben Shahn, *Miner's Wives* (see Figure F); and Varnette Honeywood, *Gossip in the Sanctuary* (see Plate 3).]

* * *

This lesson is simple enough that persons with only modest confidence in themselves could hope to be successful teaching it. The most obvious characteristic of the way it is organized is the division of information between what the teacher needs and what the children need. People at the beginning of their teaching careers have a tendency to think only of their own needs and to prepare instruction that enables them to deliver a lesson. Decisions about the information that the children need are frequently not as clearly thought through, and consequently this interferes with what they learn. The division of each lesson into two parts is designed to remind you that the children you teach need clear information just as much as you do.

The teacher's copy of each lesson begins with a brief reference to the purpose that underlies it. The children's copy usually echoes some part of this statement, but it is written at a level that the children in a particular class can read and understand. Once you have developed a fairly clear idea of why you believe art to be important in the curriculum (see Chapter 5), you may choose to insert only a brief statement of purpose in a lesson. But in the beginning you should practice writing out this statement as fully as you can, and check it when you write the instructional objectives to make sure you are being consistent.

Describing the readiness level of a lesson makes you think about the suitability of that lesson for a given group of children and how best to compose their copy of the lesson. We know something about how children typically respond to art at the different grade levels, and Chapter 6 explores this topic. But the typical behavior of children is only a partial guide. Some children are blessed by being outstandingly good at everything they do. Other children are correspondingly unfortunate. Intellectually handicapped children cannot do the same work as those who are more typical. You wouldn't dream of expecting that in reading; it is equally faulty to do so in art. The nearly blind child in art will be recognized immediately as having special needs, whereas the mildly retarded child may not be easy to identify. Art, as a subject, may even bring some children into prominence who for various reasons may be unproductive in their other studies. At the heart of all these differences is the need for you to be prepared with lesson modifications that will permit all of your children to learn as much as they are capable of from a particular art experience. A given lesson may remain fundamentally the same as far as the children in your classroom are concerned, and yet your recognition of the varied capabilities of the children may cause you to make your lesson preparations very different for each such group, even to the point of planning for individualized instruction.

The key to success in teaching art is to be as clear as possible about the art the children are to learn from a given lesson. This topic is developed in Chapter 7. Art teaching, however, presents special problems. Most subjects have school textbooks that describe the content for a given level in school. This information is not available for art except in a general way through state and school district art guides and a few textbooks.* This means that you need to think more about your objectives in art and how to write them down clearly than you might for science or mathematics. One of the tragic results of careless thinking about art objectives is concluding that because children seem happy and busy that they are necessarily learning something worthwhile. A similar problem occurs when a teacher states objectives for an art lesson in such general terms that they are meaningless. You may at first enjoy hearing that the objective for a lesson is "to make children creative" or that the lesson will help them "develop a love of beauty"; that is, until you have to decide whether a child succeeded in achieving those objectives. Such sentiments are noble, and you will certainly hope that these things will eventually happen, but they are worthless as lesson objectives. Unless you are prepared to state exactly what, for a given lesson, the class is to learn, you will probably end by telling every child that he or she did well, when many will sense it is not true, or if true the children will not know in what way they were successful. Alternatively, you may praise only the work you happen to like. Good lessons all reveal intelligent, sensitive, imaginative, and above all, clear, thinking.

If you can write clear art objectives for yourself, that is an achievement. If you can write them so the children you teach can share this information at their level of comprehension, then you are truly becoming a teacher.

Once lesson objectives have been established, the task is to decide what is the best way for children to achieve them; and strategies for art teaching are developed in Chapter 8. The possibilities are limited only by your energy, imagination, and experience. Success, in fact, is most likely when you and a class of children both become personally involved in a lesson and find the experience stimulating. In order for this to happen, you need to know what advance preparations are necessary. You also need to have decided on a title or subject for the lesson and the choice of words that will explain it to the children and motivate them. This information includes such things as directing the children to read something or look at certain pictures. It may refer to rewards of one kind or another that they might receive; or the text may be prepared in such a way as to stimulate the feelings of excitement, mystery, or anger in the children that will lead to artistic expression. If the class is to receive spoken instructions, you will want to be sure that the children have every opportunity of understanding them. A fairer way, perhaps, is to distribute duplicated instructional information or to write it out in full on the chalkboard at a level they can comprehend, so that all may read—and re-read—at their own speed. Such preparations also allow you later to study what you did and so make changes to improve it before the next time you give the lesson.

The wise use of pictures in art teaching is especially important, because

_____ *Note: A list of elementary art text materials appears at the end of the chapter.

most art is non-verbal, and children need direct visual references if they are to learn the objectives effectively. This topic is developed in Chapter 4.

The final step in art lesson design is determining how to assess what has been learned. Chapter 9 explains ways of measuring achievement in art. This is difficult to do, but no more difficult than in other subjects. The first and greatest difficulty is overcoming the common belief that art learning cannot be measured. Measuring the achievement of most art objectives can be done if the objective was originally stated clearly. The single, most important, decision to resolve is what you will accept as success for any of the objectives. In some instances you can simply observe that the class has mastered an objective. In other instances you may have to take much on faith. Sometimes you will realize that the decision is based on your personal feelings. Finally, you need to be alert for achievements to appear that you did not plan for. They deserve attention on equal terms with the objectives you included originally.

The introduction to the structure of art lessons would be incomplete without some mention of how to set about writing your own lessons. Where should you begin? One logical way might be to follow the sequence presented here. For some people, that may be the best plan. However, no one correct way exists. An idea for a lesson might be triggered by seeing a particular piece of sculpture in a museum. A surprise gift of some art supplies might cause you to design lessons to make use of them. Your science program might have just reached a point where you could unite art and science in a single lesson. All that matters is that before the lesson is delivered to a class, the various parts are present and have all been considered in relation to each other. And yet, since teaching is nothing if not a practical profession, a lesson will rarely achieve its mature form until it has been practiced several times with a class of children and has been revised accordingly.

When you have practiced writing your own lessons and have developed a sensitivity for the task, you should practice the actual delivery. In some college classrooms, instructors help by arranging for simulated teaching experiences in which students deliver lessons to their peers. Other students make presentations in front of television cameras and then, in the company of the instructor, evaluate their performance by watching a video playback of the presentation. The best experience, of course, is to have experience teaching classes of children in advance of regular student teaching, so that you have had a chance to develop some art teaching proficiency before facing children on a daily schedule.

Regardless of the method used, the best way to begin teaching is to present lessons that are likely to be successful, such as the ones in Appendix A. After that, you can experiment by designing lessons that you have written yourself in their entirety (Appendix B includes considerable raw materials for this purpose). The children you teach, an experienced classroom teacher, your college instructor, and also your peers will all be able to help with critiques of every part of your instruction, and in that way help you know how to revise your materials. Revision is the secret of success; and while frank critiques may not be the easiest thing to accept, the experience is invaluable. If none of these opportunities to face real people is available, and you are confined to seat work in a college classroom, the best thing is to explain your reasons for every choice you made in building the lesson, and then have your instructor respond and make suggestions.

The lessons in this book are all organized in the same way, and the acronym PRISM serves as a five-point checklist to ensure that nothing is omitted. As you become more experienced, you will probably modify this organization to suit your personal needs and desires; but all of the parts must be represented in some way in every lesson if it is to be complete.

SOURCES FOR ART LESSONS

A rich source for lesson ideas is to be found in the many books and magazines that have been published on art teaching.* The test of any idea you may find, however, lies in its completeness and its suitability to your needs. The PRISM structure for an art lesson provides a guide as you write your own lessons. The same five questions become a valuable checklist when studying published materials, but only infrequently will you find all five parts fully represented. If you are to use any of these lessons, you will need to complete them yourself. Most of the time these lessons are fairly complete in the strategy section. The instructions for what procedure to follow and what materials to use are normally well done, although you may find even this information to be incomplete when you try it for yourself. Statements of purpose and readiness are often buried in the information, but at best they tend to be handled casually. The neglected areas in most published art instruction lie in instructional objectives and the measurement of achievement. You will sometimes be able to identify objectives, but they are rarely stated clearly enough to know what was in the writer's mind. And information on how best to evaluate achievement is hardly ever reported clearly.

In spite of the shortcomings described above, these resources are invaluable. They provide the germs of innumerable ideas for lessons that have been successful enough that teachers—usually art teachers—have taken the trouble to have them published. The missing parts may have been present when the lessons were actually taught and simply omitted later either to conserve space or to avoid boring the reader. None of these lessons are of any use to you, however, until brought to a state of completeness consistent with the preceding lesson illustration.

Other people's ideas can be valuable, but the best ones will eventually be your own. These ideas grow out of what you know about art and what you know about children. They will improve in quality as you begin teaching and develop a sensitivity for what is appropriate for children at a particular level of development. But you must know something about art in order to teach it—even if what you are able to do is only a few steps ahead of the children you teach. Chapters 2 and 3 discuss the knowledge and skills you

———— * A list of publications that include art lessons appears at the end of this chapter.

need which, added to the art you have already learned, will provide a foundation for preparing art lessons.

Lesson Analysis Assignments

1. Select one art lesson from a magazine such as the *Instructor, Arts and Activities,* or *School Arts* that you think could be useful in an elementary classroom, and re-write it to fit the sample lesson presented earlier in the chapter. Include specific references to any visual materials that may be needed.

2. Select one art lesson from a book of elementary art lessons, and either re-write or add to it in such a way that all the parts needed in an art lesson are stated fully. Include references to any visual materials that may be needed.

SEQUENCING ART INSTRUCTION

Preparing single art lessons is an art in its own right, but often a class period of 40 or 50 minutes is not long enough for certain sets of related objectives to be achieved. This may cause you to break the content into two or more parts each of which will occupy individual lesson periods. The maturity of a class will also affect what can be done in given art periods. Children in the lower grades may be able to continue on the same subject for four or five lesson periods before they need a change, although much may depend on how each class period is organized. If each lesson in a sequence provides the children with something new and interesting to learn, then you can expect the class to be happy and to work enthusiastically in one area of art for much longer than if each lesson is little more than an obvious continuation of a single topic. The secret lies in linking related lessons together, where each is an enjoyable and identifiably different learning experience. The culmination of a sequence should bring about a natural ending to one unified experience.

Well sequenced instruction is the result of such deliberate questions as: Is there a need to provide a change of pace for a particular group in a class? Does the class need to extend an earlier topic in a more advanced way? Is the class ready to move to another kind of art instruction as part of a plan to cover a range of art learning? Should the content of a particular art lesson be linked with that of a lesson in another subject area? and so on. These questions and the responses do not deny the possibility of spontaneous decisions, but they do ensure that the foundation for what happens in most sets of related lessons is clearly understood and planned in advance.

Preparing sequences of lessons that extend over several class periods is much like preparing several single lessons, in that the parts for each unit remain the same. Considerable practice is required, however, to be able to split a large chunk of art instruction into pieces that make a good fit for conventional lesson periods. If you find yourself teaching in a self-contained classroom, you might decide to solve a particular sequencing problem by dividing the weekly allowance of time for art (between 80 to 100 minutes a week is recommended in most states) into variable time blocks throughout the week: 20 minutes; 40 minutes; 30 minutes; and 10 minutes. Each part would still be a complete lesson, and yet each would lead to the next stage in the sequence. A more conventional solution would be to break the blocks of time in two equally. No one way is either right or wrong as long as your reasoning is good. Beyond that, the best test is to try out the plan to see whether it works.

KINDS OF ART SEQUENCES

One of the most obvious kinds of art lesson sequencing occurs when a class follows a particular set of steps toward a goal that is governed by a technical process (see Figure 1). For example, children may spend one period making a face from oil-based clay. The next lesson may require the children to apply layers of papier-mâché strips over the face to make a mask. The third part in the sequence can occur only when the papier-mâché is perfectly dry, so the time separation between lessons one and two can be short, but between two and three will be much longer. Lesson three would be spent in removing the clay and painting the mask. This three-lesson sequence could be extended if the face were to be used as a puppet head. Alternatively, the mask could mark the beginning of a new sequence. The lessons fall logically into a sequence in this common and yet perfectly satisfactory method for sequencing instruction in art.

A related method of sequencing is to prepare a set of lessons that require a student to work on progressively more complex problems. Such a sequence might begin with a drawing lesson in which the class draws the main outlines of some objects. In a following lesson, they draw a set of similar objects consisting of more complex shapes, but this time they are to add the details they can see. A third drawing lesson might require the class to include all the shading they can see in and around a similar group of objects. Sets of such sequences may continue to build throughout the school year, although you would be wise not to stay with one kind of art for more than three or four class periods. Children soon tire of any experience, however interesting it may seem to be at first. Part of your skill as a teacher will be to maintain sequences just as long as they continue to be productive—and no longer. The difficulties of this task are compounded by the different personalities and capabilities of the children present in any given group of children.

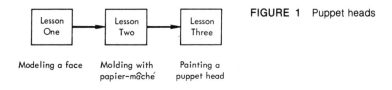

FIGURE 1   Puppet heads

The above kinds of sequences are simple to construct. Another approach is to follow related themes or techniques through a series of lessons all of which require different media. A sequence on human proportions may be carried out first in a drawing lesson and then with one in clay modeling. The emotion of anger might be developed first by means of a painting, then through a cardboard box assemblage, and finally in a linoleum print. Such bridging of art forms and materials by means of a single topic opens the door to possibilities of sequencing that are governed only by the limits of your knowledge and imagination. Similar relationships can exist where the only tie from lesson to lesson may be for students to master an objective such as symmetrical balance. Or a linkage may be established that focuses on a medium, like textile fiber, to make a sequence consisting of a lesson on weaving, one on the history of textiles, and finally a lesson on stitchery. In this way a legitimate sequence may exist and yet not closely resemble the conventional step-by-step sequencing in art. In all sequences, you should obviously be consciously aware of what you intend the children to learn, and as far as possible the children should be kept equally well informed. Moreover when a sequence is complete, it is a good idea to review with the children what it was all about.

Art is a subject where review is something that everyone can look forward to. This is the time when the art is put on display for everyone to see. You can talk about the work that has been done, and so can the children (see Figure 2). These experiences are as much a part of the sequence as the art work itself, and should be included in your planning. For example, if you want the children to practice their skills in describing the similarities and differences evident among the class work on display, then that task becomes part of the sequence. If they are to use that time for restating what was learned in the preceding lessons, then that, too, is part of the sequence and should be planned accordingly.

The foregoing examples of sequencing art instruction all assume that classes of children will be working together at the same time. This kind of art teaching requires planning, but it is not too difficult to do for the reason that the children will begin the lesson together with you in control of the presentation and the distribution of art materials. They will perform the assigned task, after which the finished work and left-over materials will be collected. All the activities are contained within a specified time and are focused on a set of predetermined objectives. This can be a most effective method of sequencing art instruction—especially for a beginning teacher—and yet lesson sequences may be much more complex and hold out the possibility of even more interesting results.

Instead of being the only person who decides what shall be learned, you may prefer that the children participate in developing their individuality more fully. Lessons where everyone in the class does the same thing at the same time obviously cannot spark individuality and initiative to the fullest. And yet, if the children are allowed to do anything they like, the results will

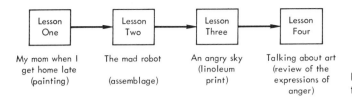

FIGURE 2   Showing anger through art

usually be frustrating; and an art program will be disastrous if it is allowed to develop in such a way. Even if you prepare dozens of art lessons or use a book that includes many different lessons in it, the results will continue to be unsatisfactory. Children need direction as they learn, and you are there to give it. As wide a range of choices as possible is desirable if you want to help develop artistic individuality; but the choices need to be organized into sequences to fit the needs and desires of the children if satisfactory results are expected. One way of doing this is to organize numbers of sequences of art lessons from which individual children can make selections. A child would then choose a lesson sequence and work through it at his own speed as an individual contract. You could expect upper level students to be better able to work on their own than younger children. But if the verbal and visual instructions are properly prepared for the student's level of readiness and if the range of choices is controlled, then younger children can benefit also. Even at the early grade levels where reading may be a problem, children can respond to simple directions, explanations, and pictures. Verbal and visual instructions can be recorded on single concept cassette tapes to overcome many verbal problems that might otherwise prevent this kind of delivery system from succeeding. In sum, planned freedom is possible at most levels of elementary art teaching, and can be particularly beneficial to the above average child who is self-motivated.

Classes of more mature students may be able to elaborate further on instructional sequences so that instead of a child following a sequence of three or four related lessons, he has the opportunity to make lesson selections at each step in the sequence. Multiple choices of this kind create "strands" of lesson possibilities from which the child may choose (see Figure 3).* The individual lesson objectives at each step in the strand are related to the objectives at the next step, but in various ways. The diagram shows the content choices in a sample strand. The child follows through the sequence as before, but has numbers of additional lessons to choose from compared with a single three- or four-step sequence. This kind of instructional organization offers great flexibility and encourages children to learn by the means that appeal to them most. Strands may be given to a class one at a time so that you

---
* See Hubbard and Rouse, *Discovery and Creating* and *Choosing and Expressing*, in the list of text materials at the end of the chapter. These books make use of strands.

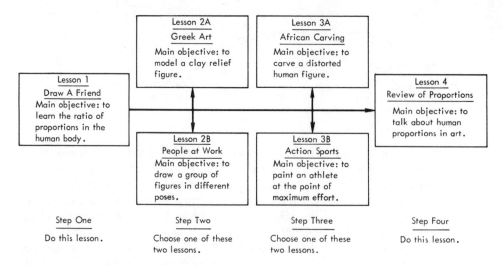

FIGURE 3   A strand

remain in fairly tight control, or several of them can be made available simultaneously, so the children could all choose to work on different lessons if they wish, and also to work at their own speeds. Before considering this approach to sequencing art instruction, however, caution should be exercised to make certain that you have learned enough about art to be able to put such strands together and that your class has mastered any basic skills that may be required. This kind of sequence takes considerable time to prepare even if you select lessons from existing books and magazines and modify them. But once the preparations are complete and the lessons have been tested, you will have a powerful instrument to work with. Revisions will naturally be needed from time to time, and you will periodically replace less successful lessons; but you will have freed yourself to spend more time with individual children, and so expand on their unique needs.

The range of possible ways for organizing curricular sequences in art can include some or all of those described here. The decision about exactly what to do will depend partly on your knowledge and interest in art and partly on the school where you teach. No one way is best for every situation, so if you prepare yourself now to handle some of these techniques, you will be ready to make use of what will work best in the school where you teach. Practice is the secret to success in most professions, and teaching is no exception. If, in addition, you have an opportunity to teach a sequence of art lessons to children—or talk to an experienced teacher as she works through a sequence—your understanding and sensitivity toward this task will expand immeasurably.

DESIGNING A YEAR-LONG PROGRAM

In a very practical sense, your task is to put together an art program that spans approximately 36 weeks. If art is included in the daily schedule, you will need to have 180 lessons. If you are expected to teach art only once a week, then 36 lessons are needed. If, in addition to your teaching, an elementary art teacher visits your room once every two weeks, the children will have an additional 18 lessons that will need integrating with your program. If you see opportunities for art to be included in other areas of the curriculum, then additional instructional objectives will need to be added to the program.

The first step will be to find out whether the school you are going to already has an art program that sets down general expectations for each grade level. Even in the absence of a formal statement, you may discover that an understanding exists among the teachers about what is to happen at particular times in the year or in the different grades. And the person who taught your class the preceding year can at least explain what happened and enable you to build some continuity into the program. Further help should be available for the asking if the school district employs an art supervisor or an art consultant. If you find that you are, indeed, on your own, the best advice is to have this book with you and to use it. You have already learned about the organization of lessons and lesson sequences, and a year of instruction is little more than a system of individual and sequenced lessons. The information and assignments in the chapters of Part II are designed to help you further expand your knowledge of the structural components of art lessons. Chapters 5 and 6 on the purposes of art teaching and the readiness of children to learn art will be particularly influential as you map the broad outlines of a program. At that time, you have to reach some general conclusions about why art is important to children's education. This decision will influence the range of art you include and the degree of emphasis placed on particular art forms or kinds of art knowledge the children will learn. A somewhat extreme position, for example, would be to declare that expressing human feelings through artistic and scientific creativity are the two highest goals for education. In that case, the art program would take a prominent position in the overall curriculum, and a wide range of experiences would be given where time and money would be required. By contrast, if a person concluded that the only contribution made by art lay in giving relief from the intellectual effort required in the academic curriculum, then the art program would be very modest and would emphasize leisure-type activities.

The decision relative to Purposes in Chapter 5 is likely to require considerable thought but will probably appear finally as a set of simple statements. The influence of the Readiness decision in Chapter 6, however, is likely to include numerous conditions and possibilities. For example, if a class is composed entirely of children classified as "normal," then the program will not have to consider those who are gifted, retarded, disturbed, or physically disabled. On the other hand, if the children came from minority families, you might find yourself needing to place considerable emphasis on works by Black American artists or on the Spanish and pre-Columbian arts of Mexico rather than on the artistic tradition of Western Europe. Likewise, the aesthetic symbols of the community and geographic region might have an important place in the art curriculum. In a city where particularly fine examples of architecture are to be found, you might want to give special attention to them in the art program. By contrast, the conservatism of some rural areas may cause you to screen certain images and assignments from a program because the children are not yet ready for them.

School traditions also affect the readiness levels for certain kinds of art. You may have personal misgivings about certain annual celebrations, but it would be difficult to imagine a school where the children did not recognize Halloween or St. Valentine's Day. Thanksgiving is another festival that affects school life. Christmas exerts considerable pressure on the school curriculum during December, regardless of the religious affiliations of the children's families. These events are joined by others such as class birthdays, Mother's Day, Memorial Day, and the first days of Winter and Spring. These festivals and events are often treated superficially or kept separate from the instructional program of the school. And yet the visual symbolism surrounding these special occasions alone warrants their consideration in the art program—both to understand their meanings and also to break the grip of visual stereotyping where twenty-five identical pumpkins line classroom walls at the end of October year after year.

Not least, your art program depends on your own experience. Chapters 2 and 3 provide a modest but adequate foundation for a beginning teacher. No one should have difficulty doing any of this work and you should be able to enjoy yourself as you learn it. Your personal feelings about art are, without question, the most important single influence on the children you teach. If you can capture this spirit while experiencing the kinds of art the children will do—more sophisticated knowledge can wait—you will be ready for the next step in designing a year-long art program.

Setting out the actual program may appear to be the final task, but it isn't. The final task is one that never ends. That is the constant cycle of trial, evaluation, and revision which you will work on continually throughout your career. However, setting out the broad outline of a year-long program marks the end of the initial preparations. You may choose to block in certain parts of the year for selected topics. The seasons may determine some of these choices where, for example, color harmony might be reserved for the fall when leaves turn all the colors from deep red to yellow. The Christmas season might be set aside for designing interior spaces. Working with clay and plaster might be reserved for the second half of the year to give you plenty of time to establish your collection and distribution routines and ensure that the children will behave properly. To begin with, make the best decisions that you can. After the first year—and preferably sooner—the process of refinement begins.

| Annual Guideline Assignments | 1. Name between six and eight dates during the school year where particular kinds of art assignments—that you could teach—would fit well. Name the assignments and, in general, the instructional objectives that would be learned. Be prepared to defend the decisions you made.

2. The period from the beginning of school to Halloween is about seven weeks. Prepare an outline of the lessons and sequences you believe could fit this period, given two lessons a week. Summarize the art you hope would have been learned by the end of this period. |

further art study

text materials for classroom use

CEMREL Aesthetic Education Kits. New York: Viking Press. Complete instructional packages for the elementary classroom in all the creative arts.

Herstein, Rosaline. *Time Out For Art:* Activities on Your Own. New York: Harcourt Brace Jovanovich, 1978. A three book program with teachers' editions designed to be used individually or in groups.

Hubbard, Guy and **Mary J. Rouse.** *Art: Meaning, Method and Media.* 6 volumes. San Diego, CA: Benefic Press, Revised edition, 1981. A structured art program for grades 1 through 6 with teacher's editions. To be used by children with help from their regular teachers.

Hubbard, Guy and **Mary J. Rouse.** *Discovery and Creating* and *Choosing and Expressing.* Westchester, IL: Benefic Press, 1977. A two volume art program with teachers' guides. While designed for junior high school use, these books can be used with advanced children in grade 6.

Ideas and Images: The SWRL Elementary Art Program: Los Alamitos, CA: SWRL Educational Research and Development, 1976. A structured art program for Kindergarten through Grade 6 for use by regular classroom teachers.

Saunders, Robert J. *Teaching Through Art.* New York: American Book, 1972. Three sets of art prints for grades 1–6 with a teacher's manual that includes art lessons.

Teaching Creative Experience through Art, Niles, Illinois: Argus Communications, 1976. A program in seven levels designed for elementary through junior high school use. Art prints, together with written information, are used to stimulate both understanding and creating art.

Townley, Mary Ross. *Another Look,* Menlo Park, CA: Addison-Wesley, 1978. A three book program with a teacher's edition designed to develop the visual awareness and creative expression of young children.

art lessons and lesson ideas for teachers

Cornia, Ivan E., Charles B. Stubbs, and **Nathan B. Winters,** *Art Is Elementary: Teaching Visual Thinking Through Art Concepts,* Provo, Utah: Brigham Young University Press, 1976. An extensive collection of elementary art lessons that can be put to immediate use in the classroom.

Hardiman, George W. and **Theodore Zernich.** *The Fourth R: Art Activities for Children.* Englewood Cliffs, N.J.: Prentice-Hall Inc., 1981. A collection of 53 lessons for use in elementary school classrooms.

Herberholz, Donald and **Barbara.** *A Child's Pursuit of Art,* Dubuque, Iowa: Wm. C. Brown, 1967. Many lesson ideas with references to supporting materials such as books, films, and records.

Laliberté, Norman and **Richey Kehl,** *One Hundred Ways to Have Fun With an Alligator and 100 Other Art Projects,* Blauvelt, New York: Art Education Inc. 1969. A source for art experiences, many of which make use of free or inexpensive materials.

Linderman, Marlene M. *Art In The Elementary School: Drawing and Painting for the Classroom.* Dubuque, Iowa: Wm. C. Brown, 1974. Art experiences for elementary children to do.

Montgomery, Chandler, *Art for Teachers of Children.* Second-edition. Columbus, Ohio: Charles E. Merrill, 1973. Includes various art experiences suitable for children.

Wankelman, Willard F., Philip Wigg, Marietta Wigg. *A Handbook of Arts and Crafts.* Third Edition. Dubuque, IA: Wm. C. Brown, 1974. A collection of simply written art lessons organized partly by media (crayon, paint, etc.) and partly by types of art (sculpture, ceramics, etc.).

Two monthly magazines on art teaching include numerous ideas for elementary art lessons:

Arts and Activities: Publishers Development Corporation, San Diego, CA.

School Arts: Davis Publications, Worcester, MA.

part

One

preparing
yourself
in art

In order to teach art, you need to know about the subject and be able to do it yourself. Chapters Two and Three introduce those two and three dimensional art forms that are most suited to elementary art programs. The chapters include art concepts and experiences that are basic to the subject, but they are written so that people with very little background in art should have no difficulty in being successful when trying them. In addition, the suggested materials are ones that are commonly found in elementary schools. The intent is to give you every opportunity to gain confidence in yourself in art and also to familiarize yourself with the materials that children in your classes will be using. The hoped-for result of reading these chapters and becoming involved with making art is a sense of pleasure that will influence children more profoundly than all of the other art teaching skills put together.

Chapter Four extends the study of pictures and objects from an emphasis on your own learning to the learning to be experienced by children. Visual materials provide basic information for art teaching. Words are important, but pictures are vital. They need to be collected or made by you and used continually in your teaching. They also need to be organized so you can find them when you need them.

In sum, Part One begins with the study of art where you are the student and ends with the study of art where you are the teacher.

2

picture making
and other
two-dimensional art

This chapter is designed to give you first-hand experience with various kinds of flat, or two-dimensional, art that elementary children can do. Picture making is the most common two-dimensional art, so more space is given to it than to the others. But all the parts of the chapter are useful, if only because you will meet children who are not successful at drawing and painting and will need your help in working in other areas. And you can only give help to children on any subject if you have had successful experience doing it yourself.

As you read, you will notice that the contents of the chapter require only slight modification to be translated into art lessons for elementary children. For convenience, the chapter is divided into five parts to correspond with the kinds of two-dimensional arts that are commonly used in elementary classrooms: drawing, painting, collage, printmaking, and textiles.

DEVELOP YOUR DRAWING SKILLS

Drawing is the most useful way of communicating ideas and information in art. Fortunately, drawing is something that children do naturally; which tells us something about its naturalness as a part of education. Most people can learn to draw, just as they can learn to read. While children learn to draw faster than adults, you can improve your own drawing if you give yourself a chance. And this ability will help you in all your teaching—not just in art.

Drawing has to do with making lines, and the first lines a person thinks of when drawing any objects belong to the outline or silhouette. This outer edge is a contour. Turn the object slightly and the outer contour changes (see

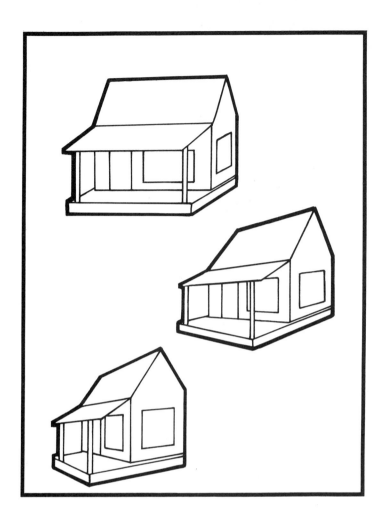

FIGURE 4 The outline of the house changes when viewed from different positions

Figure 4). Inside the main shape of an object are other contour changes that reveal themselves either through gradual shading or more sharply through lines where lighter areas contrast with darker areas. When people draw, they use lines and shading to mark the positions of these contours. Once the outer contour shape has been drawn, the task is to put in the lines showing the easy-to-see internal contours. The final stage is to put in whatever contour details and shading are wanted. Experienced draughtsmen often add or subtract parts of what they can see to create special effects.

If you draw an object once or twice, you will really begin to know it; and with further practice you will be able to draw it from memory. The practice is no different from learning a poem or a piece of music, but in order to be successful you have to practice. In a much shorter time than you think possible, you will learn to combine a growing visual memory with your imagination to invent new objects, much as a writer uses a vocabulary and remembers the ways in which people write and speak.

Four useful rules of perspective will often help when you put several objects together and want to convey a sense of distance in drawing—or any kind of pictorial art: (1) larger objects appear to be closer than smaller objects. (2) Objects that are closer will overlap those that are more distant. (3) Objects that are closer are usually nearer to the bottom of a picture than more distant objects. (4) More detail is visible on objects that are closer to the viewer (see Figures D and I). The effects of color with distance are described later in the section on painting.

Good quality drawing papers can be used, but you are advised to work on white or cream colored manila paper, because it is commonly found in elementary schools. A medium weight paper (40 to 50 lb) is better than lighter weight papers. Newsprint paper is useful for sketching rough ideas.

The most common drawing media used in school are pencils, crayons, pens, and chalks.

PENCILS   When selecting pencils for art, use the kind with fairly thick centers—but avoid the very thickest unless they were manufactured especially for elementary school use. The thickest leads of all are often so soft that they break easily and are frustrating for children to use. In contrast, any pencil with an H rating will be too hard for elementary school use. Standard pencils that are neither hard nor soft are often designated as No. 2 or HB.

Pencils make different kinds of marks depending on the shape of the point and the surface of the paper. Very sharp points make clear, thin lines, while blunt points make thicker, broader, and rougher edged lines. Drawing with the side of the pencil and not the sharp point results in a grey area that looks different when done on smooth paper compared to the same stroke on rough surfaced paper. Also, the more you press, the darker will be the penciled line or area. Shapes can be filled with pencil shading using the pencil point or the side or by smudging penciled lines and shapes with your finger. Pencils are also useful to show a gradual change from dark to light.

Pencil marks are relatively easy to erase, unless the unwanted marks are deeply embedded in the paper. Penciled areas that have been smudged may have areas and lines "drawn" with an eraser. The result is a reverse kind of drawing where you draw with an eraser over smudged areas to reveal the white of the paper (see Figure 5).

CRAYONS   Wax crayons are the commonest of all color media used for school art (see Plate 9). They are inexpensive, clean, and easy to use. Typically, children use them to draw lines on paper and to fill in areas with color. Unusual effects may be achieved by shading and overlaying one color on top of another to create a new color. Crayoning on sand paper gives a decidedly unique effect. Turpentine or kerosene can be brushed over the surface to partially dissolve the crayon to make the work look more like a painting. Crayon can be heated with a candle and dripped onto paper. Old crayons can be melted in a saucepan and then poured over a sheet of paper or aluminum to make a thin film onto which designs can be scratched. Great care should be taken whenever wax is melted to avoid any possibility of fire or burns from accidental spillage.

FIGURE 5   Some of the different ways of using pencil

OIL PASTELS   Made in sticks like wax crayons, oil pastels are much softer than crayons and break more easily (see Plate 7). They are also more expensive. However, the softness permits the color to transfer more easily to paper than wax crayons. This results in richer, more opaque colors that show up better, especially on darker colored paper. A good idea is to have some boxes of both wax crayons and oil pastels so you can experience both media and learn their different characteristics. Like wax crayons, oil pastels also dissolve in turpentine. Other, more expensive pastels are soluble in water and may be used almost like watercolor paint.

From the view of teaching art, crayon lines encourage spontaneity and rhythm much more than pencil. The wire-like line of a pencil can often be inhibiting and can encourage a kind of finicky smallness that does not give full play to your imagination. Crayon lines are coarse and force you to disregard detail in favor of broad general lines and shapes. The observation of detail is an important part of an art education, but big shapes are also important.

PENS   Pens were originally cut from quills taken from the tail feathers of turkeys and similar birds. Shaped bamboo was used in China and Japan. Recently, metal nibs or points held in stick-like holders were dipped into ink and people wrote or drew whatever they had in mind. Metal nibs continue to be excellent drawing instruments, although when younger children use them they may not be able to keep their work or themselves entirely free of ink blots. Ballpoint pens have replaced liquid ink pens for daily use. More recently felt points have been added to the choices of pens. In some ways, the effects possible with broad felt markers look more like brush work than the lines made by traditional pen nibs (see Figure L), thus blurring the separations that used to distinguish drawing from painting.

If you decide to work with the traditional metal pen and bottle of ink, be sure to avoid small finely pointed nibs. They are unsuitable for beginners of all ages. Instead, use fairly stiff nibs with slightly blunted points. They are called "drawing," "standard," or "school" nibs, depending on the manufacturer. Shading is done by grouping lines or dots in different ways (see Figures 6 and 78).

INK Ink for drawing is either waterproof or water soluble. The best looking art work is made with black waterproof ink, often called India ink. Care should be taken to prevent waterproof ink getting on clothes, since it cannot be removed. Water soluble drawing ink is thinner and more transparent, but it makes less attractive lines. Although it dissolves in water, it often leaves a stain that can be difficult to remove from clothes (herbal shampoos will usu-

FIGURE 6 Some of the different ways of using pen and ink

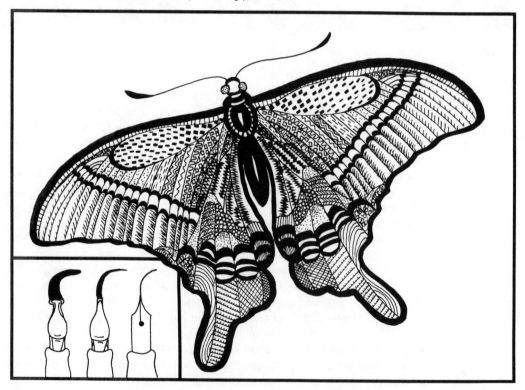

ally remove all but the most stubborn stains). The ink of felt markers is transparent and dries quickly without smudging. Felt markers are excellent for drawing but they have a frustrating way of drying out just when you need them.

COLORED CHALKS   Generally supplied in schools, they can be used very effectively for drawing. Unless the chalk is treated in some way, however, it smudges. Special fixative is sold in art stores to stop the smudging. Alternatively, you can use a solution of sugar and water, buttermilk, or a mixture of liquid starch and water in a simple hand pump spray or an old perfume atomizer. The solution is sprayed evenly over the surface of the picture to hold the chalk in place when the art work is complete.

Drawing
Assignments

1. *Simple Perspective*. Draw a view that you think looks interesting. It could be of your college classroom, your bedroom, or it could be outdoors somewhere. Be sure that some objects are close to you and others are far away. Then show that you can use the four rules about showing distance in pictures: size change, overlapping, position, and detail.

2. *Through a Picture Window*. Arrange a group of simple objects that have no shiny or transparent parts. Sit fairly close to the group. Take a sheet of plexiglass or sturdy acetate and hold it at right angles between you and the group of objects. A sheet of glass will provide support to the plastic sheet if it bends easily. Be sure the transparent "window" is kept upright and hold it still while you work. Close one eye and "trace" the outer contours of the objects on the sheet of plastic with a grease pencil or a felt pen. The lines will duplicate the contours exactly and will show how these solid shapes look when translated onto a flat surface (see Figure 7). Transfer the grease-penciled lines to paper either freehand or by using a grid, and shade in the contour changes to make a finished drawing.

3. *Contour Hunt*. Divide a sheet of paper into four. Fill each quarter with drawings of different contours selected from the insides of larger shapes. One should be of an easy-to-see, sharp-edged contour. One should show a gentle contour that can be seen only when shading is used. The other two contours should be different from the first two. The only requirement is that you think they are interesting to look at.

4. *Order from Chaos*. Use pen and ink or a ball point pen to fill a sheet of paper with a line drawing of a group of objects you think are interesting. The drawing is to be done without taking the pen off the paper. All incorrect or unwanted lines are to be painted out later, so the only concern is to make sure that all the lines or line clusters you might want are drawn in. When every part is complete, cover all unwanted lines and areas with white paint, or typist's erasing fluid. Finally, make another drawing of the same group of objects using the corrected drawing as a guide.

5. *Liberate a Rainbow*. Cover a sheet of paper with a thick layer of wax crayon in different fairly bright colors. Spread a layer of india ink or black tempera paint over the crayon (a small quantity of liquid detergent will permit the paint to cover the wax crayon). Black crayon can be used in place of black paint. When the black coating is perfectly dry, scratch a picture in it to reveal the layers of colored crayon. The work can be realistic or abstract. But

it is to include parts where very little black is removed and other parts where all the black is removed. It should also include a wide range of treatments in between the two extremes. Carpenter's nails and nail files are suitable tools. Scratch work can be repaired as desired by the addition of more black ink, which often makes the beginner feel less vulnerable. A final touch to enhance this kind of drawing is to add designs in oil pastels over the remaining black areas (see Figure 8 and Plate 11).

6. *Exploring Oil Pastels.* Select a familiar subject like St. George and the Dragon, the Crucifixion, or Star Wars and fill a sheet of paper (12″ × 18″) with a drawing that illustrates the subject. Draw the outlines for the picture with light colored oil pastels on white paper. Color the different parts of the picture with light colored pastels until most of the construction paper is covered. Press on fairly hard. Add layers of darker pastels in different colors on top of the first layers to create interesting effects. Try scratching parts of layers away to make different colored lines. When the picture is finished, you may like to paint it with shellac or acrylic gloss medium.

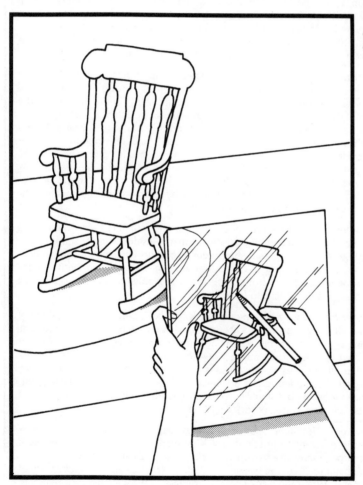

FIGURE 7 Drawing with a grease pencil through a window of plexiglas

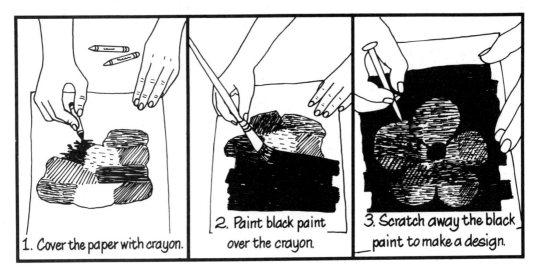

1. Cover the paper with crayon.

2. Paint black paint over the crayon.

3. Scratch away the black paint to make a design.

FIGURE 8   Crayon etching

DEVELOP YOUR PAINTING SKILLS

You will have realized by now that the terms "drawing" and "painting" are not always easy to separate. But they do identify two general areas of art and for that reason the distinction is useful. Generally, painting refers to the arrangement of areas of colored pigment to create a picture or design that conveys an artistic message. Paintings may show images that imitate nature. They may show the less realistic imagery of dreams, emotions, and fantasies. Or they may be entirely formal or nonrealistic. The general definition about what is meant by a painting is true for all of them, however. The choice of style or the way a person paints is usually a personal decision.

The study of painting focuses on the subdivision of a sheet of paper into recognizable shapes. In the painting *Pool Game* by Jacob Lawrence (see Figure E), the bodies of the nine men each make separate shapes. The heads and hands also make their own darker shapes. The pool table is divided into shapes, and so is the wall at the back. All the shapes in a painting are adjoining, each part affects the adjoining parts. The word for the relationship between one part to others in art is "juxtaposition." Colors are strongly affected by juxtaposition, in that lighter areas in a picture stand out clearly—or contrast—against darker areas. Complementary colors such as red and green contrast sharply with each other compared with more closely related colors such as red and orange. And slight variations of light colors are easier to see than slight variations of dark colors. Other colors such as greens and blues are described as "cool" and appear to be more distant than "warm" reds and yellows. Also, if you want to give the impression of distance in a painting, follow these general rules of "aerial perspective": (a) dark colors become much lighter with distance; (b) very light colors become slightly darker;

(c) bright colors become less bright; and (d) surface details become less noticeable. You can see these effects in the painting by Thomas Hart Benton (see Plate 1). The four perspective guidelines mentioned in the section on drawing also apply to painting.

Professional artists often use oil, acrylic, or casein paints; but since they are either unsuitable or too expensive for use in elementary schools, we will limit the discussion to water-soluble paints. Medium weight manila paper is suitable for most painting, although a heavy construction paper (80 lb) is also suitable, especially when working with tempera paint.

WATERCOLOR PAINT   Watercolor is transparent. It comes in tubes or in small cakes assembled in metal or plastic paint boxes. A little water on a soft brush dissolves the pigment to the point where it is thin enough to use. The color is spread over white paper as a transparent watery wash and usually looks very delicate. A problem that can arise is that it is time-consuming to mix sufficient paint from small cakes to cover large areas of paper. The best brushes to use with watercolors are round ones with soft bristles and pointed ends.

The transparent quality of watercolor depends on the whiteness of the paper underneath, and for that reason the paint should always be clear and clean. Don't use dirty water in a water jar or mix colors excessively. When watercolor paint dries, the edges of an area are clearly visible and because the paint is transparent, unwanted edges can never be covered. For the best results, therefore, watercolor should be applied fairly quickly with a soft brush and once applied it should be allowed to dry thoroughly before another color is painted over it. Each succeeding layer of paint darkens an area and alters the color. For this reason the best way to begin a watercolor painting is to cover the areas that are the palest and then work on the parts that are to be darker. In most outdoor scenes this means beginning with the most distant areas and working progressively towards the parts that are closest. However, care should be taken to allow for very light and bright areas in the foreground. In sum, watercolor painting requires thoughtfulness; but the actual brushwork should have the appearance of freedom and spontaneity (see Figures 9 and H).

Pen and pencil lines can be used effectively to accent important parts of watercolor paintings. Interesting effects can be created by first drawing heavily with a white candle and then painting over it with a thin wash. The wax and water repel each other and create an interesting effect. Rubber cement and masking tape can be used to mask out parts of the paper; these are gently removed when the paint is perfectly dry.

TEMPERA PAINT   Unlike watercolor, tempera paint is opaque. (see Figures E, F, and G and Plate 12). The color of the paper underneath is not important as long as the paint is used in a creamy consistency. Errors are also reasonably easy to cover up. Light colors as well as darker ones have to be mixed, because the paper is not used as a reflective surface. On the other

FIGURE 9   Some of the different ways of using transparent watercolor

hand, because of its opacity, tempera paintings can be begun at any point on a sheet of paper. One of the important first steps when painting with tempera, however, is to work toward covering the surface of the paper as soon as possible. Detailed work should be delayed until last. Because tempera is used more thickly than watercolor, it dries more slowly. It is therefore possible to paint to an edge more easily. When you do this, however, be sure to keep the point of the brush toward the line (see Figure 10 and Plate 4).

The mixing of tempera paint presents no problems as long as you always remember to begin with the lightest color of a mixture and add the darker colors to it gradually. For example, to mix a certain kind of green from yellow and blue, begin with the yellow and add touches of blue to it until the color is right. And always use black very sparingly; it is much more powerful than beginning students realize. While tempera is marketed in paint boxes like watercolors, that is not usually the best way to purchase it for school use. A better way is to order it as a powder, a ready-mixed liquid, or in large cakes. A cannister of powder is the least expensive way to purchase tempera paint, but the task of mixing it can be messy and time-consuming. Liquid

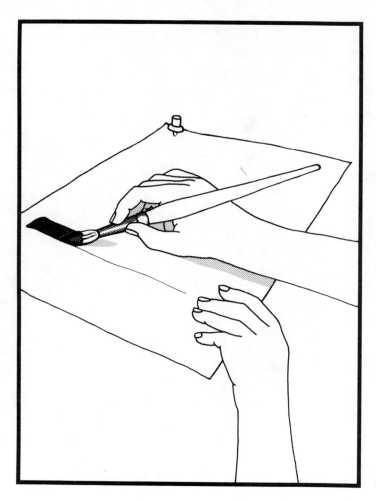

FIGURE 10 Painting to an edge

tempera in glass or plastic jars is a convenient but more expensive way of handling it. Two-inch diameter cakes of paint are convenient, although they do not as readily yield a thick creamy pigment—the best consistency for tempera—as compared with the powder and the liquid forms. The test of what you believe is best to use will only come from your own experience in art. The best kind of brush to use with tempera paint is one that has fairly stiff bristles.

FINGER PAINT Enjoyable to work with, it can be used to create highly sophisticated designs (see Figure 11). It has considerable value as a means of learning about textures, lines, repetition, and variation. Finger paint is sold in art stores, although it can also be made very inexpensively as follows: Beat together 1 cup of flour, 1 teaspoon of salt, $1\frac{1}{2}$ cups of cold water, and $1\frac{1}{2}$ cups of hot water and boil until clear; add food coloring or powdered tempera paint and stir. This mixture should be stored in a closed jar. A simpler recipe is to mix liquid starch with tempera. A specially prepared finger painting paper is manufactured so that moisture from the finger paint is not absorbed rapidly. Less expensive substitutes can sometimes be found among glazed shelf papers sold at the local supermarket; but be sure to experiment before making a large purchase. Heavily crayoned paper also makes a good surface.

BRUSHES   When selecting brushes, be sure you have a range of sizes to correspond with the size of paint areas to be covered. Low numbers indicate small sizes. The largest size is usually number 12. If you cannot paint a line of fairly watery paint across an area to be covered without having to refill the brush with paint, the brush is probably too small. Nothing is more frustrating than working with a brush that is out of proportion to the work that has to be done. This obviously means that a brush could be either too large or too small for a painting. Oriental bamboo brushes are also good to have in your collection. They make different kinds of lines from the usual round and flat designs and are not expensive.

Care of brushes is also important. They can easily become damaged and unusable unless washed carefully and gently pressed into shape before storing. Brushes should be stored either flat or with bristles pointing upwards. When given reasonable care, brushes can last for years.

FIGURE 11   Child's finger painting, Colombia, South Amercia. Courtesy, The International Collection of Child Art, Ewing Museum of Nations, Illinois State University.

Painting
Assignments

1. *Creative Perceptions*. Soak a sheet of white paper with clear water and paint areas quickly with watercolor to create random designs. When the paper is dry, drop several large blobs of dark paint on to the paper, and make additional designs by blowing the blobs of paint with a soda straw. While the paint is drying, study the combined designs to determine what the images remind you of (see Figure 12). During this process the paper can be turned around and even looked at through a mirror. Complete the task by drawing and painting whatever details seem necessary. Erase parts as well. A useful test of your idea is to involve a friend in deciding what the picture is about.

2. *Spontaneous Brushwork*. Use a fairly large soft brush and watercolor to paint a bowl of flowers. Work quickly to try and capture the character of the stems, leaves, and blossoms. Avoid any kind of meticulous attention to detail. Allow yourself no more than 10 to 15 minutes before either painting another plant or moving to a different position for a different view of the first plant (see Plate 13 and Figures H and N).

3. *The Grey of Colors*. Find a colored picture that you can draw fairly accurately. Draw the outline contours to fill a sheet of paper. Complete the picture using tempera paint, but limit yourself to mixtures of black and white. The task is to translate the colors in the original into appropriate shades of grey, as in black and white photography.

4. *Symbols with Color and Shape*. On a white sheet of paper use water color paint to represent the concepts of Goodness and Purity. On a blue or black piece of paper use tempera paints to represent the concept of Evil. Most of the area of the paper in each case is to be covered with paint. The choices of colors and shapes will be determined by the meaning to be communicated (See Plates 2 and 5).

5. *Historical Transformation*. Artists are continually being influenced by the art of other times and places. This problem requires you to study any historical work of art reproduced in this book—it does not have to be restricted to painting—and to transform part or all of it into a painting of your own creation. Keep the main shapes of the original in your work.

DEVELOP YOUR COLLAGE SKILLS

Drawings and paintings are completely flat. Collage is a form of picture making that departs slightly from a flat surface but not enough to be called sculpture. The artistic ideas involved in collage are the same as in drawing and painting. Collage pictures are made by gluing flat materials, usually paper, rather than covering areas with paint.

Library paste is a solid white vegetable adhesive that is well suited to collage work. Other common glues and pastes include white (Elmer's) glue and rubber cement. Unlike the liquid pastes and glues, rubber cement does not wet paper and cause it to wrinkle. It can be used as a temporary adhesive or a permanent one. If a coat of cement is applied to paper that is then stuck down, the process is temporary. If cement is applied to both sheets and

FIGURE 12   College student's soda straw paintings

allowed to dry before pressing together, the bond is permanent. You can also mix your own paste out of liquid or powdered starch and water.

Scissors are the most usual tools used for preparing the pieces for collages, although they can be torn or cut with a knife. Very young children may need to work with blunt-ended scissors, but you will want to work with pointed scissors because they permit the cutting of more intricate shapes. For your own use in school, a pair of general purpose shears should be available.

The art of collage became known as an art form during the early part of this century as a result of experimental work done by such European artists as Pablo Picasso, Georges Braque, and Kurt Schwitters. The American, Romare Bearden, is one of the best known collage artists today. Collage is well suited to beginning students of all ages. It is particularly useful where individuals feel self-conscious about their seeming inability to draw or paint realistically—if that is considered to be important. It can help a person develop a sense of design. And it can be useful for encouraging free experimentation with a variety of paper and paper-like materials, such as colored tissue paper, corrugated paper, metal foils, pieces of cloth, sheet plastic, cellophane, and leaves from trees (see Figure 13 and Figures O and P).

Photomontage is the name given to a collage made from parts of photographs; it is an appropriate medium for this century with its profusion of photography. The artistry of photomontage lies in assembling recognizable images to communicate an idea or emotion (see Figure Q). Another variation of collage occurs when shapes are cut out of dark paper and arranged on a light surface to create silhouette pictures. Yet another variation is called

FIGURE 13 College student's collage of natural material

FIGURE 14 Paper mosaics on a box, by children in Grade 3

décollage, where areas of a sheet of paper are cut or torn out to reveal layers of paper and other interesting materials beneath that complete the design. A simple form of décollage is to remove parts of the upper layer from corrugated cardboard to reveal the corrugations. Lastly, mosaics can be created with collage materials where the pieces are cut into small, similar shaped pieces and pasted on to a sheet of paper to make a picture or design where each square almost touches the next one (see Figure 14 and Figure R).

Collage Assignments

1. *Symbolism*. Make a collection of different kinds of paper. Select the pieces that you believe will go together best in a design. Tear some pieces and cut others to make the shapes of as many kinds of familiar symbols as you can remember, such as hearts, suns, moons, stars, nonverbal road signs (steep hill, deer crossing, etc), man, woman, religions (Christian cross, Star of David, etc), and well-known trademarks (Chevrolet, Shell Oil, etc).

Glue large pieces of paper to completely cover a paper or cardboard base. These pieces of paper should contrast in color with the torn and cut symbol shapes. Practice arranging the symbols into groups on the base paper to create an attractive asymmetrical design. When you have decided on the best arrangement, glue the symbols in place.

2. *Laughter*. Search for magazine photographs and parts of photographs that suggest a particular kind of laughter—a giggle, a bellow, a snicker, etc.—and design a well-balanced montage where the kind of laughter is clearly communicated to other people. All of the base sheet is to be covered with pieces of photograph glued securely in place. One part of the design, however, is to be more important or dominant than the others. It can be anywhere in the design *except* on the vertical center line. Test the quality of your communication by having fellow students describe what they believe was the particular kind of laughter you were communicating, and explain why your work suggests this type of laughter.

DEVELOP YOUR PRINT MAKING SKILLS

Three kinds of printing useful for classroom teachers to know are the stamp print, which is often made from a potato; the collograph, which is like printing from a collage; and the linoleum block print. All designs for printing are made in reverse so they will print the right way. Drawing paper can be used for printing, but it is often too rough surfaced. Newsprint paper is quite adequate for most school purposes because it is smooth and absorbent. Cloth can be used if you use oil-based printing inks rather than water-based inks. Cloth should be washed and ironed before being used as a printing surface, however. For the best results, all printing should be done over a perfectly smooth, firm pad of paper.

STAMP PRINTING Many objects have surfaces that will make a print when painted or inked and pressed on to paper, including leaves, keys, paper clips, bottle caps, old toys, corn cobs and even fish—not to mention fingers and hands. One of the simplest forms of block printing is made by slicing a potato or similar root vegetable in half and cutting a design into the exposed surface with a knife or nail file. A drawing pen nib pushed into a penholder in reverse makes an excellent and safe cutting tool for school use. Inking a potato block is done by either saturating a small piece of thick felt with paint or by painting the surface of the block with tempera paint. The block is then pressed or stamped onto a sheet of paper resting on a flat pad of newspapers (see Figure 15).

The mechanical task of stamp printing is easily mastered. The creative part of the task occurs when deciding what prints will make an all-over repeating pattern that links each unit together in the most attractive way. This is the problem that textile designers face continually. A block can be printed simply and also attractively; and yet as your experience grows you will search for more elaborate arrangements. The simplest of motifs can become a source for the most sophisticated print arrangments (see Figure 16).

COLLOGRAPHS This kind of printing is like making a print from a collage. One way of making a collograph is to cut out some shapes from fairly thin cardboard (1/16″ thick) and stick them to a thick cardboard base. Printing ink is rolled over the entire block with a rubber roller called a brayer. The preparation of printing ink is accomplished by squeezing either water-based or oil-based printing ink onto a flat surface. While water-based printing ink is

FIGURE 15   Potato printing

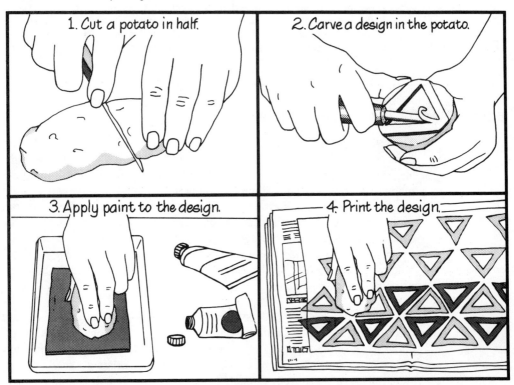

1. Cut a potato in half.

2. Carve a design in the potato.

3. Apply paint to the design.

4. Print the design.

FIGURE 16 Child's potato print design

best for most school situations, you are advised to use oil-based ink and its solvent, turpentine, with your exercises so as to be prepared for school situations where only oil-based ink is available. A sheet of plate glass is best for the flat surface, but a plastic or metal cafeteria tray is quite satisfactory. A brayer is used to spread the ink into an even film. All of the collograph block is then inked in readiness for printing. A sheet of paper is placed over the inked block and rubbed with the bowl of a spoon. The resulting print is of the entire block, but like all prints the design is reversed. For letter shapes to appear the correct way when printed, for example, they have to appear in reverse on the cardboard block. This kind of print can also be done on smaller blocks of cardboard with thicker cardboard glued on to make a design. Prints are then made in the way described for stamp printing (see Figures 17 and 18).

Similar blocks can be made by gluing cut pieces of cardboard or rubber innertube on to a small piece of plywood. Pieces of styrofoam, sponge, or pencil eraser can also be cut to create shapes for printing. A flat piece of wood or cardboard wrapped with string also makes a block. Yet another kind of block can be made by impressing a design into the bottom of a styrofoam meat tray with a pencil and printing with the whole meat tray.

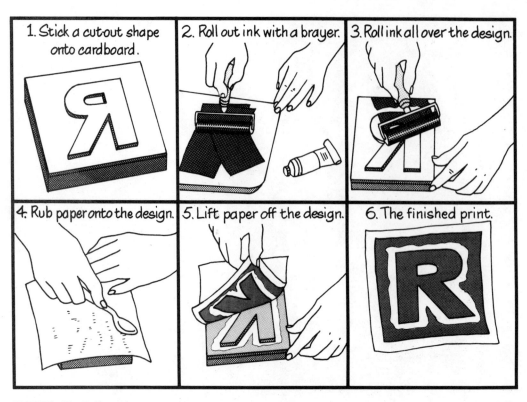

1. Stick a cutout shape onto cardboard.

2. Roll out ink with a brayer.

3. Roll ink all over the design.

4. Rub paper onto the design.

5. Lift paper off the design.

6. The finished print.

FIGURE 17   Collograph

LINOLEUM PRINTING   The most finished looking prints are made by cutting into blocks of linoleum. To do this, linoleum cutting tools are required. These are sold in kits consisting of a handle and several different kinds of sharp blades. The blades are designed to cut when either pushed or pulled. Linoleum may be purchased locally or from an art supply company. The best blocks come glued to a piece of plywood to make a firm base, but such blocks are expensive to purchase. Be sure that the linoleum you use is fairly soft and thick. The best kind for printing is often called "battleship" linoleum.

Here is the process of linoleum printing design and printing on a block. (1) Draw a simple picture on paper to fill an area the size of the block and paint it with black ink. Some parts will be solid black while the rest will remain white. Mistakes can be corrected with white paint. (2) Paint the linoleum with white paint. Add black so the result looks exactly like what you did on the paper. (3) Cut the linoleum away in only those parts where the white paint shows. Cut fairly deeply, but do not cut through the linoleum. Always make sure the tools cannot slip and cut you. If you are not sure what to do in any part of the design, leave it alone. You can always cut the linoleum away later; but it can never be replaced once it has been removed. Lastly, (4) make a trial print or proof before all of the cutting has been done. Wash off the white paint and dry the linoleum. Apply printing ink with a brayer. Lay a sheet of fairly thin soft paper over the block—newsprint paper will do. Gently rub the paper with the bowl of a spoon while making sure that the paper remains perfectly still on the block. Gently peel the print off the block, starting at one corner. (5) Look to see whether you have cut into the linoleum deeply enough, and whether you have cut enough of the block away to make the printed picture show up clearly and attractively. (6) Paint the uncut surface of the block again with white paint. Use pencil or ink to mark the places where you need to do more cutting. (7) When you are satisfied that the cutting is finished, repeat the process described in (4) for making a print (see Figures 19, 20 and 21).

Interesting variations can be made by rubbing colored chalk into the paper before printing on it or gluing pieces of colored tissue over some areas. Prints made with oil-based ink can be painted with clear water color to make them look more interesting. Wait until the ink has dried before painting. Prints can be framed. They can also be stuck on to the fronts of personal greeting cards. Small prints can make attractive headings for notepaper.

FIGURE 18 Japanese child's collograph. Courtesy, The International Collection of Child Art, Ewing Museum of Nations, Illinois State University.

FIGURE 19   Preparing a linoleum block

FIGURE 20   Repeat lino print by a child in Grade 5

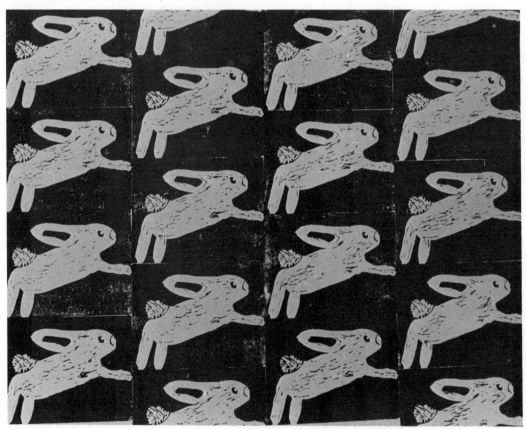

FIGURE 21   Lino print picture by a child in Grade 5

OTHER KINDS OF PRINTING   You may want to try your hand at other kinds of printing, such as *stenciling* and *monoprints,* as you prepare yourself to teach. Before attempting them, however, you may want to experiment with a brayer as a way of painting pictures (see Figure 22).

The kind of stenciling done in school is the parent of a widely used technique of silk screen printing. A stencil is based on the idea that ink or dye can be controlled so that it covers areas that are parts of cut designs and is prevented from covering uncut areas. For example, if you cut a heart from the center of a sheet of paper and use a sponge to dab moist paint over the cut shape, the paint will mark an underneath sheet of paper with a heart (see Figure 23). Even with this simple approach to stencils, they can be built up in several colors and can be repeated and overlapped in different ways to make patterns. Pictures can also be cut out to make stencils. The best paper for stenciling is stiff and waxy. Because of the waxiness, it does not soften when wetted with paint during the stenciling process. Since it tends to be expensive, you may prefer to use thin cardboard, especially if the number of prints you plan to do is not large enough for the cardboard to soften and break up.

A monoprint is literally unique in that it is a one-time print. Ink is rolled out on a sheet of glass or a tray. A design or picture is then drawn onto the film of ink. The drawing can be done with a pencil, knife, or stick—in fact anything is suitable that will scratch ink away. If at any point the drawing is not pleasing, it can easily be obliterated with a brayer and begun again. When the drawing is satisfactory, a slightly damp sheet of paper is laid on the inked surface and pressed down gently to pick up the ink. The resulting print will show the lines of the drawing in white and the remainder of the print will be the color of the inked plate (see Figure 24).

FIGURE 22 College student's brayer painting

FIGURE 23 Stencil printing

1. Cut a design in the center of a piece of paper.

2. Dab color all over the cutaway area.

3. Remove the stencil to show the finished print.

1. Scratch a design in ink that has been rolled out on a flat surface.

2. Gently rub paper onto the scratched design to make a print.

FIGURE 24   Monoprinting

Printing Assignments

1. *Designing for Textiles*. Design an animal or bird shape to fit a piece of linoleum measuring about 3″ × 5″. Remove the linoleum you do not want to show in the finished print. Make test prints to be sure the block is just as you want it. Then fill three large sheets of paper with good clear prints. The prints should just be touching each other, with no gaps between, and no overlapping. Each sheet of prints should be arranged differently. Decide which arrangement of prints would be most successful for a shirt or dress.

2. *Reversal in Printing*. Cut out different sized letters and numbers from thin cardboard and arrange them to fit on a piece of thick cardboard measuring about 3″ × 5″. Glue the shapes in place when you think the design looks attractive. Some of the letters and numbers should be the right way round. Others should be turned over to show in reverse. Now print the collograph. Notice how the reversed shapes print the right way round and the ones that are the right way round on the block print in reverse. This is a fundamental rule in all printing.

3. *A Print-making Sampler*. Every print is a surprise when seen for the first time. Listing the various objects that can be printed may be useful, but it does not compare with making prints from those objects yourself. This assignment is directed at collecting objects, printing with them, cutting out the best ones and mounting them. Keep brief notes about the objects that are useful for printing and those that are not. An introductory list of objects appears at the beginning of the section on stamp printing (p. 39).

DEVELOP YOUR TEXTILES SKILLS

Textiles provide an approach to art instruction that is very similar to what can be accomplished in drawing and painting. The common concern for accurate realism rarely if ever presents a problem in the textile arts, however.

The subject of printed textiles has been introduced already (p. 39). So this section will address the textile arts of weaving, stitchery, and macramé that are constructed from yarns or enriched by them. The basic processes in each area are simple. The opportunities for creative work to occur is when weaves, stitches and knots are combined to produce unique designs. If a problem exists with textiles for school use, it is the tendency for them to become routine and repetitious where the basic construction skills are taught and creative involvement is neglected.

The textile arts are not imitational (or realistic) but abstract. They present line and shape problems. Yarns are lines that are built together to make shapes. Fabrics and yarns also have varied textures and colors that must be thought about when making designs. Fabric construction also tends to exploit the repetition of simple motifs in both regular and irregular patterns.

The three forms of textile art introduced here offer many opportunities for elementary school application. Weaving is basic to the construction of cloth. Stitchery involves embroidering and appliqué. Macramé is a decorative construction process based on knots rather than weaving.

WEAVING The basic principle of weaving is that yarn interlocks when lengths of yarn are made to go over and under other lengths of yarn stretched at right angles to the direction of the weaving. The stretched yarn, called the warp, is held in place on a frame, called a loom. The threads crossing over and under the warp are called the weft (or the woof).

Looms for school use can be made of cardboard that has been notched at the top and bottom to keep the warp in place. A simple wooden frame with nails spaced at regular intervals at each end is also satisfactory. Probably the simplest loom of all is made by cutting slits in a sheet of construction paper. Soda straws may also be used to make the warp threads stiff so that weaving can be done (see Figure 25).

Materials for weaving consist of any long, thread-like material. Beginners and young children will be more successful when using thicker yarns. Generally the warp needs to be of tougher material than the weft. Moreover, since warp threads are usually not visible in the finished product, less colorful yarn or string can be used.

The weft creates the woven design, and selections may range from strips of paper, natural and synthetic yarns, raffia and dry grasses to plastic tape and strips of aluminum foil (see Plate 14).

STITCHERY Embellishing the surfaces of cloth is called embroidery or stitchery. Children are likely to be more successful working on burlap, thick paper, or on plastic foam meat trays, with large-eyed needles and fairly thick yarns. But you may want to work with fine textured cloth and a variety of yarns ranging from those that are thin and silk-like to those that are thick and bulky. A limited range of stitches is recommended for general school use, although—again—you may want to add to them quite considerably in your work (see Figure 26 and Figure S).

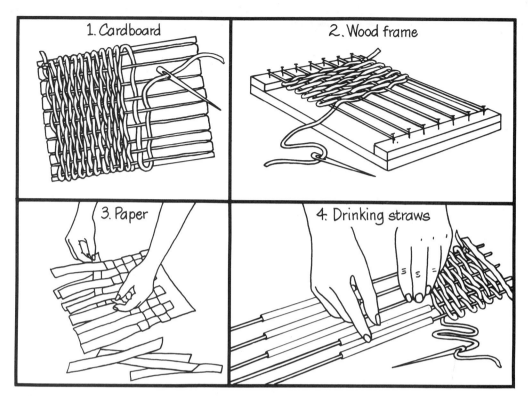

FIGURE 25   Simple looms

When small pieces of felt or cloth are stitched to a larger piece to create a picture or design, the result is *appliqué*. Appliqué is an extension of both stitchery and collage (see Plate 8 and Figure U).

UNUSUAL USE OF YARN   Yarn painting is a Mexican-Indian invention (called a nearika) in which lengths of yarn are stuck to cardboard or wood to create a picture or design. The yarn is stuck spirally with no spaces between the threads, to fill all the spaces on the board. While the yarn in Mexican originals is attached by pressing it into a layer of bee's wax, the sparing use of white (Elmer's) glue is more practical for your use (see Figure T).

MACRAMÉ   The basis of macramé is the knotting of cord to create a lace-like textile. The knots themselves are simple, but when combined in different ways they can produce intricate and original fabrics that may be useful or decorative. Macramé products may be flat or, with the help of a framework, may become three dimensional. Beads and medallions can be integral parts of macramé designs. As with other textile arts, macramé offers an invitation to be original, and yet all too often it never rises above copying ideas invented by other people.

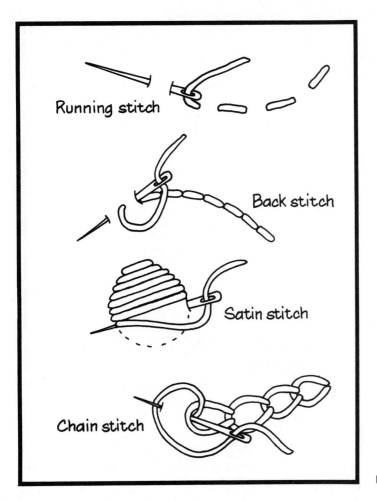

Running stitch

Back stitch

Satin stitch

Chain stitch

FIGURE 26 Simple stitches

While many kinds of string or yarn can be used in macramé, the best is any fairly stiff, tightly constructed cord that once knotted will hold together. Silky cord tends to be limp and to lack friction. Thin cord is often waxed to assist in the tying of very small knots. Very thick jute yarn does not need to be waxed, because it is easy to manage. A cord measuring about one-eighth inch in diameter is a good size for a beginner to use.

A good first step is to tie a set of lark's head knots along a strip of wood with considerable lengths to the tails to allow for the knotting to occur. The basic knots are then tied in different arrangements to make a finished product. The ends of the cord are knotted to hold the piece secure. The loose ends are sometimes untwisted to make a fringe (see Figures 27 and 28).

Textile Assignments

1. *A Decorative Table Mat.* Make a loom out of thick cardboard measuring 10″ long and 6″ wide and set up the warp threads. Weave a repeating design with yarns of different thicknesses, colors, and textures that look attractive to you. Put into words your reasons for thinking the design is

attractive. As you weave, be sure that the piece does not get narrower toward the middle.

Remove the weaving from the loom by cutting the warp threads. Knot them at the point where the weft begins and fringe the ends.

2. *Lines and Shapes.* Cut out a series of shapes from colored felt. Attach the felt pieces temporarily on a piece of cloth with smears of rubber cement. Create a pleasing design. Add to the design by stitching with various yarns in any organization of "lines" that enhance the piece. Complete the design by rearranging the felt pieces and by adding more yarn until the product satisfies you.

3. *An Alternative to Pictures.* Macramé lends itself to being made into decorative wall hangings that fulfill the same function in a room as a picture. The size of a wall hanging depends on the space to be filled and the design you choose, although the length of the cords should always be at least four times as long as you expect the finished piece to be. This particular piece is to be done for a particular place in your own home.

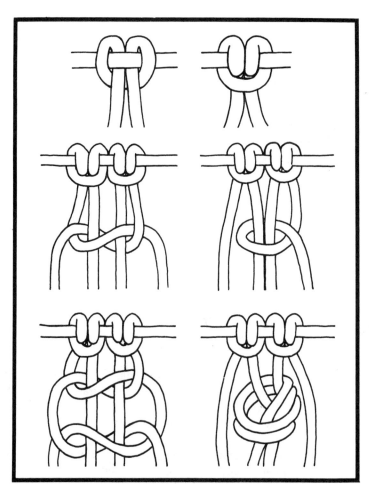

FIGURE 27 Macramé knots

FIGURE 28 College student's macramé

further art study

This brief introduction to the pictorial arts should give you a sufficient foundation to be able to start your own elementary art program in these subjects. However, you will benefit greatly if you enroll in art courses that specialize in some of the same kinds of art. And the children you teach will also benefit.

In addition to taking art courses, you may want to study books that go into these art forms in greater depth than is possible here.

Albenda, Pauline, *Creative Painting with Tempera.* New York: Van Nostrand Reinhold, 1970. A useful book for learning to paint and also to help in planning painting lessons.

Baker, Leslie A. *The Art Teacher's Resource Book.* Reston, Virginia: Reston Publishing Co., Inc., 1979. A comprehensive, well-illustrated source book on school art materials and techniques.

Clark, Gilbert and **Enid Zimmerman.** *Art/design: Communicating Visually.* Blauvelt, New York: Art Education, Inc., 1978. An art text designed for high school use that can also be of assistance to future elementary teachers in expanding their own art.

Hersk, Bernadette. *The ABC's of Batik.* Philadelphia: Chilton, 1975. Good instructional illustrations and clear instructions make this a useful book for beginners.

Kampmann, Lothar. *Creating with Crayons.* New York: Van Nostrand Reinhold, 1967. An introduction to the various ways of using crayons.

Kent, Cyril. *Starting with Relief Printmaking.* New York: Watson-Guptil, 1970. A beginner's book on printmaking.

Laliberté, Norman. *Pastel, Charcoal and Chalk Drawing.* New York: Van Nostrand Reinhold, 1970. An introduction to drawing techniques using these media.

Meilach, Dona S. *Macramé: Creative Design in Knotting.* New York: Crown Press, 1972. A thorough introduction to macramé for the person who wants to work in depth.

Morein, Shirley. *Stitchery, Needlepoint, Appliqué and Patchwork.* New York: Viking Press, 1974. Includes basic needlework techniques. Very well illustrated.

Newman, Thelma, *et al.* *Paper as Art and Craft.* New York: Crown Publications, 1973. Includes all forms of paper usage in art.

Ocvirk, Otto G., Robert O. Bone, Robert Stinson, and **Philip Wigg.** *Art Fundamentals,* 3rd ed. Dubuque, Iowa: Wm. C. Brown, 1975. Develops the language of art for college students and includes exercises that offer opportunities to develop art skills.

Palmer, Frederick. *Introducing Monoprints.* New York: Drake, 1975. Includes the basic processes and also many innovative ideas.

Portchmouth, John. *Working in Collage.* New York: Viking Press, 1974. Presents various collage techniques and materials in a clear manner.

Wilson, Jean. *Weaving Is Fun.* New York: Van Nostrand Reinhold, 1971. A useful guide on various kinds of weaving, including weaving for children.

3

sculpture making
and other
three–dimensional art

A measurement along a straight line is a dimension. The addition of a second dimension of breadth to length creates a flat surface, such as a sheet of paper or a desk top. In Chapter 2 you were introduced to art tasks that are all executed on flat, two-dimensional surfaces. However, much art—for example, sculpture, jewelry, and architecture—is three dimensional. It fills space, that is, it has depth in addition to length and breadth.

Working with solid materials has special significance that extends beyond the goals of art teaching. School curriculums concentrate on learning *about* things that are solid, through drawings, photographs, diagrams, formulas, or verbal descriptions that avoid direct exposure to the objects themselves. And yet, three-dimensional information and problems face children and adults every day. Moreover, the ability to solve three-dimensional problems is required not only by artists but also by mechanics, surgeons, dentists, athletes, astronauts, engineers, and many others.

Some teachers are fearful of the mess that often accompanies three-dimensional art lessons. Also, the bulkiness of materials creates difficulty in storing partly finished work in most classrooms. For some teachers this is enough for them to eliminate most of such work from their art programs. The hope here, however, is that as you do some of the work described in this chapter, you will overcome these tendencies to neglect this important part of elementary art education.

Artistic objects can be divided into two basic groups: those made mainly by additive methods and those made by subtractive methods. Thus, three-dimensional art is made either by joining pieces together to produce an object, or by starting with a large mass from which parts are cut away. Both forms of three-dimensional art may stand freely on a table or floor, and sometimes they may hang from the ceiling. Alternatively, they may be attached to a wall. When this happens, the art is described as *relief* sculpture. It is three dimensional but remains a part of the flat surface.

Additive sculpture is the most versatile kind of three-dimensional art suitable for school use, and the chapter opens with information and experiences that introduce you to modeling and constructing. Subtractive sculpture is represented by a section on carving. Molding and casting follow; and the chapter ends with a brief statement about sculptural environments that refers to both additive and subtractive methods.

DEVELOP YOUR MODELING SKILLS

The most immediate results in sculpture happen with modeling, and for this reason it is extremely effective for elementary school art, particularly at the lower grade levels. The major task in art is always transforming artistic ideas from your imagination into a material that can be seen and touched; and modeling is perfect for this purpose. The forming steps are more a matter of technical skill and with practice you can learn these skills.

Modeling objects so they look realistic can sometimes be important, but it is a mistake to think that is the only standard of excellence, especially for people who expect to work with children. Many excellent artists disregard imitational sculpture because they know that artistic feelings show themselves best when changes are made to the way things appear when we look at them normally. Children may be impressed by imitational art, but they themselves are not usually concerned with it as a goal in their own work until they approach the end of school. For your purposes, therefore, it is best to develop a sense of familiarity with modeling so you can help children with their art and by means of your own pleasure and confidence encourage them in their work.

CLAYS The most common modeling medium is clay, although papier mâché and various home-made doughs are useful. Clay has a magnetic appeal, because if can be easily squeezed and pulled to take on virtually any shape. It is a form of finely powdered earth that is mixed with a binding material, the most common of which is water. Water-based clay dries hard and can be baked, or fired, in a kiln to make pottery. Oils and glycerine are also used to bind clay. This kind of mixture makes non-hardening clay that can be re-used indefinitely but cannot be fired. Both kinds of clay can be purchased in a ready-mixed form for immediate use. Some kinds of clay are specially made to be fired in a domestic oven, while others dry hard when exposed to air. Clay powder is by far the least expensive to purchase, but mixing it with water can be messy and time consuming. Whatever you choose to use, be sure to have plastic sacks and ties available when any clay needs to be kept moist.

Moist clay needs to be thoroughly mixed to remove any hard or soft spots and also any air bubbles. This process is called *wedging* and is performed by thoroughly kneading the clay in the same way you would knead dough. The best way to maintain the moisture of clay, during this process and also while working with it, is to keep your hands continually wet. In this way, the water is dispersed evenly throughout the clay. Clay that is too wet will soon dry out if you manipulate it with dry hands.

You can prepare clay substitutes, but none of them is as good as clay, although they do make three-dimensional art projects possible. A salt dough can be made by mixing two cups of flour with one cup of salt and adding water to the mixture until it reaches a good consistency. A sawdust dough can be made by mixing two cups of sawdust with one cup of flour and one tablespoon of water soluble glue or paste. Add water until the dough reaches a good consistency. The actual quantities will depend on how much dough you need. Other dough recipes exist, but these were selected because they do not call for boiling the mixture as part of the process.

Additive clay sculpture is made by sticking pieces together until it takes on the shape you want. Very large pieces of sculpture may need internal support to prevent the clay from collapsing. These internal supports are called *armatures* and can be made of wood or thick wire, although balls of wadded newspaper can often fulfill the same function (see Figures 29 and

FIGURE 29 A wire armature

89). Another additive technique is to flatten a lump of clay on a piece of burlap or the back of a piece of oil cloth. Two strips of wood, between 1/4″ and 1/2″ thick are placed on either side of the clay and it is rolled into a slab of even thickness with a wooden rolling pin (see Figure 30). The clay slabs then are cut into pieces and stuck together to make sculpture (see Figure 31). Slabs can also be made into masks or Christmas tree ornaments, either with designs and textures scratched into the surfaces or objects pressed into them to make designs. A slab can be draped over some object to give it the desired curvature.

If a clay model is to be allowed to dry out, and particularly if the piece is to be fired in a kiln, all of the places where one piece joins another have to be bonded together in a special way to prevent their separating when the clay dries. This is done while a piece is being constructed and the clay is moist. The two surfaces are roughened and before being joined are painted with a creamy mixture of water and clay known as *slip* (see Figure 32).

POTTERY   The techniques for modeling are the same for making pottery. Pottery is an ancient art and continues to be popular. Three basic hand-built pottery forms exist. They are the pinch-pot, the coil-pot, and the slab pot. The following illustrations show the steps to be taken in constructing each type (see Figure 33). An interesting variation to coil-building occurs when coils are built vertically to make the walls of a pot.

Pottery is also made on a revolving wheel, but wheel-thrown pottery is likely to present problems in elementary schools, partly by the expense and space required for wheels, and partly by the children's lack of physical strength. For these reasons, no instructions are given here on wheel-thrown pottery.

FIGURE 30   Rolling a slab of clay

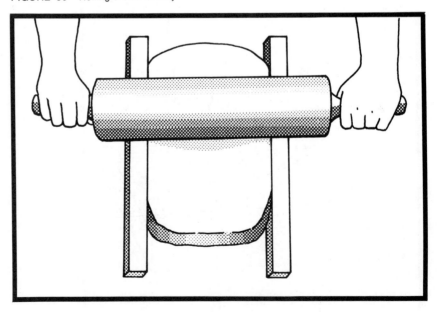

FIGURE 31 "Tower of Birds," by Richard Peeler. Courtesy of the artist.

FIGURE 32 Joining clay

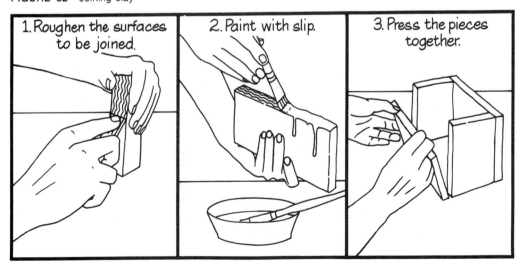

1. Roughen the surfaces to be joined.

2. Paint with slip.

3. Press the pieces together.

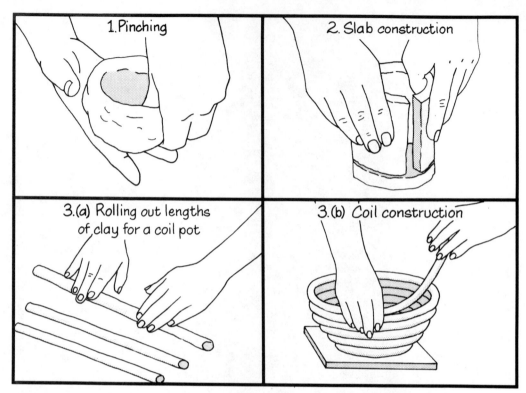

FIGURE 33 Pottery making techniques

If you can get access to a kiln before starting to teach, you should practice firing at least one piece of clay pottery or sculpture. Schools sometimes possess kilns, and children enjoy having their work transformed from the easily breakable clay into permanent ceramic. If you do not have an opportunity to fire a piece now, the following three hints are worth remembering for the future. First, be sure you wedged the clay thoroughly so that all irregularities of moisture and any air pockets have been eliminated. Air pockets burst during the firing process and will damage or destroy the piece. Second, be sure the piece is not solid; and that the walls are of fairly even thickness and nowhere thicker than 1/2″. Solid and thick-walled pieces are inclined to warp out of shape or break during the firing process. Third, be sure the clay is thoroughly dry before firing. A good test for dryness is to feel the piece. If it feels cold, then moisture is still evaporating from it. If it feels about the same as room temperature, then it is dry enough to fire. At this stage the clay is called *green*. The actual process of firing is not difficult, but on the first occasion you should ask someone to show you how a particular kiln is operated. Finishing a piece of pottery once it has been fired—this stage is called *bisque*—is done by painting it with a glaze and firing it again. Alternatively, a finish can be given by applying shoe polish or by painting the surface and sealing it with a coat of shellac.

PAPIER-MÂCHÉ   This is a useful material for modeling. It was originally a French solution to re-cycling at an earlier time when paper was too valuable to destroy. Because of its durability, papier-mâché was made into furniture as well as decorative objects, numbers of which still exist after being in existence for several hundred years. Papier-mâché is still used for such things as egg cartons because of its strength and light weight, as well as for making decorative objects.

The two common ways of using papier-mâché are with strips and pulp. You can model with pulp, while strip is best used for molding (*see* p. 79). Papier-mâché can substitute for clay, although it is not as easy to manipulate. It is made by soaking small pieces of paper in paste until the mass is thoroughly softened. Pulp may be used by itself or built over existing forms composed of objects such as boxes or bottles. Prepared forms of pulp can be purchased that give excellent results, but they are likely to be more expensive than most school budgets will allow. The more usual way is for newspaper to be torn into very small pieces and first soaked in water before being squeezed and saturated with wheat paste. Pulp papier-mâché can be prevented from smelling with the addition of a few drops of oil of cloves, wintergreen or lysol. An interesting addition to papier-mâché is to mix the wet pulp with plaster of Paris and wheat paste (see Figure 34).

FIGURE 34   College student's papier-mâché mask

1. *Adding Decoration*. Make several elongated pinch or coil constructed pots, two of which are to be larger than the others. Turn them over so that the opening is flat on the table, and transform these pottery shapes into a group of people or animals. Pieces of clay can be attached to the pots, the surfaces can be altered, and parts may be cut away to achieve your objective in the most creative way possible. Household pets can be added to a family group if you so desire (see Figure 35).

2. *Dreamland Tower*. Roll clay into a large slab and then cut it into smaller slabs of various dimensions. The problem is to build a tower of a kind that could only exist in your dreams. The only stipulations are that the tower show innovative construction ideas and that it be sturdy. Naturally, you should find it pleasing to look at from every direction.

3. *Opposites*. Washington Irving's character, Ichabod Crane, was a fragile little man who was scared of his own shadow. By contrast, the mythical figure of Paul Bunyan was larger than life and incredibly powerful. In this assignment, create two clay models to stand side by side to bring out this large-small, strong-weak contrast. The models may be people or animals or they may not resemble anything at all. Armatures may be needed, especially for the big figure. Your success with this message will rest mainly on the reactions of the people who see your models and especially with the way they respond to the creative way in which you solved this artistic problem.

4. *Personal Adornment*. Make three $1\frac{1}{2}''$ wide bracelet-sized loops with folded newspaper. The shapes of the loops should be evenly curved. Bind each loop with 3–5 layers of strip papier-mâché. The last layer should be made from smooth white paper. When the paste is dry, glue one or more layers of colored tissue paper over the entire surface with white (Elmer's) glue. Add surface decorations, such as string, solid shapes made from wadded tissue paper and white glue, felt marker, pen and ink, pieces of metal foil, etc. Each bracelet should be different from the others, but all of them should look as though they belong in a set. A coat of clear lacquer or acrylic gloss medium will give the finished pieces a professional look that will please you (see Figure 36).

5. *Jigsaw Relief*. Visit a wood shop and ask to collect small scraps of waste wood. These are usually burned. Select only the pieces measuring up to $3''$ in any direction. Search for interesting shapes, various colors of wood, and those pieces with unusual markings on them. Arrange the wood pieces to fill a rectangular piece of plywood at least $12'' \times 15''$ to create an interesting relief design. The pieces will project from the surface of the plywood in various ways depending on how they are arranged; and this is where you are to test your creativity.

When the arrangement makes the most creative arrangement you can think of, glue all the pieces in place with white (Elmer's) glue. Lastly, nail or glue thin strips of wood around the edges to make a frame (see Figure 37).

6. *Puppet Heads*. Prepare a ball of pulp papier-mâché the size of your fist or slightly larger. Press a hole fairly deeply into the ball for your index finger. Model the papier-mâché into a comic cartoon character that could be used as the head of a puppet.

As you work on your head, be sure that the eyes are placed about halfway down the head. You may find yourself putting them too high on the head.

Distort parts of the head such noses, eyes, ears, to make them very prominent and help represent the character clearly. When the model is complete, let the papier-mâché dry thoroughly, and then paint it to bring out the character even more clearly. Yarn can be added for hair. A coat of shellac applied rapidly over the painted areas will protect the paint and give a shiny finish.

You may want to complete the puppet by making clothes for it. Puppets like these can captivate children. They can be used for art and also as aids in teaching other subjects.

FIGURE 35 Mexican pottery

FIGURE 36 College student's papier-mâché jewelry

FIGURE 37 College student's wood scrap relief

DEVELOPING YOUR CONSTRUCTION SKILLS

Constructed sculpture was first made in this century by sculptors who called themselves "constructivists." Their work was done in flat wood and sheet metal. Construction materials for school use, however, include such things as paper, cardboard, wire, boxes and cartons, bottles and cans, metal foil, plastic foam products, pine cones, sea shells, pebbles, and so on. This kind of additive sculpture differs from work done in clay or papier-mâché in that the shapes of the materials are not easily altered. For convenience, the following information groups materials by their similarities, although in practice you may find that mixtures are more useful.

STICK-LIKE MATERIALS Included are soda straws, popsicle sticks, tooth picks, strips of balsa wood, lengths of dowel rod, metal piping, stiff wire and dead twigs. They all possess considerable strength for their size and can be joined together very much like a human skeleton or the web of steel beams found in tall buildings. Sculpture of this kind is like line drawing; but instead of drawing on flat paper with a pencil, it calls for assembling lines in three-dimensional space.

Several methods of construction exist. One is to assemble sections of a constructed piece on a flat surface. Kites are best made in this manner. Another is to build a structure from the base upwards. Toothpick sculpture is often built in this way. A third method involves holding the piece in your hand as it is made. This is best suited to wire sculpture where the products tend to be quite small (see Figure 38).

Heavy, strip-like materials, such as piping, thick wire and larger wood strips lend themselves to more massive constructions. The pieces can be held together by binding them with thin wire, string or tape, or perhaps gluing them. Such a framework can be painted or left as it is. Alternatively, it can be wholly or partly covered with either plaster of Paris or plaster impregnated bandage (see Figure 39).

FIGURE 38 Alexander Calder, *The Hostess* (1928). Wire construction, $11\frac{1}{2}$" high. Collection, The Museum of Modern Art, New York. Gift of Edward M. M. Warburg.

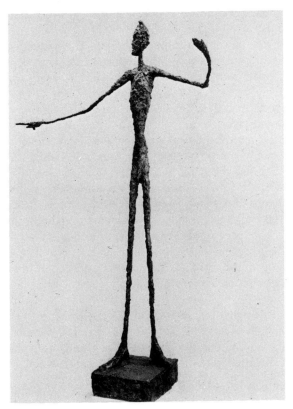

FIGURE 39 Alberto Giacometti, *Man Pointing* (1947). Bronze, $70\frac{1}{2}$" high, at base $12 \times 13\frac{1}{4}$". Collection, The Museum of Modern Art, New York. Gift of Mrs. John D. Rockefeller, 3rd.

SHEET-LIKE MATERIALS Stiff paper or cardboard have different qualities and result in unique sculpture. Paper or cardboard bends easily, but if it is folded like a concertina it behaves like corrugated paper: it is flexible in one direction and rigid in the other. When a sheet of paper is bent in several directions, it becomes completely rigid. Added rigidness occurs when bent sheets are joined together. Paper and cardboard sculpture is glued or stapled, while metal sculpture is welded, bolted, or riveted; but the result is the same.

The ply-rating given to art cardboard in catalogues is a helpful guide both to thickness and price. For example, 4-ply board is light-weight, bends easily, and is comparatively inexpensive. A 10-ply board, by contrast, is heavy, stiff, and expensive. The names given to cardboards can vary quite considerably, but suitable types of board for school use are often called Bristol board or Posterboard. If in doubt about what board to order, request samples from a supplier.

An effective way of making sure that paper or cardboard will bend sharply at one place is to indent it (but not cut through) with the point of a pair of scissors. This is called "scoring." Scored lines may be made by using a rule or freehand. Paper or cardboard will bend naturally along the scored line and depending on the direction of the line, the paper will take on a new form (see Figure 40).

A way of giving stability to thicker cardboard is to slot it. A sheet is cut part-way across and the resulting slot is slid over another sheet at an angle. Slots may be cut into both pieces of cardboard where they intersect to make a more complete join. Complete sculptures can be built using just this technique (see Figures 41 and 42).

For decoration, paper can be cut into strips and curled. This technique requires that drawing paper or construction paper be pulled sharply at right angles across the blade of a pair of scissors. The dragging action makes the paper curl (see Figure 43).

Intricate shapes are best cut with scissors (if you are left-handed, you may want to use "Leftys") or small X-acto knives (see Figure 44). Shears, mat knives, and paper cutters are most useful when cutting larger, straight-edged pieces. But be sure not to try to cut more than four or five sheets of paper with a paper cutter because the paper will tear.

The American sculptor, Alexander Calder, invented another kind of constructed sculpture that hangs from the ceiling and is called a "mobile" (see Figure 45). It can be used very successfully in elementary schools for teaching design and balance in three-dimensional space. Mobiles are especially appealing because they move. The technique of making a mobile is relatively simple; the work becomes more interesting once you depart from the basic construction and begin to explore alternative ways of achieving physical and aesthetic balance.

The basic procedure is to hang two interesting objects, which may or may not be identical, to a length of stiff wire by means of thread. It is important to be sure that the thread will not slip along the wire and upset the balance. A dab of glue on the knots will usually prevent slipping. A length of

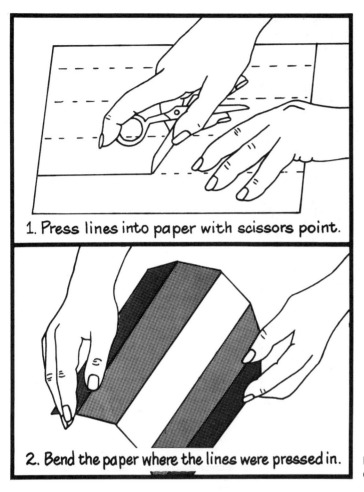

1. Press lines into paper with scissors point.

2. Bend the paper where the lines were pressed in.

FIGURE 40 Scoring paper or cardboard

FIGURE 41 Slotting paper or cardboard

1. Cut slots.

2. Join pieces together.

3. Complete the details.

FIGURE 42 College student's slotted sculpture

FIGURE 43 Curling paper strips

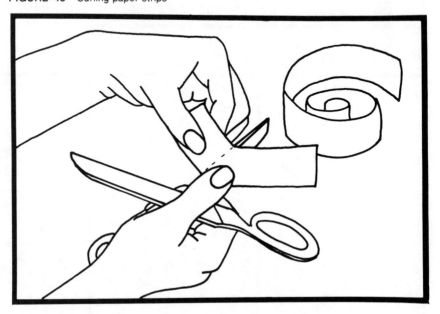

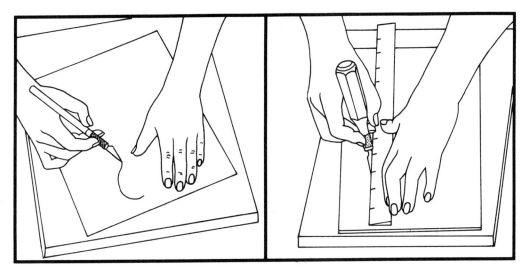

FIGURE 44 Cutting with an x-acto knife

FIGURE 45 Alexander Calder, *Lobster Trap and Fish Tail* (1939). Hanging mobile: painted steel wire and sheet aluminum, about 8'6'' x 9'6''. Collection, The Museum of Modern Art, New York.

thread is then attached to the wire at the balance point. This process is repeated to make a similar or dissimilar unit. The two units are themselves suspended from a third length of wire. The process continues until the artist judges the mobile to be finished (see Figure 46).

BOXES, CANS, AND BOTTLES They can be tied, taped or glued together to create forms. While some may be cut with scissors or knives to modify them, they generally remain much as they were originally. Since the surfaces of these objects often carry advertising, the finished sculpture looks better if it is painted. Aluminum paint is opaque and can be sprayed on in well-ventilated areas to cover most surface designs with one coat and make a base on which designs can be painted or stuck (i.e., paper mosaic and collage). Tall, box-like constructions can be made stable by filling the bottom container with sand (see Figures 47 and 48).

A related construction task is to stick varied solid objects together. These materials can be wood scraps from a carpenter's shop, pieces of old toys, used flash cubes, ball point pens, egg cartons, centers from toilet tissue

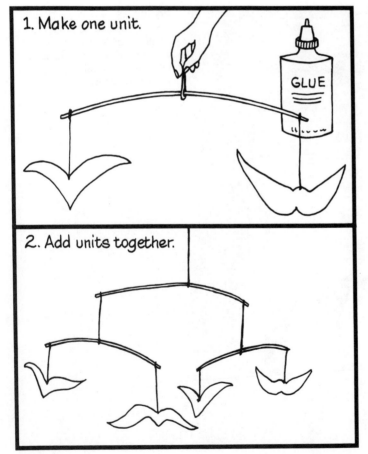

FIGURE 46 Building a mobile

1. Make one unit.

GLUE

2. Add units together.

FIGURE 47 David Smith, *Cubi XVII* (1963). Stainless steel. Dallas Museum of Fine Arts, The Eugene and Margaret McDermott Fund.

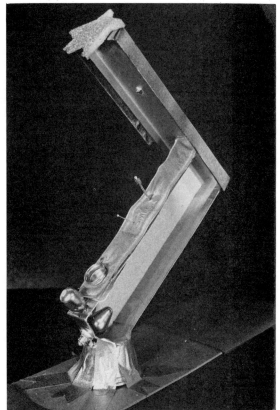

FIGURE 48   College student's box construction

71

rolls, and similar items. Some of these scrap materials were used earlier for making reliefs (p. 62). If the surfaces are all at the same level, the art work can become a mosaic by filling in the cracks between the pieces with plaster. Dry sand can be used if the mosaic is to remain flat. When plaster is used this way it is called *grout*. White casein (Elmer's) glue is best for sticking things on to porous surfaces, while cellophane, masking tapes, and string are useful for joining larger pieces and non-porous materials.

Construction Assignments

1. *The Medium is the Message.* Assemble a collection of empty food cartons and cans of all shapes and sizes into a piece of free-standing or relief sculpture that captures the feeling of a subject that you find emotionally stimulating. Such subjects might include: "The Political Prisoner", "The Twenty-First Century", "Pregnancy", etc. When finished, light the piece, using a spotlight in a darkened setting (a flashlight is satisfactory) to display it at its best.

2. *Creative Perception.* Pablo Picasso looked at some bicycle handlebars and a saddle and transformed them into a bull's head (see Figure 49). Artists engage in this kind of thinking regularly and you need as much practice as you can get in order to help children develop their own aptitudes for perceiving creatively. This assignment requires that you hunt through what most people would call trash or junk, and salvage such items as old light bulbs, old spray cans, egg cartons, and plastic spoons. Then put the pieces together to make an attractive yet surprisingly different object, like an animal or flower. Practice is the only way that this kind of thinking can be stimulated.

3. *Mardi-Gras.* Both children and adults enjoy dressing up in disguises. A disguise that is commonly used in schools consists of a brown paper sack placed over the head with holes cut for the eyes. The difference will be that your transformation of the paper will be both adult in conception and more sophisticated in execution than can be expected from children. The image, itself, is to reflect one or more of those thoughts that exist inside everyone but are not permitted to be expressed publicly—except in the fantasy-like setting of a mardi-gras parade or a fancy dress party.

The embellishments to the paper sack mask are to be done exclusively with paper as a test of your ingenuity. Just a few of the many possibilities include curling it to make beards and eyelashes; folding it or scoring it to make earrings; and rolling it to make cigars and eye-brows. The list of possibilities is extensive. You may use white paper only or a mixture of white and colored paper and also various textures of paper (see Figure 50).

When the disguise is done, list all the different ways in which you used paper. Each one of them will then consciously become part of your art teaching resources.

4. *Capturing Empty Space.* Thread a length of yarn through a series of whole drinking straws or shorter sections of straws. Manipulate the straws until they create an interesting three dimensional volume. You will have to

tie the yarn at the points where the straws join for it to hold its shape. Single straws—or sections of straws—may now be tied to the joints in the structure, either to support it or to improve its appearance. Decide on the point from which it should be suspended. The finished sculpture should be attractive when seen from all points of view (see Figure 51).

5. *Asymmetrical Balance.* The drawings that show how a mobile is constructed only illustrate a symmetrical organization, that is, where an object is identical to the one that it balances. The photograph of the mobile by Calder shows one that is asymmetrically balanced. This assignment requires you to make a mobile where the pieces are all arranged asymmetrically. The finished sculpture should reflect a particular feeling or message such as "Orbiter", "Dove of Peace", etc. Choose your own title and display it with the mobile.

6. *Modular Sculpture.* Decide on a simple shape to be made from toothpicks or popsicle sticks, like a triangle or rectangle. Use white casein (Elmer's) or airplane glue. Airplane glue is excellent, but be sure to work in a well-ventilated area. Make 20 identical shapes or modules on the desk top. When the glue is dry, stick colored tissue or cellophane over five of the modules. Assemble all 20 modules to create a three-dimensional structure that you think is interesting to look at from all directions.

If, when all the modules have been used, you feel the sculpture would be improved either by the addition of more modules or by the addition of individual pieces, then make those changes.

FIGURE 49 Pablo Picasso made a bull's head with bicycle handlebars and a saddle

FIGURE 50 College student's
paper bag mask

FIGURE 51 College student's
paper straws construction

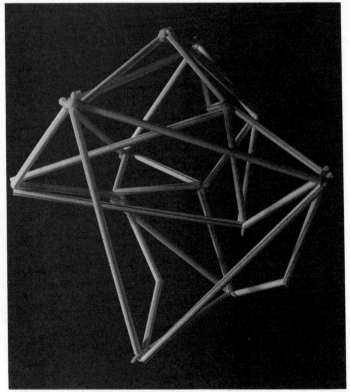

DEVELOP YOUR CARVING SKILLS

Additive sculpture offers the easiest first step toward three-dimensional art experiences in school. Subtractive sculpture is an equally important part of art and belongs in the elementary art program, but it is unlikely to be as prominent as the various additive methods.

The art of removing materials from a solid block is called carving. The best material for beginners to carve is clay, since the waste is re-usable and the beginner almost always cuts away too much of the block. A clay block may be allowed to dry out completely before you start to carve; or it may be carved while the clay still has a stiff, soap-like consistency (called leather hard). Artists often make drawings or clay models of what they will carve to begin with to help develop an idea. A side view is then drawn or scratched on the block and the excess is carved away until that silhouette shape is achieved. A similar drawing is made on the top of the view from above and the block is reduced to that shape (see Figures 52 and 53). The roughed-out form is then refined to make the finished sculpture. Plaster can be used in the same way but should be first poured into a milk carton or similar kind of box to make a block. Vermiculite and saw-dust may be added to modify the texture and hardness of plaster.

Another way of doing carving is to take an irregular block of hard clay or plaster. Plaster can be poured into a plastic sack and molded into any desired form before it sets (see p. 78 on how to prepare plaster). When dry, the sack can be torn off to let you carve the plaster with a kitchen knife or similar tool to make an appealing new form. The piece will grow as you work on it, rather than from any preconceived ideas (see Figure 54). As always in carving, one of the key concerns is to avoid removing any part that you might want to retain in the final work. You can rarely attach pieces that have been carved away either deliberately or accidentally.

FIGURE 52 Carving

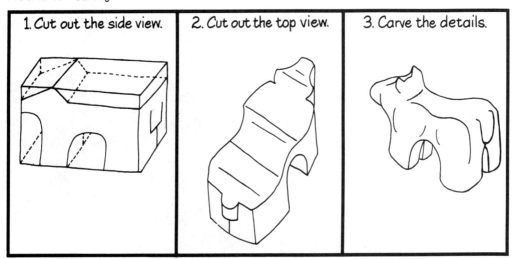

| 1. Cut out the side view. | 2. Cut out the top view. | 3. Carve the details. |

FIGURE 53 Constantin Brancusi, *The Kiss* (1908). Stone, 22$\frac{3}{4}$'' high. Philadelphia Museum of Art: The Louise and Walter Arensberg Collection.

FIGURE 54 Jean Arp, *Human Concretion* (1935). Original plaster, 19$\frac{1}{2}$ x 18$\frac{3}{4}$''. Collection, The Museum of Modern Art, New York. Gift of the Advisory Committee.

A word of caution deserves to be made about carving in soap. It is an attractive medium, especially for meticulous work, but it is more difficult to do than it appears. Try white ivory soap yourself before letting children do it. And before beginning, open the package and let the soap dry for a week or so.

<table>
<tr><td>

Carving
Assignments

</td><td>

1. *Deciding What Is Really Important.* Cast a block in plaster that has been tinted with paint. A milk carton makes a well-proportioned block. While the plaster is setting, take some clay and sketch several designs for a carving to be done in the block. The problem will be to cut the least amount of the block away, while making an attractive piece of sculpture of a clearly recognizable person or animal.

When the plaster is perfectly dry, cut the milk carton away from the block. Translate what you have done in clay onto the plaster. As your work unfolds, make any changes to the design that seem necessary.

2. *Individual Hand Magic.* Cast a block of plaster or prepare a block of water-based clay and let it set solid. The task is to carve away the block until it feels good when held in your hands. The decision that something feels good is very personal. To some people this would mean it is smooth and round. Others would declare that for an object to feel good it must have flat surfaces and crisp edges. Individuals vary considerably; but your task is simple: to please yourself thoroughly. All that is asked of you is that you do it; and insofar as you are able, that you put into words what there is about the piece that enables you to say that it feels good.

3. *Lighting and Composition.* Pour a slab of plaster in a cardboard box measuring about 7″ × 9″ × 2″ and set a wire loop near the top so it can hang on the wall. Allow about 1/2″ all around for a border or frame. Use the inside space for a carving that shows the main message in either a well-known nursery rhyme or a moral (an Aesop's Fable, one of the Commandments, the Golden Rule, etc.).

The design should make use of all the space inside the frame. In parts of the carving, go to at least 1″ below the surface of the block and if you wish, and are careful, go up to $1\frac{1}{2}$″. Periodically, hold the carving in a vertical position to check on the effects that lighting from above has on the different surfaces and textures. The relief should not only fill the space well, it should look its best when lit from above. Since plaster cannot be replaced when once removed you may want to try ideas out on a practice slab or in a piece of clay.

</td></tr>
</table>

DEVELOP YOUR MOLDING AND CASTING SKILLS

Molding and casting are techniques used for reproducing objects, but they can also be used imaginatively for creative art. A mold is a hollow object into which fluid material such as wet cement or liquid jello is poured. The mold is lifted away from the dry cement or solidified jello to reveal the exact form of the inside of the mold. An object made in a mold is called a cast. Molds can be built over clay sculpture and the clay removed. Liquid metal or plaster is then poured into the mold which, when solidified, makes an exact copy of the original sculpture in a more permanent material than clay.

While this process may not be used in schools exactly in the way described, molds and casts made with plaster and papier-mâché have a place in the elementary art program.

Plaster of Paris is excellent for making exact copies of objects and has been used for this purpose for centuries. This white powder can be purchased at a local building supplies store or through an art supply company. It is inexpensive but must be kept perfectly dry to prevent spoilage. Plaster is prepared by filling a container 2/3 full with water and quickly sprinkling the powder into the water until it appears above the surface. The mixture is then gently but thoroughly stirred by hand. The creamy liquid quickly thickens to become a white solid (see Figure 55). Vermiculite or sawdust can be added to plaster before the mixture sets to give the surface an interesting texture. Both are available at the same sources as the plaster. Powdered tempera can also be added to tint the plaster. Do remember, however, that plaster should never be allowed to wash into the drains either in the powdered or solid forms. Care should be taken to prevent the powder from tracking across floors and, more importantly, from getting into your eyes. If it gets into anyone's eyes, flood the eyes immediately with clear water.

A simple technique is described here for use with plaster to make casts of original designs pressed into sand. Sand casting is used extensively in iron foundries and the school technique is substantially the same except that plaster is used instead of molten metal. A movie on what happens in a foundry, or better still a visit to one would be most appropriate—for social studies and science as well as art.

The task calls for some fairly fine-grained sand that is damp enough to cling together and be pressed down firmly into a box to make the foundation for a mold. A cardboard box can be used for school use because it will remain stiff for long enough that the process can be completed. Objects are

FIGURE 55   Mixing plaster

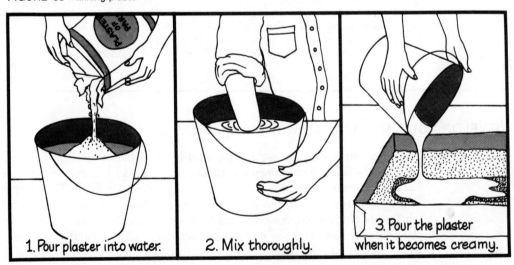

1. Pour plaster into water.   2. Mix thoroughly.   3. Pour the plaster when it becomes creamy.

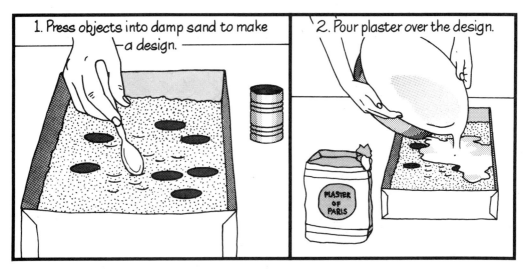

FIGURE 56   Sandcasting

then pressed into the sand to various depths to leave as clear a set of impressions as possible. A banana, a pine cone, a seashell, a shoe, a hand, a horseshoe, or a pair of scissors may all be used to make impressions. When a design looks complete and the edges of the impressions are fairly sharply defined, the box is carefully filled with liquid plaster of Paris. When the plaster has set hard, carefully peel or tear the cardboard away from the plaster. Brush the excess sand from the surface. The plaster cast will show the design of objects that were pressed into the sand, but they will now stand out to make a relief (see Figures 56 and 57).

While molding is normally the foundation for a cast, it can also be used to create near replicas. This is done best with strip papier-mâché or with cloth that has been soaked in starch or plaster of Paris. Strips of soft paper—usually newspaper—are soaked in wheat paste and laminated over a predetermined form, usually made of clay. Five or more layers of newspaper are usually enough to make a fairly tough shell. You may have difficulty remembering how many layers you have put on and whether each layer has been applied evenly, so you might want to practice alternating layers using two colors of paper. The first layer can be regular newspaper, for example; the second layer can be either from the colored comics or paper towels; and so on. Alternatively, each layer of strips can be applied at right angles. Large sculptures are made by first constructing an armature using chicken wire, tightly rolled newspapers, or wood. The strips are draped over the form as before (see Figure 58).

Several artists have become famous using the same technique to reproduce people. This approach to molded sculpture gives you an opportunity to do something like that—if not quite as ambitious. Have a person offer their hand, foot or face for you to cast. First, press soft wet paper towels or thin plastic wrap over all the surfaces of the model and especially into the crevices. This will prevent the plaster from sticking to the hairs. If you are casting a face, either leave the nose free or place two straws in the nostrils

FIGURE 57 College student's
sand casting

FIGURE 58 Strip papier-mâché

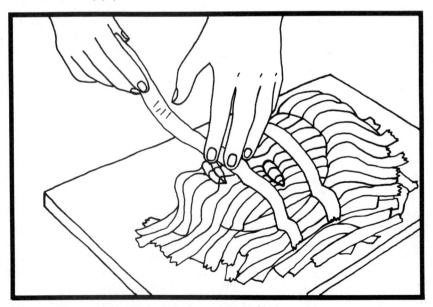

to permit breathing. Put a single layer of plaster impregnated bandage or strips of thin cloth soaked in wet plaster over the model and let it dry thoroughly. When the cast is removed, it will need trimming and perhaps some final touching up. You may want to paint or decorate the cast, or you may prefer it left the way it is (see Figures 59 and 60).

FIGURE 59 George Segal, *Bus Riders* (1964). Plaster, metal and vinyl, 69 x 40 x 76'. Hirshhorn Museum and Sculpture Garden, Smithsonian Institution.

FIGURE 60 College student's plaster mask.

| Molding and Casting Assignments | 1. *Dramatic Play.* Teachers have long known the value of puppetry in the education of children, and more recently television has capitalized on this knowledge. This assignment requires that you make a puppet head in a different way from the one using pulp papier mâché. Model a head in clay, preferably in the non-hardening, oil-based variety. The head should be at least 4″ high and be a forceful caricature of a particular personality type; such as a hero, glamor girl, gangster, etc. Be sure that the head is given a neck. The model is to be covered with strip papier mâché. When dry, the head is to be cut in half vertically just behind the ears and the clay dug out. The head is then taped back together and painted to bring out to the fullest the personality of the character (see Figure 61). |

The puppet can be completed by making clothing to fit the character being portrayed and a dramatic routine invented.

2. *Group Portrait.* Work with several friends to make mask portraits using plaster impregnated bandages. When the portraits are complete, glue them to a plywood panel in an attractive arrangement and spray the entire work with gold or silver paint. Then write your names beneath your portraits.

If this group portrait is framed, it will look most attractive, and you will enjoy having it on the wall. It will also make an excellent model for the same assignment in school. A portrait like this of your whole class will cause a sensation in school (see Figure 62).

3. *A Message Without Words.* Make a sand casting in the way described above. The design and the objects you use to press into the sand should be interesting to look at; but together they should all convey a message to anyone looking at it. Sometimes artists think of the message after their art work is complete. Sometimes it comes before they begin. In this sand-cast relief, decide on a message *before* you begin work. It could be as simple as a title of what is shown, such as "Butterfly"; or it could be more abstract, such as "Springtime" or "Greediness."

The test of your success will be the ease with which people realize what the message is, so write the message on the back of the plaster cast so it cannot be seen. And then ask your friends (and perhaps those who are not so friendly) what they think the message is.

ENVIRONMENTS

All of the three-dimensional objects in this chapter so far have been made to be seen from the outside, and yet three-dimensional space includes inside space as well. The stage of a puppet theater is a specially designed inside space. The art of decorating a room for a party or simply moving tables and chairs around to make the place more attractive is also a form of sculptural construction. The insides of boxes can be used as environments for space-filling problems where the task is to enhance the appearance of all the space in the box. Dioramas for Science and Social Studies can also fulfill similar artistic functions, but only as long as you continue to think consciously of the artistic, space-filling problems that exist.

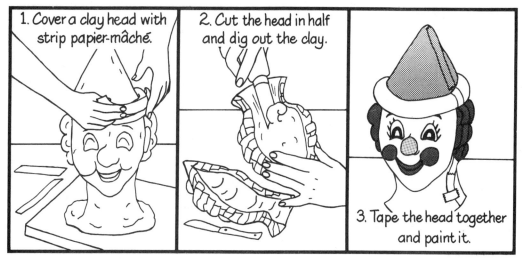

1. Cover a clay head with strip papier-mâché.

2. Cut the head in half and dig out the clay.

3. Tape the head together and paint it.

FIGURE 61   Making a papier-mâché head

Larger environments such as cities also occupy space. They present major social problems for designers today. Model making can be linked to this kind of design, both for you and for the children you will teach. Designs for gardens, national parks, and amusement parks (such as Disneyland) also have a place in this kind of art study.

FIGURE 62   A class portrait in plaster

CLASS OF 76

Environmental Assignments

1. *A Spectacle in Miniature.* Spontaneous exclamations occur when a person enters a lavishly decorated home or when the curtain rises at the theater to display a spectacular setting. And yet creative ideas are more important than size and expense. The key to success, as always, is imagination. With this in mind, you are to transform the inside of a shoe box into a miniature spectacle when seen through a single peep-hole at one end. The interior may be made to look like a place you know well, or it may be designed to play optical tricks on you with mirrors and strange lighting. However, once the lid is down it will be your environment, and the only light admitted will be through holes you have placed to achieve the special effects you have in mind.

2. *A Private Place.* All people enjoy privacy. Some of us never had enough when we were young, and perhaps for that reason we enjoy private places more than other people. Wanting to be private is natural; and being private in an attractive setting can be highly rewarding. In this assignment you are to make such a private place for yourself.

First, find a packing case or refrigerator carton large enough to hold you. Decide whether you want the carton to be standing on its end or lying on its side, and also decide how you are to get in and out. After that, let your imagination take over. You may just dream until ideas begin to flow; or you may be the kind of person who writes notes or draws plans. Do whatever is necessary to make the interior of the carton a pleasing place for you. What is pleasing to you, of course, may mean exciting or quiet and restful. The choice is yours.

3. *Landscape Architecture.* Some artists make design decisions about the best use of outdoor environments. They are called landscape architects. The closest to this work you can get is to make a model. This one is to be a land development for recreational use. A sheet of plywood or masonite makes a good base. Wood strips need to be glued around the edges to protect the design. Next, mix some plaster of Paris and model a landscape that has the following parts in it: a level area, a creek bed, a cliff or some steep slopes, and a pond or small lake. This is the basic environment, to which will be added a thickly wooded area, a marshy area, a rocky area, and a grassy area. A creative problem here is to make trees, reeds, and grass and to build or carve rocks. At this time, mark where North is.

The final task is to fit a campsite into this natural environment. Parts may have to be cleared of trees and a cabin built and perhaps some tents shown. The swimming area should have the benefit of maximum sunshine but not be marshy. A nature trail may need to be made—and so on. Each decision is the result of reasoning, and explanations should be prepared as well as the changes to be made to the site.

Compared with painting and drawing, three-dimensional art calls upon different thinking abilities when solving problems. Moreover, some of the problems that children face in their drawings tend not to be problems when working with sculpture. As mentioned earlier, teachers may perceive disadvantages in that this kind of work tends to be messier than two-dimensional art studies after exploring the three-dimensional art forms introduced in this and be noisier than usual. But the educational advantages of working in three dimensions far outweigh the disadvantages.

further art study

As with the chapter on picture making, you may want to continue your art studies after exploring the three-dimensional art forms introduced in this chapter. Enrolling in art courses will offer the best opportunities for improving yourself; but if that is not possible the contents of the following books will help you.

Baker, Leslie A. *The Art Teacher's Resource Book,* Reston, Virginia: Reston Publishing Co., 1979. A comprehensive, well-illustrated source book on school art materials and techniques.

Beecraft, Glynis. *Carving Techniques.* New York: Watson-Guptil, 1976. Many of the materials and techniques are suitable for elementary school use.

Clark, Gilbert and **Enid Zimmerman.** *Art/design: Communicating Visually,* Blauvelt, New York: Art Education, Inc., 1978. An art text designed for high school use that can also be of assistance to future elementary teachers in expanding their own art.

Farnsworth, Warren. *Beginning Pottery.* New York: Van Nostrand Reinhold, 1974. A clear, well-illustrated introduction to pottery techniques.

Kenny, Carla and **John B.** *Design in Papier Mâché.* Philadelphia: Chilton, 1971. A good instructional manual for elementary teachers.

Portchmouth, John. *All Kinds of Papercraft.* New York: Viking Press, 1972. Well illustrated instruction using varied kinds of papers and paper techniques.

Stribling, Mary Lou. *Art From Found Materials: Discarded and Natural.* New York: Crown Publications, 1970. Includes useful information on a wide range of materials.

using pictures and objects
for teaching

Art is unique in the elementary curriculum in that its content has to do mainly with visual knowledge and its imaginative use. Words are useful for developing understanding, but artistic ideas and information cannot be properly communicated, except by seeing art and making it (as we did in the last two chapters). The importance of pictures in teaching art is so great, in fact, that the information about how to collect suitable visual materials and also find them again when they are needed requires a separate chapter.

PICTURES

Visual images provide ideas and information. Children learn to recognize particular examples of sculpture and architecture by looking at the real objects or at pictures of them. A photograph of a Model T Ford provides information that enables a child to draw an old-fashioned car. Fifth graders learn what colors they can use for weaving more quickly if they first see some pictures—or better still, if they look at and handle some examples of weaving (see Plate 14). A sequence of pen and ink illustrations can explain the process of making an embroidery stitch better than a page of written explanations (study the illustrations used in Chapters 2 and 3). A photograph of Eero Saarinen's arch in St. Louis, "Gateway to the West" (see Figure 63), will introduce children to an important American architectural monument. Information is also communicated when a picture introduces a child to an emotional feeling or heightens a feeling that already exists. The painting by the American Indian painter Blackbear Bosin (see Figure B) shows the great fear of fire that all animals feel.

FIGURE 63 Eero Saarinen, "Gateway to the West." Courtesy, St. Louis Regional Commerce and Growth Association

Our society is powerfully visual, but because we are so bombarded with images, we often see only a very small part of what is there. We defend ourselves against too much of anything by mentally ignoring it. The alternative would be to have a nervous breakdown. Your task, however, is to put to good use whatever you can find that is useful for teaching art. The first step is to unchain yourself from the defense of not seeing, so you can learn to enjoy looking for pictures that will help you in your teaching. All this takes practice, but it is enjoyable from the beginning; and it gradually opens up vistas of knowing that you did not realize existed. What follows is an invitation to join in this expansion of your visual self and at the same time to prepare yourself better as an artist and as an educator of children.

REPRODUCTIONS   A reproduction is a printed picture of a painting, drawing, engraving, or lithograph. It is usually smaller than the original art work. Some are almost identical to the originals and are correspondingly expensive. Large reproductions are well worth framing and hanging on walls in classrooms, school corridors, and cafeterias, and of course your own home. They are invaluable in teaching art because students become familiar with good art works in the best way possible—by living with them. Since people tend to "tune out" images they see continually, good teaching requires that children's attention be directed at pictures for purposes that apply to specific instructional needs. It may be that you want the class to use paint thickly or brightly and the reproduction shows this. Or you may want the children to talk about how artists show distance in pictures. This can also be illustrated by a reproduction.

A collection of good reproductions either framed or stored in a folder can thus be most useful. Picture resources of this kind are also what PTA and PTO groups can often be persuaded to buy for the school.

Less expensive postcard-size reproductions can be purchased in museum stores and bookstores and serve the same purposes. These small reproductions are sometimes printed in color and sometimes in black and white. Reproductions are also to be found in magazines and art books. Many of us have been brought up to believe that it is wrong to destroy or deface magazines, so we periodically bundle them up for permanent storage in basements. Or we banish books to bookshelves. We don't destroy them. What we do is worse: we never use them. Many magazines from time to time have articles on artists and usually show reproductions of several of their works. Certain magazines specialize in the visual arts.

Take courage! If you know what pictures you need for your teaching, cut the relevant pictures out and keep them at school where they can be made useful. No one would suggest dismembering an excellent art book—a book can be a thing of beauty in its own right—but if you visit a second-hand bookstore, you will frequently discover adequate art books that may be purchased for a modest price. (Publishers and printers may sometimes be a source of loose proofs.) Cut the pictures out that could be used in class and throw the rest away. Alternatively, if the book is really more useful in one piece, add it to your classroom art library. The only problem with pictures in books is that they are not usually in the sequence you want them in for teaching. Also, there are often so many things of interest in an art book that children—and you too—end up spending valuable class time just turning pages and enjoying the pictures.

PHOTOGRAPHS Photographs are so varied and plentiful that the problem lies in knowing where to look first. Books and magazines are good sources if you don't mind cutting them out. Other sources include discards from family albums and out-of-date shots taken by local newspaper photographers. The secret is to decide in advance what you need and focus your attention on that. If you also hang a little loose, you will not miss those gems that only appear by chance; but at least you will have direction in your search. When you find what you need, you will feel good; and when you discover something unexpectedly, you will feel elated.

As you pick out photographs, constantly try to put yourself in the place of the children. Researchers tell us that children's aesthetic preferences are not like those of well-educated adults, so as you search for suitable photographs, give some thought to the images most likely to be enjoyed by children. They will then learn more easily what you have in mind. If at the present time you find this advice confusing, don't be overly concerned. All you need do is watch the children's response to the pictures you use, and you will rapidly develop a sense of what is appropriate. The natural curiosity of children can even be harnessed to help you in making a collection of photographs. You will be amazed at what they will unearth if given clear directions and if suitably motivated. Such activities can often become learning experiences in their own right if carefully thought through in advance.

Photographs are taken of all kinds of objects and events. Famous buildings are photographed regularly, and you are sure to have a need for such photographs in your teaching. Examples of industrial design, such as automobiles or airplanes, are often photographed, and these will also be useful. You may want to collect photographs just because they are excellent examples of photography; and you will want your class to learn to enjoy good photography as much as you will want them to enjoy good paintings.

On the other hand, you will need to make available pictures of different objects just to provide children with information about their appearances. Such a collection could include a French horn, a motorcycle, a racehorse, a thundercloud, a spaceship, a shark, a camel, and so on (see Figures 64 and 65). No one can ever know enough about the way different objects look, so if you are to assist children to develop an understanding of them, you need to be able to see them; and a photograph is the next best thing to having the real object to study.

EXAMPLES OF ART AND DESIGN   Mothers periodically throw away drawers full of old clothes. Drygoods merchants sweep out unsalable ends

FIGURE 64   Photo of a French horn

FIGURE 65 A Kawasaki motorcycle, photo by Len Peak

from bolts of cloth. Decorators destroy wallpaper samples when new lines are introduced. Gifts are wrapped in decorative papers which are then thrown out with the trash. Travel agents display lush posters to invite people to travel. This list could go on and on; but the point is that actual examples of potentially useful art and design can be found wherever you live. They can be used to enhance your teaching; and in most instances will cost nothing at all.

CHILDREN'S ART WALLS The usual product of an elementary art lesson is a painting or drawing or similar piece of work. Much of this work is eagerly taken home and comes to a final resting place on the door of the family refrigerator. But you may only have to ask for it to be left behind, or make a call to a parent for it to be returned. You can thus begin assembling one of your most important collections of pictures. Photographs have their uses in teaching art, and so do reproductions of work by professional artists, but the most direct visual reference for learning in art is a successful piece of work done by another child. Any fears that children will copy what they are shown can be quickly dispelled. Unless coerced by you or unnaturally repressed, children will rarely be satisfied by copying something done by another child. They may begin by copying but will soon introduce their own modifications. If this possibility worries you, then collect varied lesson products to show future classes. The more diverse the interpretations of a given lesson, the less will be the likelihood of copying.

ILLUSTRATIONS AND DIAGRAMS You can demonstrate repeatedly how to mix plaster or how to do lettering, but you will discover that explanatory drawings and diagrams will also be very useful. Modern photocopying makes the task of collecting this kind of information very simple, and items can be enlarged or reduced to whatever size you need. Alternatively, you may want to trace an item or make your own freehand drawings. The key to any visual information of this kind is clearness. Photographs may show everything with perfect realism and yet not be nearly as easy for a beginner to understand as a line drawing. As you become experienced as a teacher you will be able to judge the kinds of visuals to use for the best results. For now, the task is simply to realize that illustrations and diagrams can be very useful. You might also prepare some samples of your own.

*SLIDES** While a great many important works of art are available as 2″ × 2″ slides, the typical elementary school budget does not permit extensive purchases; although as suggested before, you may be able to interest the PTA and PTO in sponsoring the purchase of the slides you need. A word of caution is due, however. If you plan on purchasing a set of slides, have it sent on approval first, to be sure that the slides are all usable in your program. It is one thing to have a comprehensive collection purchased for the school; it is quite another to have developed skill in using it. Sometimes schools or school districts have cameras and copystands, in which case you can make slides from illustrations in books for the price of the film and processing. The families of some of your children make another good source for slides—as with photographs. A holiday slide may not flatter Aunt Molly and yet may be an excellent illustration of how overlapping in pictures conveys a sense of distance.

A problem with using slides in the classroom is that the room usually has to be darkened for them to be seen properly. For small group presentations, however, the inside walls of a large cardboard box can be lined with black paper and the bottom lined with white paper. When tipped on its side, this becomes a satisfactory hooded screen and the rest of the room can remain fully illuminated (see Figure 66).

The word "slide" is also used for the familiar overhead transparency. Slides of this kind usually are made for specific learning tasks. Very few are prepared for teaching art so you will probably have to make your own. The nice thing about overhead slides is that you do not have to darken a room to show them, and you can arrange and rearrange them more easily than is possible with a tray of 2″ × 2″ slides.

FILMSTRIPS† Filmstrips, as their name implies, cannot be rearranged; the sequence is fixed. A number are suitable for elementary art teaching. If a topic suits your needs, especially if it has a synchronized sound track, then a filmstrip can be very useful. In some cases, a filmstrip is of no use to you in its

_____* A list of slide sources suitable for elementary art is given at the end of the chapter.
_____† A list of filmstrip sources suitable for elementary art is given at the end of the chapter.

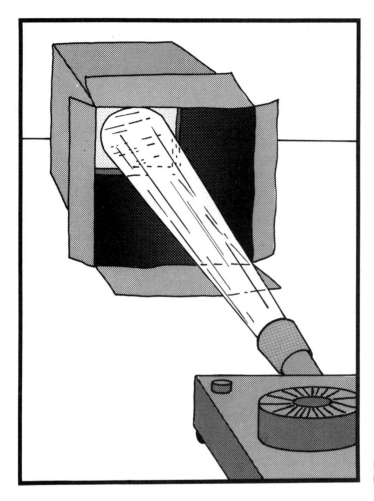

FIGURE 66 Projecting a slide into a lined cardboard box

published form. The best thing to do then is to cut all the frames apart and put them into plastic or cardboard mounts as slides. People often experience the same feeling at the thought of doing this as they do at the prospect of cutting up a book for the pictures. And yet, if this inhibition can be overcome, you may develop a much more serviceable set of visual resources than otherwise. Damaged filmstrips are excellent candidates for this kind of treatment.

MOVIES, TELEVISION, AND VIDEOTAPE Immensely rich visual resources exist in these media, especially in film. If a school district has a Learning Resources Center, you will be able to discover what exists for art and order it through the Center. And some organizations transmit televised classes, sometimes in art. Particularly good television programs can be played into your classroom and even recorded for use later when you need them, if videotaping equipment is available. And since almost all children watch television, commercial and public television is a continuing point of reference for information and an excellent source for motivation.

While television commercials may not possess much in the way of desirable content for teaching, numbers of them are technically and artistically very good. If you can find a television station in your area that will give you outdated commercials for use in school, you will have a good source for the study of the way motion pictures are made, and even ideas to stimulate children in art lessons. Since television films are played on 16 mm projectors, all you need is a typical school movie projector to show your discarded commercials, and even to splice sections of different films together to make new and often humorous movies of your own.

Picture
Collecting
Assignments

1. Study all the color plates in this book and decide which ones would help children most as they prepare to paint a picture that is to convey a sense of excitement or adventure.

2. Select four pieces of art you have done (from Chapters 2 and 3 or elsewhere) and explain how each of them could be helpful for teaching art.

OBJECTS TO SEE AND FEEL

Pictures are important partners with words in the art program, but objects are also important. Children draw and paint objects on paper, but the original objects themselves are solid. While reproductions and photographs can be very useful, they are flat and the information they contain is not nearly as complete as that derived from studying the real things. For example, a collection of different kinds of rocks aids the teaching of art as much as of science, in that children can experience various surface characteristics and colorations by feeling them as well as by seeing them. This information can be applied to the improvement of drawing skills, to modeling in clay, and to color mixing. Objects exist everywhere in classrooms. Rooms are furnished with chairs, tables, desks, and wash basins. Children's attention can be directed at the edges of tables so they can study what happens to light and shadow on surfaces that are at right angles. A picture of a chair can help in understanding how a chair is constructed, but feeling the parts of a real one is better still. You may want to collect objects for your room where the shapes will be useful for one lesson sequence while the textures and colors will be useful on other occasions. Such a collection might include a bicycle, an old hat, a pair of roller skates, large sea shells, pine cones, dress-maker's dummies, an umbrella—and even live turtles, hamsters, and plants. Objects—especially bigger ones—do not exist by themselves in a classroom, however. They stand on floors, are pushed against walls, and hang from ceilings. All of them have a place in a room. Some of them are designed to be moved while others are fixed. The child who is doing the looking may sit or stand normally and the room will look one way. But, if the same child lies on the floor and looks at the ceiling, she will be amazed at how different the same tables, sinks, and light fixtures appear and how much more there is to see. A room, then, is a small environment that in addition to people contains furniture, equipment, and perhaps a special art collection. It is a rich resource for teaching art. The same is true of the school in general and also the views to be seen through the windows.

NATURAL AND MAN-MADE OBJECTS Different kinds of objects can be used to help teach art. A vase is man-made. The flowers in it may be natural or synthetic. Both usually go together very well. They improve the places we live in, and they provide information to students about the flexibility of flower petals and the rigidity of the glazed surfaces of vases. Children can hold a vase of flowers—or each flower singly—and explore as much with their hands as they can with their eyes. You may bring to school some large conch shells or smoothly worn pebbles that you collected while on vacation. The children can feel the glass mouth and the rough-textured exterior of the shell but also listen to the rushing "sea" sound inside it. If your school is in a desert area, you may want to display a bleached skull of a cow or a cactus in bloom (not to touch); or just because the school is in the desert you may want to grow plants that live in more temperate areas. All of these objects provide ideas and information for particular art assignments and also mental images to draw upon when solving future art problems.

Man-made objects are as interesting to see and touch as natural ones. The carburetor from an automobile (thoroughly cleaned), or a mechanical clock with its mechanism exposed, or an old camera with its back removed can be valuable subjects of study—either in one piece or in many pieces. The list can be expanded to include old radios, telephones, outboard engines, and similar items that are more fascinating for some children to draw and model than natural objects. Originals and reproductions of works of art and design are special kinds of man-made objects and include old but well-designed household appliances and even model replicas of classic cars. Good pottery reproductions of ancient Mexican art can be purchased at modest prices. Miniatures of large pieces of sculpture and of famous buildings are often for sale in museums. A local architect may even allow the model of a building to be brought to class once the building has been constructed. A local sculptor or—if you are very lucky, the school's artist-in-residence—might be equally ready for examples of her work to be on temporary display and also to be handled (as long as hands are more or less clean). Members of the local high school orchestra can be invited to visit so that the children may actually feel the shiny spirals of a French horn or the glossy boxiness of a cello. Rugs and soft sculpture can all be made a part of an ever-changing program of direct physical experiences that is integrated with the specific instructional objectives to be accomplished in the art program.

The list of possibilities is much more extensive than you might at first believe. To what has already been mentioned can be added articles of interesting clothing, costume jewelry, shoes, suitcases, and other similar items of a more personal kind, not to mention the children themselves. Children with curly hair will never know what straight hair feels like unless they can touch it and vice versa. The children could also be encouraged to experience, through their father or grandfather, the feeling of wrinkled cheeks, a roughly bearded chin, or a smooth bald head. As a nation we are often inhibited when it comes to bodily involvements such as those described; but if you teach in a school where such acts are not eyed suspiciously, you will provide experiences that can have a profound effect, for example, on how the portrait of an older person might be drawn or painted; and this develops understandings of a kind that could remain with the children throughout their lives.

A similar kind of learning experience is possible from handling a pet cat (nonscratching), a dog (friendly), a rabbit, or a turtle that one of the children might bring to class. Our social attitudes are usually as open toward handling animals as they are closed when it comes to handling other people; and while you may deplore this, it is a fact to be lived with if you hope to be a successful teacher. Children's pets provide an excellent source for tactile information that can be applied to art lessons. They can be supplemented by more exotic animals if a nearby zoo will cooperate. An alternative that loses in vitality but is likely to be less hazardous is to find a friendly taxidermist who may have some small stuffed animals such as owls, snakes, or lynxes for the children to handle. This kind of collection is best begun now—if only in a limited way—and not deferred until you find a job. If you wait until then you will probably be too immersed in work to ever get around to doing it.

Your classroom will permit only a certain number of objects to be displayed at any one time. Others can be kept in a storeroom, brought from home, or scheduled from their owners for a stay of a limited duration.

| Object Collecting Assignment | Since objects are bulky to carry around, make a list of at least fifty man-made and fifty natural objects that could be collected for use in teaching art. In each instance, make a brief note of how it could be used. |

ORGANIZING VISUAL INFORMATION FOR TEACHING

People are often very good at collecting materials but very poor at finding things in their collections when they need them. It is no help to Nick if he is looking for a picture of an African chief to draw, and you know you have one in your picture collection of 500 items—somewhere, that is. Hand in hand with the task of collecting, then, goes the equally important task of organizing the collection so that it is easy to use. Think of a library. A collection of books is not very useful unless you have a catalogue to help you find what you want. The pity is that picture libraries don't exist in the way book libraries do, so you have to be your own organizer.

The easiest kind of collection to maintain is one of flat things like pictures, photographs, and children's art. Because they are flat, they take up very little space and can be stored in boxes or file drawers. Three-dimensional objects are not nearly as easy to store, and consequently the number of such items you will collect is likely to be limited. You may even be able to remember all the three-dimensional items in your collection and not need a system for retrieval. But once the collection of flat images increases, you need a system to help you make use of it efficiently.

FILING BY LESSON   The simplest way to collect useful pictorial information for teaching art is by individual lessons. You decide on the images that go with a lesson and put them all together. The lesson, the images, and the folder are all given the same number or title and can be stored in a file drawer or similar container. If any slides are to be used with a lesson, they are best kept in clear plastic sheets that contain twenty small pockets for slides. Alternatively, slides may be numbered to correspond with lessons and stored in a slide box. References to filmstrips, books, outsize prints, and other bulky items should be noted in the lesson and identified by number; but the items themselves will need to be numbered and stored in some accessible place.

Such a system can mean that your entire art program consists of a series of file folders, each of which includes all the verbal and visual information needed for every lesson. A master list referring briefly to each lesson will provide you with a method of finding any lesson when you want it. This list can be organized by type of art lesson, alphabetically, or by a year-long sequence (see Figure 67).

The limitation of this system is that each of the pictures has only one use. A photograph of a basketball player in the act of scoring a goal will belong to one lesson only—probably one having to do with action in sports. For lessons on drawing the proportions of the human body, another picture

FIGURE 67   Filing pictures by lessons

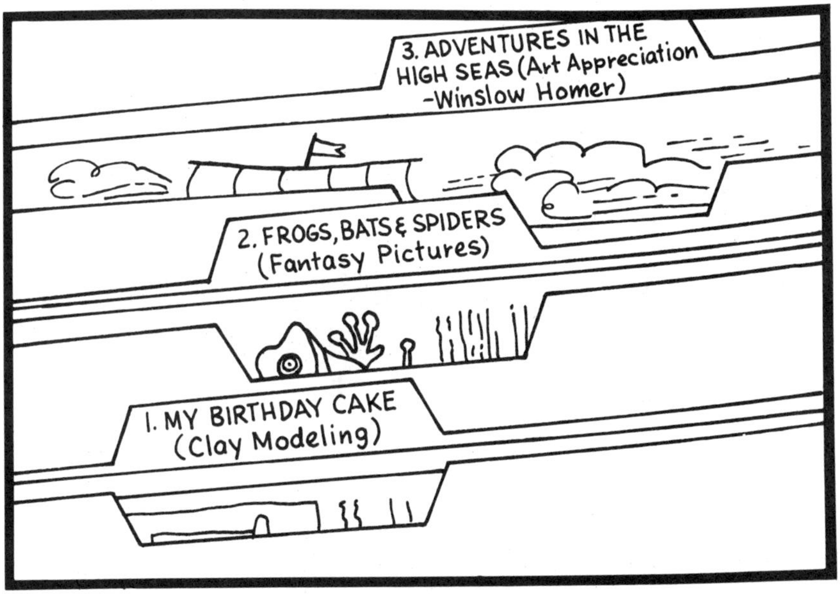

97

will have to be found, even though the basketball photograph might serve the purpose very well. This system of filing is thus easy to build and to use, but it is not as flexible as other systems; and such collections can take up considerable space in a file drawer because of the need for many separate examples.

FILING BY TOPIC Photographs and reproductions can be filed according to topics you know will be useful in your art program. Instead of filing pictures with their corresponding lessons, you file them under headings such as birds, skyscrapers, jewelry, airplanes, and so on. When children need to understand what a particular object looks like, you or the children can go to the files and search for a picture under the most suitable title. The choice of titles is affected by the lesson material included in the art program. For example, if the instruction emphasizes individuality in drawing, the collection will include drawings done by artists with very different styles. Eventually, when you have taught the program for a year or so, you will also have added some highly individual examples of children's drawings.

The kinds of pictures tend to follow the choices of lesson topics, but the collection can also influence the choices of lessons. For instance, if the only pictures you can find on landscape painting are by British and French artists, this could lead you to teach more about British and French art than you had originally intended. If, however, you do not want this emphasis to continue, you may deliberately add pictures on Oriental landscape painting.

A collection of visuals like this can be kept in a box or file drawer and will require that you write self-explanatory headings on the file folder tabs (see Figure 68). Alphabetical arrangements are probably best. As parts of the

FIGURE 68   Filing pictures by object category

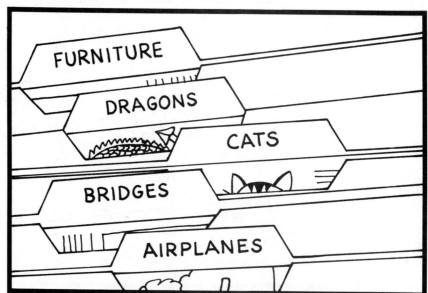

collection expand, you may consider subdividing topics to avoid confusion and time wasted in searching for particular images. For example, if your collection of pictures of household pets becomes very large, you may want to break it into more manageable parts under such sub-headings as dogs, cats, turtles, canaries, etc.

FILING BY NUMBER   By far the most flexible system of storing visual information is one where you number the pictures as you collect them. As each piece is collected, you decide what useful part it can play in your art program. What objective does a picture of a famous building fit in with? The new East wing of the National Gallery of Art in Washington, D.C., for instance, is an example of modern architecture (see Figure 69). If you had objectives in certain lessons of your program that had to do with modern buildings, then this picture might be useful. Elsewhere in your program you might have a drawing assignment where the children had to show how the different sides of a building are shaded differently. Still another possibility might be in a lesson in which the children learn about constructing buildings having large expanses of flat masonry and build a tower out of clay slabs. The same picture of the National Gallery could be used equally well in all three cases. All that would be necessary is for the number of the picture to be written on 3″ × 5″ file cards that had titles such as Modern Architecture; Light Falling on Flat-sided Shapes; and Building Construction: Stone Walls (see Figure 70).

FIGURE 69   A view of the exterior, East Building, National Gallery of Art, Washington, D.C. Architect: I. M. Pei Associates

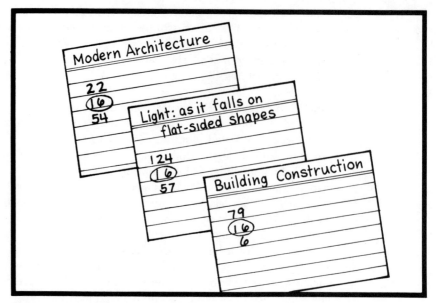

FIGURE 70   Filing by art content

This system is useful for helping teachers select pictures that illustrate particular objectives or lessons. Older elementary children can be taught to use it themselves. It is more immediately useful than filing by topic and it makes better use of pictures than filing by lesson; but it is more complicated for children to use. No one way is perfect. What you need to do while still in college, however, is to begin a collection of visuals following one of these systems. If what you do now is not suited to the teaching situation you eventually find yourself in, the collection will not be so large that you cannot reorganize it fairly easily.

For most of this work, the only tools needed are keen eyes and sharp scissors. But you must know what you are looking for. When an item has been located and cut out it should immediately be put into one of the filing systems. Otherwise you will lose it, or forget why you chose it. An explanation of how to make and preserve visuals appears in the next section of the chapter.

Organizing Assignments

1. Make three sample visual files to correspond with the three systems of filing: by lesson; by topic; and by number. Each collection is to consist of ten colored pictures. Develop a statement from your own experience and also the written material in this section to explain the good and bad points of each.

2. Select one system of filing from the three described and make a collection of at least thirty items, together with an appropriate system of retrieval for the effective use of those pictures.

Here are some of the simplest possible ways of preparing your own visuals. Such work is an educational specialty in its own right, and if you need additional assistance, most school districts employ skilled people who will be pleased to help you. If you master the described techniques here, however, you will be able to satisfy most of your classroom needs.

DRAWING YOUR OWN ILLUSTRATIONS If you can draw and paint some of your own visuals freehand, then do so. If not, then use one of several drawing aids to help you. Tracing paper, ditto-master, carbon paper, as well as the use of opaque and overhead projectors are useful when you want to transfer an image from an original to a sheet of paper and perhaps duplicate copies so all the class can have one. Drawings on paper can also be transferred to acetate for use as transparencies with an overhead projector. Photomechanical methods have revolutionized the task of reproducing pictures; but they will not be discussed here. Where a school has such a machine, you will soon discover how to operate it. But most teachers do not have free access to this kind of equipment and need to know how to prepare visuals using equipment that is almost certain to be available.

TRACING Tracing paper can be placed over an image and a drawing made on it of the parts of the underneath shape that are wanted. The tracing paper is turned over and the lines redrawn on the underside with a soft black pencil. The process is completed by turning the tracing paper over and placing it on a sheet of clean white paper. The original lines are then re-drawn with a sharp pencil. The black lines on the underside will transfer to the clean paper and should now only need darkening for the process to be complete (see Figure 71).

Tracing can also be done with typists carbon paper. Carbon paper is placed *face down* on the clean paper and the picture is clipped in place on top. All that is then needed is to trace the lines on the original picture and they will transfer to the clean sheet of paper. This process is quick and easy. Problems arise with carbon paper, however, if you want to erase the carbon line for any reason or if it is important for the traced image not to smudge. Alternatively, most schools have spirit duplicators. You follow the same process with a ditto stencil as you did with regular carbon paper. The traced image can then be duplicated so each child in the class can have a copy. A problem can arise when tracing in the last two ways in that you have to press firmly. It should be done, therefore, only when the picture to be copied is on thin paper and not of great value.

GRIDS This procedure requires that you mark the picture you want to copy into squares. If the picture is too valuable for marks to be put on it, then draw the grid of squares on a piece of transparent acetate and clip it to the picture. Next, mark out a sheet of paper into the same number of squares as on the original picture. If you want a reduction then the squares will be smaller than on the original. If you want an enlargement, they will be bigger.

1. Draw a picture onto tracing paper.

2. Re-draw the picture on the back of the tracing paper.

3. Draw on the front of the tracing paper again with clean paper underneath.

FIGURE 71 Tracing

The task is then to draw that part in each square on the paper which appears in the corresponding square in the original picture. The result will give you the desired enlargement or reduction (see Figure 72).

PROJECTIONS   The usual problem with visual information in books is that it is too small to be seen by all the class at one time. And you may not want to go to the trouble of duplicating it for every child. An effective way of making large reproductions of such items that will communicate with an entire class, especially line drawings, is to use an opaque projector. The image is placed in the projector and projected on to a large sheet of white paper or cardboard that has been pinned to the wall. All you do, then, is to draw over the lines as they appear on the paper with a pencil, felt marker, brush, or crayon. Crayons or paints can then be used to add color if needed.

PRESERVING VISUALS   Pages from magazines are flimsy and easily damaged. These and other kinds of visuals can be protected best by mounting them on paper or cardboard. Paper is less bulky and for that reason is generally to be preferred over cardboard, especially if you have a large collection. On the other hand, cardboard is best if children will be handling the visuals regularly. In both instances, mount the pictures on standard-sized sheets and allow for a border all the way round. One size of sheet will prevent smaller sheets from slipping down and being damaged. A border allows for corners to be damaged without affecting the pictures: pictures can often be remounted more easily than replaced.

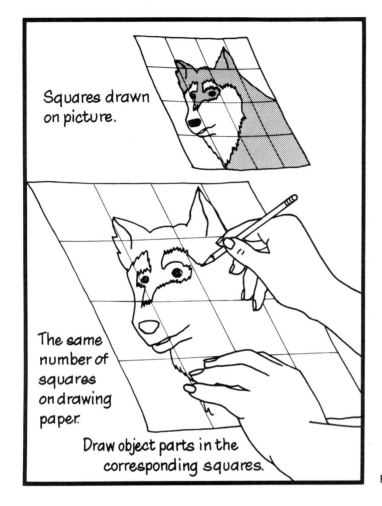

Squares drawn on picture.

The same number of squares on drawing paper.

Draw object parts in the corresponding squares.

FIGURE 72 Using a grid

PASTE AND RUBBER CEMENT The most common school adhesive is paste. Wheat paste and white glue (Elmer's) tend to wet visuals and make them wrinkle, so library paste or rubber cement is often preferred. Library paste is white and has the consistency of butter. When vigorously brushed while in the container, it liquifies. It may also be thinned with warm water.

The procedure for mounting pasted visuals is as follows: (1) Turn the picture face down on a sheet of clean newspaper. (2) Brush paste on to the back of the picture. The brush should have fairly stiff bristles and the strokes should begin near the center of the paper and extend outwards over the edge of the picture and on to the newpaper. Ensure that the paste reaches all the corners of the picture. The paste on the picture should be free from lumps and blobs of paste. (3) Lift the picture carefully and place it in the desired position face upwards on a sheet of paper or cardboard and gently smooth it down to ensure contact. (4) Allow the mounted picture to dry thoroughly by placing it between sheets of dry absorbent paper under gentle pressure. The paper having direct contact with the face of the picture should not have any printing on it that might soil the picture (see Figure 73).

The procedure when using rubber cement is different from paste in that the cement is applied both to the picture and to the paper on which the picture is to be attached. Both are allowed to dry before they are joined. Because of this, rubber cement does not cause any wrinkling. Rubber cement is a contact adhesive, however, so you may want to take the precaution of placing two sheets of waxed kitchen paper between the picture and the paper until the positioning is correct. Then one sheet of wax paper is rolled away to permit the two cemented surfaces to adhere. The second sheet of wax paper is then removed.

Since rubber cement dries very rapidly when exposed to air, be sure that it will flow easily before applying it. Add rubber cement thinner (solvent) to bring it to the proper consistency. Also, as you apply cement be sure to avoid brushing over areas that are not quite dry, since that creates rough spots that can leave unsightly marks on the finished work.

DRY MOUNTING   Many schools have dry-mounting presses and if not an electric iron is a satisfactory substitute. Dry mounting is an excellent method for preserving visuals. It is a heat process, however, so do not try to mount original crayon art or any similar heat-sensitive material this way.

The process is as follows: cut a piece of permanent dry mounting tissue the same size or slightly larger than the picture you want to mount; lay the picture face down and fix the tissue in several places with a tacking iron or an electric iron that is heated to the point where moisture boils on contact. Trim the tissue exactly to the size of the picture. Place the picture on the mounting

FIGURE 73   Mounting a picture

1. Paste the back of a picture.

2. Place the picture onto a sheet of paper and smooth it down.

1. Fix tissue with a tacking iron. **2. Insert into a dry mounting press.**

FIGURE 74   Dry mounting

surface and fix the tissue in place to the mounting surface with a tacking iron. Cover the surface of the picture with a sheet of clean paper when you have checked that it is perfectly clean. When the press has heated to 225°F, insert the picture and the attached mount, for the period of time recommended by the manufacturers (see Figure 74). In the event that the school does not possess a press, an electric iron can be used in a continuous spiral motion working outward from the center. When the process is complete, the mounted item should be allowed to cool under pressure to prevent buckling.

STORAGE   Your collection of visuals will be a valuable art teaching resource and should be suitably protected. If you choose a size of sheet that corresponds with a notebook and a conventional letter-size file drawer ($8\frac{1}{2}''$ × 11''), you will have no difficulty in finding a suitable storage. On the other hand, that size will probably be too small for art teaching. At grocery and liquor stores, however, you will almost certainly find cartons that will take a larger sized visual. If all else fails, go to an appliance or furniture store for a large carton. With careful cutting and taping you can adjust a container to fit any particular needs. In most instances, you will want to cover the box to obliterate any printing.

Making and Preserving Assignments

1. Draw an enlargement of a picture or diagram you could use for an art lesson using the grid technique. The finished work should be large enough to be easily visible from all parts of a typical classroom.

2. Mount a picture using rubber cement in the way described in this section.

LETTERING

Lettering is an indispensable skill in teaching and is perhaps of greater importance for art than for other subjects, because art is expected to look attractive. In some situations, you may even want to have children learn to do lettering, although lettering is usually better suited to secondary art teaching. The purpose of this final section on visual resources, however, is to enable you to communicate with your classes quickly, legibly, and attractively. When mastered, lettering has numerous applications in your art program, such as identifying items in your collection of visuals, putting names and titles on displayed art work, and making lists of art objectives that children are to remember. It is worth adding that nothing spoils a display of art work more completely than poor lettering.

Professional-looking lettering can be made using commercially produced stencils or transferring pre-printed letters to paper with a rubbing action (often referred to as press-type), but these methods are slow and expensive. The lettering described here is both inexpensive and quick to do, and while it may lack a slick professional finish, it is much more serviceable for the everyday needs of a busy classroom teacher.

Letters made with a single stroke are the best for general classroom use. A broad felt pen with a chisel-shaped point is satisfactory, although a steel lettering pen and India ink will give much better results. Both instruments are held so that the angle of the thinnest line is held constant between 30° and 60°, depending on whether you want to have strong vertical strokes or horizontals and verticals of equal weight (see Figure 75). The

FIGURE 75   Lettering pens

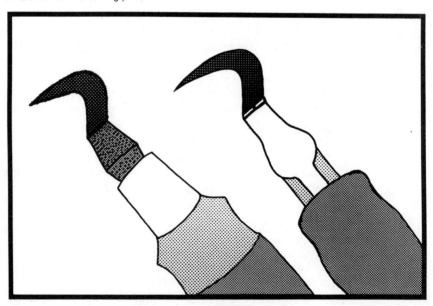

strokes are always begun at the point where the line is thinnest, and are pulled toward you. No lettering can be successful if you push the pen or marker away from you. When you use pen and ink, the results will be better if you work on a sloping surface to prevent the ink from flooding to the point of the pen.

The key to good lettering, once the instrument can be controlled, is to practice from an alphabet of well-formed letters. The one shown here (see Figure 76) is deliberately very simple. Beginners have a tendency to make letters decorative and in doing so to make them less legible. This model restricts you to the study of the basic structure. When that has been mastered, you may want to make your own modifications.

FIGURE 76   A simple single stroke alphabet

ABCDEFGHI
JKLMNOPQ
RSTUVWXYZ
abcdefghijklm
nopqrstuvwxyz
123456789

Before beginning to make letters, however, you are advised to master the basic strokes of lettering: the verticals, diagonals, and horizontals; and the two curves. After that, practice the capital letters and numerals. They are simpler to do than the lower case letters. When you feel ready to do some lettering of your own, select a fairly broad pen and find the best height for the pen point by making the most satisfactory letter S that you can. All the letters will then be that height. Also, decide on the distance separating one line of lettering from the next. No rule exists to say how far apart they should be, but beginners usually make them too close together. If in doubt, increase the space between lines more than seems necessary.

Lettering Assignments

1. *Name Tag.* Letter your own name, using the model alphabet. Do it first in all capital letters and then in initial caps and lower case.

2. *Reinforcement.* Select a set of objectives from a lesson in Appendix A of the Data Bank (pp. 214–249)—preferably one you plan to do yourself. Letter a sheet of paper with those objectives. The letters should be of a suitable size to be easily readable from anywhere in a typical classroom.

further art study

Minor, Ed, and Harvey R. Frye, *Techniques for Producing Instructional Media.* New York: McGraw-Hill, 1970. A practical, clearly illustrated text covering all forms of visual media. An excellent book for any teacher to have.

Shrank, Jeffrey. *The Seed Catalog: A Guide to Teaching/Learning Materials.* Boston, MA.: Beacon Press, 1974. A source book.

Wurman, Richard S. *Yellow Pages of Learning Resources.* Cambridge, Mass.: MIT Press, 1971. A source book.

Reproductions

Art Education, Inc., Blauvelt, N.Y. 10913. Sixty-four full color prints, with a manual to assist teachers in their use.

Shorewood Reproductions, Inc., 475 Tenth Avenue, New York, N.Y. 10018. Large but inexpensive reproductions of paintings.

University Prints, 15 Brattle Street, Harvard Square, Cambridge, Mass. 02138. Inexpensive post card reproductions in color and black and white.

Van Nostrand Reinhold, 450 West 33rd Street, New York, N.Y. 10001. Sets of high quality, sturdy reproductions of two and three dimensional objects organized around art concepts.

slides: each of the following offers a full collection from all periods

Americal Library Color Slide Collection, 222 West 23rd Street, New York, N.Y. 10011.

National Gallery of Art, Extension Service (free loan programs), Washington, D.C. 20565.

Prothmann Associates, Inc., 2795 Milburn Avenue, Baldwin, N.Y. 11510.

Sandak, Inc., 180 Harvard Avenue, Stanford, Conn. 06902

filmstrips

Hausman, Flora and **Jerome.** *Visual Sources of Learning.* Stanford, Conn.: Sandak. Famous art works and a teacher's manual that includes activities.

Mandlin, Dotty and **Harvey.** *Art World Series.* Revised edition. Glendale, CA.: Bowmar, 1977. A multimedia art program directed at awareness and expressiveness.

three-dimensional replicas

Alva Museum Replicas, 30–30 Northern Boulevard, Long Island City, N.Y. 11101.

Joseph W. Foraker Associates, Inc., 520 Speedwell Avenue, Dayton Building, Suite 116, Morris Plains, N.J. 07950.

part

Two

prism:
a guide to
preparing
art lessons

Theory often comes first in textbooks on the assumption that a person must understand what to do and why it should be done before doing it. But in this book the more practical sections have been placed at each end and the more theoretical material is sandwiched in the middle.

The guidelines presented in the following chapters provide the key to successful art teaching. Each topic is related to the others. The sequence of *Purposes, Readiness, Instructional objectives, Strategies,* and *Measurement* follows logically, and yet no particular sequence is actually required. The word PRISM was chosen deliberately, however, to help you remember each of the different parts of the task of teaching art. No one, for example, should ever teach who cannot explain why a subject is important for people to learn; so Chapter 5 is appropriately placed first. Since numerous points of view exist about the place of art in the elementary curriculum, you should develop your own position and be prepared to defend it when challenged. Readiness governs what children are capable of learning; but since children are full of surprises, you can again expect your initial position to modify with experience.

The last three topics account for most of the daily events that will occur in the classroom. First, your choice of instructional objectives determines what children will be expected to learn; and since this is a complex topic for people who are not specially trained in art, objectives are broken down into three categories—Seeing, Knowing, and Doing—to help you remember them. Chapter 8 describes some of the more useful ways of communicating art objectives to children. While much of art teaching calls for reasoned intelligence and knowledge, strategies of teaching depend for success on the quality of a teacher's imagination. The measurement of achievement comes last; but since the results of learning affect what needs to be taught next, it also marks a new beginning to the cycle of instruction.

The process outlined in Part II is intended to help you remember the parts of art lessons. However, the sequence followed by the letters that spell PRISM does not describe the interrelatedness of the parts as children learn art or as teachers teach it. The sequence of stages does not have to follow the order in which the parts are presented here, yet at first you will probably find this sequence useful. When you are more experienced, you will probably adopt an approach that suits your own personal needs. But every part of an art lesson will always have to be presented somewhere in all your teaching.

PLATE 1
Thomas Hart Benton, "Arts of the West." Courtesy, New Britain Museum of American Art, Harriet Russell Stanley Fund.

PLATE 2
Joseph Stella, "Battle of Lights, Coney Island." Courtesy, Yale University Art Gallery. Gift of Collection Société Anonyme.

PLATE 3
Varnette Honeywood, "Gossip in the Sanctuary." Courtesy, Taylor Art Gallery, North
Carolina Agricultural and Technical State University.

PLATE 4
Frank Stella, "Singerli Variation IV."
From the Collection of Mr. and Mrs.
Burton Tremaine, Meriden,
Connecticut.

PLATE 5
Abraham Rattner, "Place of Darkness." Oil. Courtesy, Indiana University Art Museum.

PLATE 6

William Michael Harnett, "After the Hunt, 1885." Oil on canvas. Courtesy, The Fine Arts Museum of San Francisco. Gift of H.K.S. Williams to the Mildred Anna Williams Collection.

PLATE 7
Norman Laliberté, "Apocalypse." Oil pastel. Courtesy of the artist.

PLATE 8
Barbara Kensler, "Oregon #2."
Stitchery and appliqué. Courtesy of the artist.

PLATE 9
Primary girl, Austria. Wax crayon. "My Friend."

PLATE 10
Primary boy, New York City. Chalk. "New York."

PLATE 11
Intermediate boy, Hong Kong. Crayon
etching. "Botanical Garden."
Courtesy, International Collection of
Child Art, Ewing Museum of Nations,
Illinois State University.

PLATE 12
Primary girl, New York City. Tempera.
"My Family."

PLATE 13
Primary girl, University City, Missouri. Watercolor. "Flowers."

PLATE 14
Intermediate girl, Indianapolis, Indiana. Weaving.

p = purposes

why art is important in the elementary school

All thoughtful statements about educational goals include some reference to the need for art. And yet, while teachers and parents quite rightly have no doubts in their minds about the importance of reading and mathematics, they are not nearly as clear about the importance of art. The predicament of art is that while it is likely to be included among the desirable goals for elementary education, only rarely are convincing explanations given for the reasons why it is worth including; and even less is said about how those goals might be achieved. As a consequence, art instruction is not given a high priority in most elementary schools. And even where it is a regular part of the program, teachers often experience difficulty when asked to give reasons for its importance.

Imagine for a moment that an aggressive parent at a well-attended PTA meeting were to ask you to explain how instruction in art might benefit her child. Could you provide a convincing answer? Such an event may never occur, but if it does and you have thought the answer through in advance, you will be better able to communicate it to parents and others. The ones who benefit most of all from this thinking, however, will be you and the children you teach. If you have a clear idea of the value of art in education, you will teach it better and the children in your charge will experience the added benefit of being exposed to your sense of conviction that art is a worthwhile subject of study.

But where should you begin? Your personal experience with art may suggest that a few children are naturally talented but that most are not. And yet if you have been around children very much, you will have noticed that almost all of them enjoy art, and any differences in talent do not seriously affect this enjoyment until later childhood. You may also have discovered that in all areas, children show different strengths. Some can read more efficiently than most. Others can run faster. And a number can draw better than most. In contrast, some children are much less capable than others in various subjects. However, we teach mathematics to all children, not because they are talented, but because we believe that all people need to be able to calculate in order to live satisfactory lives. The possession of basic writing skills can lead a person to become a professional writer; but few children will actually be poets, novelists, or journalists. Likewise, children should know some science and social studies to satisfy the needs of daily living, and not because they are preparing to be physicists or economists. This view of the basic character of human beings leads to the conclusion that all people are capable of some achievement in all areas of knowledge. The important emphasis in this view of people is not of their limitations, but of their possibilities for achievement, given a suitable opportunity to learn. Naturally, the specially gifted in art will excel, and eventually from that group will come the professionals. The highly gifted are always important, but they are few and far between. The fundamental task of public elementary schools is to serve all children as fully as possible; where all learn to advance their art knowledge and performance inasmuch as they advance in other school subjects.

Even if you now believe that all children are able to learn art, you may still be unsure of the ways in which art contributes to a child's education. One way of reaching an answer to this question is to study the two-pronged educational tradition we have inherited and show the relationship of both prongs for art instruction. One tradition supports the pursuit of knowledge for its own sake. The other is directed toward the achievement of knowledge that is useful in daily life. Some people interpret these two sets of purposes for education as opposed to each other, while others believe they are complementary.

The problem to be faced in this chapter is to determine where the educational contribution of art belongs, and more particularly, what your personal point of view is. For this reason, the topic is divided into sections that first of all introduce art education as a part of the need for individual development. This is followed by a statement outlining the social benefits of an art education. These statements are then followed by the views of professional educators and with a brief review of what actually happens in many schools. Lastly, you will be asked to prepare your own statement regarding the purposes of art in elementary education.

ART FOR INDIVIDUAL DEVELOPMENT

Americans believe that individual freedom is a basic human right. However freedom does not just happen. People have to be educated to know what freedom is and how to use it wisely. The first step toward individual freedom occurs through the sense of sight, hearing, touch, smell, and taste; with the sense of sight being the most important. Vision is thus one of the principle channels by which information of all kinds reaches the brain. Only when that information is gathered and interpreted can we have any knowledge of it.

Children, like all young animals, use every means at their disposal to explore their environments. They want to understand the world around them. It is not a luxury for them, but a necessity; and yet children think of it as exciting exploratory play. However, children differ from animals, in that this kind of behavior can continue and expand throughout life if it is nurtured. In fact, the greatest of human achievers are renowned for their efforts at continually exploring and searching for answers to problems—spending their lives, in effect, engaged in the kind of exploration that is best described as serious play.

If pleasure and play lie at the heart of human life and learning, then you would expect schools to strive for children to achieve highly in those areas. In spite of the evidence, that is not what typically happens. Schooling is often viewed as a humorless necessity; and the natural enjoyment that is apparent in art lessons is likely to be cited as evidence that art is a less substantial area of study than some others. Teachers who make use of children's artistic desires in their lessons are putting this natural tendency to use. Drawing, painting, and modeling are reflections of this irrepressible urge to explore; and through it children are not constrained in their development by the prior need to read or write or compute. However, art experiences are not confined simply to gathering visual information. They open the way to the development of the uniquely human aptitudes for creative imagination and expressions of feeling. These qualities are as necessary to fully developed human beings as are conventional academic subjects, if human accomplishments throughout history have any meaning. And as with all abilities, they develop most fully when systematically encouraged during the formative childhood years.

The structure of the brain, itself, gives added support to the importance of art in education. Recent research indicates that the two halves of the brain fulfill different intellectual functions.* The left side appears to perform primarily those tasks associated with the academic subject matter traditionally emphasized in school. The right half of the brain appears to specialize in intellectual behaviors we describe as creative. It also handles thinking about shapes and about objects in space. Thus, the right hemisphere seems to be responsible for those kinds of behaviors often described as artistic. Both hemispheres are linked, and the brain works as a single unit; but the different functions of each half are clearly apparent. While we do not yet know enough about the structure of the brain to make final statements regarding art education, a satisfactory education clearly involves developing the capabilities of the entire brain and not just part of it. And yet in practice this is all too often not done. Schools focus their efforts almost exclusively on left-brain functions, while right-brain intellectual powers are given only token encouragement. This has occurred because our educational tradition has disregarded ideas that were known and valued as long ago as ancient Greece.

_____* Information on this topic is developed in the Further Reading section at the end of this chapter (see Sagan, *The Dragons of Eden*).

Art is thus a way of learning, and some children learn better in one way of learning than in another. And if for no other reason than that, art has a well deserved place in the elementary curriculum. A nation may, of course, choose not to attempt the full development of children, but when the purposes of education are said to include the development of all intellectual powers, as they are in this country, then any disregard of art is dishonest.

Within this broad view of intelligence and education lies the need to realize that the art of children is not the same as the art of adults. Children's art is more an expression of a unique kind of developing intellect that shows itself during this important period of maturation. It is a particular form of thinking that derives primarily from the visual sense. Like language, art consists of symbols; that is, of shapes that have meaning; but unlike language and most other school subjects art involves organizing visual symbolism that does not follow a step by step sequence from beginning to end. All of a completed work of art is there to be seen at the same time. The philosopher Suzanne Langer (see Further Reading at the end of this chapter) separates art from most areas of study by using the words "discursive" for academic school subjects and "non-discursive" for art. Both are ways whereby children can know and express themselves and both are necessary if children are to have an adequate knowledge of the world around them and be able to use that knowledge. Both kinds of intellectual activity deserve equal attention. The highest level of achievement from this point of view is to be found in the ideas expressed by such people as psychologist and humanist, Abraham Maslow (see Further Reading, Wilson). As a consequence of his researches, Maslow concluded that fully developed people (educated, that is, in the full sense of the word) unite all the rational and emotional qualities they possess and live with greater intensity than is possible otherwise. Maslow described this enhanced human condition as "self-actualizing" and declared art education to be among the few areas in the school curriculum where such a sense of heightened awareness is likely to develop.

Art also satisfies that part of an individual's needs which recognizes the feeling of achievement. The simple fact of knowing that something is successful is important in the education of everyone. And achievement in art extends far beyond obedience to predetermined rules to a sense of personal worth that every child can experience. Human beings possess the unique power to be creative. It is an essential part of basic humanness, and for that reason it deserves to be nurtured. Seen from this perspective, art belongs in the curriculum because it promotes self improvement for its own sake—a person is not complete without it. Art is a form of serious play in which people manipulate art materials and make images. The result is a sense of well-being that has nothing to do with any practical or useful product—the activity is rewarding for its own sake and reinforces the importance of individual decisions. It is enjoyable. The popular belief which declares necessity to be the mother of invention, for example, is in fact the opposite of the truth. Inventions have always been the products of people at play, where the motivation lies much more in the process of doing something than in the achievement of the product itself. When people must attend only to what is necessary, they generally have little energy to spare for imaginative daydreaming. Great ideas came from the minds of the masters of slaves—and rarely from those who are slaves. And that is as true today as it ever was.

If people derive such satisfaction from purposeful self-stimulation, then an education that claims to help people realize their full potential should deliberately include such activities in the curriculum. And art is a natural subject for this kind of educational service in the elementary school. Reading, writing, and calculation are tool skills that develop important ways of thinking and also make other kinds of learning possible, and they must be learned before the kinds of exploratory play described above can occur in academic subject areas. However, these tool skills take time to learn and insofar as children are obliged to learn them first, they are forced to defer their exposure to exploratory play. And yet, children possess the need to develop all their aptitudes concurrently. The desire for purposeful play is present everywhere in their behavior; but, because of the social pressures that call for academic achievement, these important educational needs are all too often neglected—unless the school has a strong art program. Among school subjects art is unique in that on her first day in school a girl may behave toward the imaginative exploratory purposes of education in the same manner that a seasoned artist or mathematician would do.

If teachers hope to develop individuality to its fullest—and they regularly say that they do—they must direct their attention to organizing experiences that will lead children to that kind of achievement. Education happens by design—not by chance. And it never occurs by neglect. *If the qualities of imaginativeness, exploration, and a sense of individual self-worth are to flourish, then they must be cultivated.*

ART FOR THE BENEFIT OF SOCIETY

Dividing art education into individual and social purposes is useful for helping understand why the subject should be included in the elementary curriculum, but the two are by no means neatly separated. You will probably find it much easier to think of the art program serving the individual development of children than providing social benefit; just because art is a subject that focuses so heavily on individual decision-making. Some of the reasons for having art in the curriculum may clearly have underlying purposes designed to benefit society, and yet they are more likely to be learned by children for the personal pleasure they give. Moreover, the purposes of individual development in art may also have social benefits. Throughout history, aesthetic curiosity has been at the root of discoveries that have dramatically affected the way of life of people. Most minerals were first discovered and put to use as paint; their utilitarian properties were discovered much later. The cultivation of flowers for enjoyment came long before useful agriculture. The alloying of metals developed as an outgrowth of artists searching for better ways of making jewelry and sculpture.* Art for individual development has in it, therefore, the seeds of social benefits that cannot be anticipated, simply because discoveries are more likely to emerge as a result of aesthetic curiosity than as a result of deliberate attempts to be useful. The single-minded attention often given to academic tool skills may often blind teachers to the real reasons for having a usefully educated population. These reasons are essentially creative and aesthetic rather than practical and utilitarian, and yet they lead as much to practical ends as those which emphasize individual development alone.

In a more direct sense, art is useful for developing a child's pride of belonging to a particular social or ethnic group. Children can be exposed to important works of American art where the intent is to develop in them a sense of pride in the creativeness of American artists and designers. Familiarity with such works is likely to encourage children to value them and eventually to acknowledge them as cultural symbols with which they identify. All systems of education have as one of their purposes this continual reaffirmation of the culture. Art has a special part to play in this task in that each piece is unique and original.

Art also performs an educational service when it is used to provide children with skills that will be useful in their future careers. From ancient times it was thought to be necessary for doctors, soldiers, and architects to be able to draw. Words are useful, but they are often quite inadequate as communication compared with drawings. Compare the effectiveness of a house plan, for example, with a written statement that is intended to communicate the same information. The drawing is far more useful. Benjamin Franklin was well aware in the eighteenth century of the practical desirability for everyone to be able to explain themselves by means of drawing; and the large-scale introduction of art into schools in the late nineteenth century was done to satisfy the practical need for designers and draftsmen in industry. Skill in drawing, however, calls for much more than a set of techniques. It also requires that visual memories be trained in order to develop a "vocabulary" of images that a person may use as needed. People can learn to draw houses, cars, and people from different views and to recall those shapes from memory. Talented people, of course, will excell; but everyone can learn to do it if given the opportunity.

The nurturing of outstanding talent also falls into this category of social purpose, for the reason that artists and designers fulfill special functions in society. The insights of architects, graphic designers, and painters transform the appearance of homes, offices, and all kinds of manufactured products from typewriters to airplanes. The talents of gifted people in all fields—art included—continually create new jobs and modify old ones. The vocational benefits from art education abound, and the abilities that lead to this happening are best developed when children are young. However, elementary art

_____* Cyril Stanley Smith, "On Art, Invention, and Technology," *Technology Review* (Vol. 78, No. 7). June 1976, pp. 36–38.

instruction should not be obviously vocational; although the intent—the purpose—is there: to prepare children to be able to step into such work if and when the need arises. Those that do not elect to be artists and designers may still benefit from many developed skills and interests that permit them to continue their interest in art avocationally. In sum, the intent underlying art instruction is quite comparable with instruction in every other subject in the elementary curriculum. All people have a right to be fully prepared to take advantage of developed talents, and the initial development must occur in the elementary school if it is to occur at all.

The future trends toward increased leisure present another area where art fulfills a social function. Teachers need to re-evaluate such traditional educational purposes as preparation for work. More and more, people are facing reduced working weeks. Educating people in art for a world in which leisure time will occupy an increasing proportion of each day is thus as necessary for the well-being of society as educating them for the traditional work-a-day world of the present. The personal satisfactions to be derived from art have already been mentioned; and yet these personal satisfactions also satisfy social needs.

In addition, our society exerts tremendous pressures on people to succeed when only a handful will have an opportunity to actually realize success. The stress of this situation can be psychologically very damaging. The uniqueness of art is such, however, that almost all people can enjoy success through these experiences, and not only in the elementary art class. While the intent is again for individual betterment, the result contributes to the mental health of the nation.

Art may also be used to provide needed support with children for whom academic achievement is delayed or denied. Under these circumstances, art becomes a vehicle for helping children progress educationally to the best of their ability. Retarded children, for example, often find in art the reward and encouragement they need in view of the slower and more limited school progress they experience compared with typical children. Where children suffer disabilities in verbal communication, art can be used as a means of sharing thoughts and emotions. The physical dimensions of art facilitate motor skills, while basic knowledge about objects to be seen and touched can be aided by art instruction. This dimension of art education is of such importance that numbers of teachers have become specialists in it. However, the growth of mainstreaming can be expected to require all teachers to be better prepared to use art in educating the handicapped than in the past.

Not least, the development of children's sense of sight through art has important practical benefits. Advertising embraces all of us and much of it is visual. If art education did no more than sensitize children to what they see, in order that they become better critics of what is presented, then the presence of elementary art programs would have been worth the effort and expense. Thomas Jefferson believed that an illiterate population could never be free; and while he was referring to verbal literacy, the same claim may be said in this day of television regarding visual literacy. And the only school subject that even begins to treat this problem is art.

Teachers have a special interest in making clear what their professional purposes are, and the associations that represent teachers go to considerable trouble to make their positions clear, not only to their members, but also to the general public. The educational organization with the greatest investment in the teaching of art is the National Art Education Association. Although the membership is made up predominantly of specially trained art teachers rather than elementary classroom teachers, the overall point of view adopted by this organization may help you clarify your own position. For this reason, the underlying rationale of an official statement published in 1973 by the NAEA is included here in its entirety for you to study.

The professional organization that represents most elementary classroom teachers is the National Education Association. The Education Policies Commission of the NEA published a statement in 1968 about the contribution to be made by art in elementary schools that included six reasons or rationales for teaching art. The main features of this report are also included in their original form for you to study as you develop your own statement.

These two statements reflect the views of different groups of educators and as you might expect they interpret the purposes of art instruction somewhat differently. Nevertheless, considerable overlapping is evident in each and also with the position about art taken in the first part of this chapter.

THE ESSENTIALS OF A QUALITY SCHOOL ART PROGRAM
(A Position Statement by the National Art Education Association)

The Rationale: Introduction. The growing national interest in the arts combined with the new challenges confronting education make it imperative that the National Art Education Association, a voluntary professional association of teachers of art, set forth the essentials of a quality art program and the requirements for implementing such a program in the elementary and secondary schools of the United States.

Art and the Individual. Both when he produces works of art and when he contemplates them, man uses the arts to help him understand himself and the world around him. One of the traditional and unique functions of the arts has been to emphasize individual interpretation and expression. The visual arts today continue to be a means whereby man attempts to give form to his ideas and feelings and to gain personal satisfaction through individual interpretation and expression. The visual arts today continue to be a means whereby man attempts to give form to his ideas and feelings and to gain personal satisfaction through individual accomplishment. The growing complexity of our contemporary culture, including its visual aspects, also requires of every individual a capacity for visual discrimination and judgment.

Art and the Community. Through the ages man has used the arts to build and enrich his personal and shared environment. Art experiences should help him understand the visual qualities of these environments and should lead to the desire and the ability to improve them. An art education program which consistently emphasizes the ability to make qualitative visual judgments can help each citizen to assume his share of responsibility for the improvement of the aesthetic dimension of personal and community living. Acceptance of this responsibility is particularly important during periods of rapid technological development and social change.

Art and the Culture. The visual arts contain a record of the achievement of mankind, since the values and beliefs of a people are uniquely manifested in the art forms they produce. A critical examination of these forms can lead to a better understanding of both past and present cultures.

Art in Education. If art in education is to contribute effectively to the development of personal expression, qualitative aesthetic judgments, cultural understanding, and visual discrimination, then professional imperatives need to be continuously redeveloped as the society changes. This reassessment should, within the context of current professional goals, be concerned with content of the curriculum, qualifications of personnel, and instructional arrangements and facilities. Professional organizations such as the National Art Education Association have a continuing responsibility for giving leadership in the development of quality school art programs.

Art and the School Art Program. Art has four aspects: *seeing and feeling* visual relationships, *producing* works of art, *knowing and understanding* about art objects, and *evaluating* art products. A meaningful school art program will include experiences in all of these areas. A planned program in art should be provided at all educational levels from kindergarten through high school. At each grade level, art experiences should be selected and organized with different emphases and different degrees of intensity and complexity so as to result in a broadened understanding in all four aspects of the art subject: perceiving, performing, appreciating, and criticizing. For all these aspects, certain common objectives of the school art program can be specifically stated, and certain basic experiences can be provided to help achieve them.

Objectives. Art in the school is both a body of knowledge and a series of activities which the teacher organizes to provide experiences related to specific goals. The sequence and depth of these experiences are determined by the nature of the art discipline, the objectives desired, and by the interests, abilities, and needs of children at different levels of growth. As a result of the art program, each pupil should demonstrate, to the extent that he can, his capacity to: (1) have intense involvement in and response to personal visual experiences; (2) perceive and understand visual relationships in the environment; (3) think, feel, and act creatively with visual materials; (4) increase manipulative and organizational skills in art performance appropriate to his abilities; (5) acquire a knowledge of man's visual art heritage; (6) use art knowledge and skills in his personal and community life; (7) make intelligent visual judgments suited to his experience and maturity; and (8) understand the nature of art and the creative process.

Content. To achieve these objectives, the school art program must provide experiences consonant with the interests and the intellectual, social, and aesthetic maturity of the student. Not all of the experiences will receive the same emphasis at each grade level or with each child; all, however, are appropriate to the total school art program. The art program should provide experiences in: (1) examining intensively both natural and man-made objects from many sources; (2) expressing individual ideas and feelings through use of a variety of art media suited to the manipulative abilities and expressive needs of the student; (3) experimenting in depth with art materials and processes to determine their effectiveness in achieving personal expressive form; (4) working with tools appropriate to the students' abilities in order to develop manipulative skills needed for satisfying aesthetic expression; (5) organizing, evaluating, and reorganizing work-in-process to gain an understanding of the formal structuring of line, form, color, and texture in space; (6) looking at, reading about, and discussing works of art: painting, sculpture, constructions, architecture, industrial and hand-crafted products, using a variety of educational media and community resources; (7) evaluating art of both students and mature artists, industrial products, home and community design; (8) seeing artists produce works of art in their studios, in the classroom, or on film; (9) engaging in activities which provide opportunities to supply art knowledge and aesthetic judgment to personal life, home, or community planning. Although many experiences would be planned with the broad major objectives in mind, an individual lesson or unit might be organized about a specific goal which would, in turn, contribute to the development of the capacities desired. For example, it would be quite possible and in certain situations highly desirable for students to have intense involvement with color per se, since an understanding of the structural and expressive values of color would contribute to a realization of any of the stated objectives. Conversely, in expressing ideas and feelings creatively with art materials, it would be desirable to consider manipulative skills needed, suitable materials and processes, and overall organization of the visual statement. Student needs and abilities would determine emphasis and depth of the art experience.

THE ROLE OF THE FINE ARTS IN EDUCATION
(A Statement by the Educational Policies Commission of the NEA)

1. *Historical Rationale.* Artists and art educators lean heavily on the idea that "Art has always been important. There is much evidence that many civilizations, past and present, have greatly valued artistic experiences. Since art, then, is important in life, and since education is designed to prepare people to live well, art must be important in any educational plan." This is a very attractive thought. It attaches to artistic endeavors a familiar and genuine importance as a transmitter of cultural heritage. It places the question of artistic experiences and their importance in a context which reminds one of the high level of importance which other cultures have placed and still place on art. It makes art important by association. Although this notation does not explain in detail why people throughout history and in every culture practice many kinds of things which we call *art*, nonetheless the universality of art in time and in space—even with no explanation to enrich or embellish it—is a compelling partial argument in its favor.

A correlate of this argument is that art is a part of mankind's cultural heritage and it is the duty of schools to impart that heritage. Therefore, an education which does not teach art is deficient because it does not teach the culture.

2. *Art-for-Art's-Sake Rationale.* Another attitude common among artists and art educators is a disdain for any attempt to consider the arts as having values outside themselves. "Art is an end in itself," they say, implying that one who sees the arts as having utility demeans them. This is a tempting notion. The joys of artistic experience are manifest in many lovers of the arts. Such responses should not be taken lightly; they are positive, attractive feelings which many persons clearly need and welcome. Indeed, one of the bases of the belief that art is a universal phenomenon is the view that all people everywhere through all of time have found joy in it.

3. *Therapy Rationale.* One reason for using the fine arts in education is well documented and fully accepted; this is the use of the fine arts in various kinds of therapeutic situations. Persons in prisons, hospitals, mental institutions, homes for the aged, and similar places have frequently been shown to be greatly benefited through the use of artistic experiences. There is some evidence that similar therapeutic gains can come to persons who are disadvantaged, who might drop out of school otherwise, and who are retrievable, from a school's point of view, only by maximizing the school's attentions to their artistic interests. There is a strong possibility that the same kinds of values and benefits exist for all people, rather than just for those who need therapy.

4. *Creativity Rationale.* "Creativity" has recently become a popular topic. It is also a very important subject. Despite unclear and distorted meanings which the word has picked up during its popularity, it is still a good word, and it refers to a vital aspect of human abilities. "Creativity" has been getting serious attention from scholars in recent years with results which have significant implications for education in the arts. Research on creative thinking abilities has shown that the arts generally provide better settings than do other fields for exercising and stimulating imagination. One reason for this is that the fine arts can be more easily taught in a playful manner and creativity continually shows a relationship between playfulness and creative behavior. Similarly, it is possible in art instruction to avoid judging a student's production of ideas and objects. This practice may not be universal, but it is at least possible, and that may offer important values. This kind of free-expression opportunity is highly valuable in building up the kinds of psychological prerequisites (such as self-confidence, willingness to make mistakes and to fail, and the valuing of unconventional responses) which appear to be linked with creative abilities.

5. *Acceptance-of-Subjectivity Rationale.* A newly emerging rationale in favor of the arts suggests that they provide a setting in which people can learn to accept their own limited abilities to be totally objective about anything. This may seem at first to be either unimportant or unwise. It may be felt that acceptance of one's own irrationalities is not such a good thing, if it means no longer trying to be more rational. The strains of argument here are delicate, and they often are discussed in a self-defeatingly garbled manner.

Most will agree that no man is perfectly objective about anything, and is likely to be quite nonobjective about himself. This realization, however, seems to be insufficient to keep some people from trying always to be as objective as they can about everything. They consciously submerge everything uncontrolled within them in order to squeeze out one more degree of objectivity. This battle is apparent in the fields of behavioral science. There, many research devices invented for the physical and biological sciences are being taken over wholesale, without enough critical appraisal of the present suitability of these devices for studying people. Some behavioral scientists believe that their researches inevitably become more and more reliable and useful as they strive harder and harder (and therefore more and more successfully) to wipe from their awarenesses and consciousnesses the uniqueness of themselves, the imperfections of their objectivity, the quality which makes them unlike machines.

There are many kinds of intellectual jobs in which no subjectivity is necessary. Adding two and two requires of one nothing but objectivity. It can be done by imperfectly objective people only because two plus two is simple enough that one's emotional and personal responses, while they do exist, do not get in the way.

Science, mathematics, and various aspects of many fields are built mostly upon impersonal, objective mental operations. It may be necessary to use the idiosyncrasies of one's mind in order to develop Einstein's formulas, but even those formulas can be understood (in the kinds of ways that two plus two can be understood) without necessarily calling upon the emotional, idiosyncratic, and incompletely understood aspects of one's intellect.

Successes in science and mathematics have often seemed to follow on generalized efforts to be objective and to ignore as irrelevant, or even as counter-productive, all those aspects of intellect which have to do with personal and emotional idiosyncrasies. Thus a group of practitioners has come into being who feel that because these irrational hidden aspects of one's makeup can interfere with accurate recording of data and manipulation of concepts—and because there doesn't seem to be any use of them—objectivity can rightfully take over as *the* ultimate intellectual virtue.

The physical and biological sciences have not seemed to be harmed by this takeover. They deal with the kinds of data which are least affected by human whim, and therefore they have successes and they progress although their practitioners are imperfectly objective. Even in these fields, however, many theorists now feel strongly a need to begin stressing the valuable contributions to creative thinking and insight which come from relaxing and making friends with the nonobjective aspects of one's mind. This is not a rational hold on one's irrationalities. It is rather a mature, calm acceptance of the realization that one will continually be doing, thinking, feeling, being, and becoming things which could not possibly be predicted, controlled, or avoided. Some of these effects are pleasantly surprising; many are not. Some of them are necessary for creative thinking.

Many of the most impressive gains in scientific thought have come from insights which can hardly be termed logical or objective. Newton saw in a falling apple the idea that the rules which govern motion in the heavens might also govern motion on earth. Men had been bathing for thousands of years before Archimedes drew his famous lesson from a bath. To use the term *rational* is not to deny the emotional or the purposive or the purely personal. Rational responses must still be responses of whole human beings, complete with all the emotional, intuitive, and subjective elements of personality.

Here then is a unique place for the fine arts, for they deal directly with emotional, intuitive, and subjective responses.

6. *End-of-Work Rationale.* In an age when machines are ever more quickly assuming the roles and functions formerly performed by men, there is no persuasive argument which shows where this takeover will stop. Admittedly, machines which are but improvements, however extensive, of today's computers cannot be used to plan an economy or to take over any of the kinds of jobs which are now being done—above a purely mechanistic level. Neither can they be doing the doubtless much more complex jobs which the future will bring into being. It is probably a mistake, however—and one which is becoming more dangerous as it continues to be made—to assume that future machines will be mere linear improvements of the same basic kinds of computers that now exist. This mistake is easy to understand, for it permits the people who are making

predictions to feel that machines will "never do it all," and that people will always have a degree of superiority of a kind over machines in intellectual matters.

Those people who are now most expert in the field of computer design are, it would appear, most adamant in their insistence that computers "can never go beyond . . ." and will *never* attain more than a certain level of complexity, but will, of course, continue to be able to do more, faster. The Commission feels that this position, while psychologically comfortable, is unjustified. Computer specialists are qualified in many ways, perhaps, to predict the future of their profession, but of all people in the world, they are most completely, daily, and forcefully aware of the present limitations of the particular machines they work with. Their pessimism (one might call it optimism) in predicting a definite limit to the abilities of possible future machines is understandable.

Consider the situation, however, if a nation should find itself with all its people fed, clothed, and quite liberally cared for and without an opportunity or need for most people to work toward the achievement of upkeep of this state of affairs. If machines do things better than people can, then machines will be doing them and people will not. It cannot merely be assumed that the machines will always be simpleminded. They need not repeat forever the kind of gross blunders and inhumanities which people today associate with machines. The highly frustrating ways people are now "treated" by machines are actually the responsibility of shortsighted, mechanistic planners. There is nothing inherent in machines which reduces people to numbers. It is the people who wish to save money by overusing machines while those machines are still quite primitive and inflexible who willingly and dangerously sacrifice people's individualities.

A future world, let us speculate, might find no one with any kind of material want. Each person would have plenty of room, food, shelter, and the possibility of human companionship and intellectual stimulation. There would be few places for human beings, however, in the upkeep of this system. Machines would be doing everything more humanly, more excitedly, more diversely, more uniquely for each person and according to that person's wishes than humans could.

If this idealized situation approaches and the usefulness of men begins to wane, what will be men's reactions? Will they destroy their machines and begin to revert to older times when they felt less comfortable but more useful? Probably this will happen sporadically; but finally there will likely be a change in men's values. Some groups in our society are already toying with the idea of renouncing what they think of as the Puritan ethic. Their whole philosophy may be self-defeating or pathological, but their disbelief in the ennobling value of work reflects changes in the real world. If work cannot seem noble while one is doing it, and if work is not always going to be possible, much less necessary, why work now? It is easy to blame such attitudes on the absurdities which accompany the redistribution of wealth in the United States. The Commission believes that the growing alienation of American youth from the valuing of work is more than a lazy reaction to the existence of welfare. It is partly, also, a reaction to the realization that the benefits advertised for working hard are becoming unrealistic.

Projections into the future, however serious, often foresee people sleeping happily and dreaming away while machines have taken over and let the people do what they wish. It would seem that many who predict the future have held a residual belief that work is an ultimate good value. They feel that a future world where machines do everything will be boring: people in that world will probably escape it or choose oblivion. A better choice may be to give up the value of work. This seems reasonable for a world where work is becoming impossible because it is pointless.

In a future without work or usefulness, in the accepted sense, what does become important? If war and boredom are avoided—and this is a big if—then a resulting society without work might be made up of individuals who concern themselves with each other, with themselves, and with whatever expressive endeavors might meet their taste. Science might be appreciated in the future society for the excitement that comes with exploration, discovery, and invention rather than for its usefulness. In such circumstances, art would be vitally important, for it would be the kind of thing which people would be doing, for themselves and for each other. In a sense, it is through this kind of psychological, emotional, creative, expressive, and intellectual exchange that "usefulness" in such a future society will be felt.

BELIEFS IN ACTION: THE STATUS OF ELEMENTARY ART

While scholars and educators may state what they believe to be the place of art in education, the true test of the value people place on art is to be found in what actually happens in schools. American schools belong to the people in a more direct sense than many other social institutions. In part at least, local monies pay for their operation. Schools are governed by locally elected school boards. Choices of textbooks are typically made at the community level. Parent groups tend to be active in the life of the schools, particularly so in elementary schools. Self-contained classrooms predominate in elementary schools, so that teachers tend to be relatively autonomous. In sum, the attitudes of local people toward art have a profound effect on what is possible in the art program, regardless of pronouncements made by outside experts. You will soon be a part of such a community and you need to prepare yourself for some of the attitudes you will encounter.

The adult population regularly determines what will and will not be done in a given school or district. These people are taxpayers, parents, employers, politicians, and workers. The kinds of opinions they hold about art affect the attitudes and values of the children. Some of the more common expressions voiced in support of elementary art are as follows: Art is a good relaxation for children after the discipline of academic study, especially for primary children. Art is good for developing small muscle coordination. Art is good for children who are not academically inclined, because it gives them an opportunity to experience success. We should educate children to enjoy the finer things in life, of which art is one. Children should have art because they enjoy it. Artistic talents like all other special abilities should be encouraged.

This list could be extended; but these statements will prepare you for some of the more commonly stated reasons supporting art. However, the visual arts do not presently occupy a place of high prestige in schools, so you should be prepared for an even larger number of negative or neutral statements, although the greatest condemnation occurs when art is simply ignored!

Here are some of the more common negative statements: Public funds should not be spent for the benefit of the few children who are talented. Art talent develops naturally so there is no point in having art classes. Art is elitist and is no help to children who will have to work for their living. Art takes valuable time away from the important school subjects. Art materials are too expensive for the subject to be taught. Children like art, but they cannot make livings as artists.

In general, however, local populations will behave uneasily and inconsistently toward art, because they sense that it has a value but do not know enough about it to express themselves on the topic. The task of making decisions regarding art in curriculum is thus left very much to the discretion of administrators at the district school levels. Most school administrators are well aware of the public relations value of art, but they often have little comprehension of the value of art to the over-all curriculum. Consequently, whenever a district or a school faces financial problems, elementary art teachers and consultants are among the first to be dismissed. In contrast, certain school principals make a point of building admirable art programs that may include the presence of art teachers and ensure that sufficient funds are ear-marked for art. Other administrators will give considerable support for art but see no reason for it to be taught by special teachers any more than specialists are needed for reading or social studies.

Regardless of local prestige, however, elementary art programs are rarely organized to build cumulatively from year to year so that by the time children move to secondary schools, they will be in possession of a specific body of art knowledge and skills. Local convictions about art are sufficiently uncertain that this is not required, although children would benefit immeasurably were such a policy adopted. Consequently, elementary school educators are usually allowed either to encourage art or to treat it with lip-service only. The presence of a special art teacher may provide a more substantial program than a classroom teacher can present, and yet these specialists are unlikely to know the children as well as the regular teacher; and unless the art teacher and the classroom teacher collaborate, the specialists' efforts may easily result in a token art program that occurs once a week or less frequently and is divorced from the rest of the children's school experiences.

The prosperity of all elementary art programs hinges in one way or another, therefore, on the professional commitment of classroom teachers; which is all the more reason why you need to have a well-developed understanding of the value of art education before entering on your teaching career.

PREPARING YOUR OWN POINT OF VIEW

You may find some of the contents of this chapter match your personal philosophy of education. Alternatively, what appears here may stimulate you to search for an alternative position. *The choice of what you teach in art and the way you teach it will be governed by the point of view you develop.* Perhaps the best test of your convictions, however, is the degree to which you are willing to declare yourself publicly.

This chapter opened with a reference to an event where a parent challenged you. Are you now prepared to make a convincing response to that questioner? Do you feel confident enough to speak out and state your position about art—even when it is not asked for? Will you fight for money and time in the school day to make the achievement of your art teaching purposes possible? The willingness to act in support of your convictions is the final test that you possess convictions. For this reason, you are now asked to prepare a statement about the purposes of elementary art education.

Think of the task as a guide for action rather than a passive term paper. Think of it also as the first statement you will make about art rather than the last one. As your career unfolds, you will periodically want to modify this statement in the light of your experience. This present effort, however, will provide you with an initial point of view. Moreover, changing an existing statement is much easier than preparing a new one from scratch; and as busy as you may believe you are now, you will be much busier when once you begin teaching. What you prepare in response to this assignment will serve as a reference for the future; and if you share what you write with other students you may have an opportunity of having it evaluated in a friendly setting before putting it to the test with people who may not always be sympathetic.

further reading

The following selection of readings supplements the text of this chapter and is included in the hope that you will explore the purposes of art education further, as you prepare your personal statement of purposes.

Arts, Americans and Education Panel. *Coming to Our Senses: The significance of the Arts for American Education.* New York: McGraw-Hill, 1977. States that the sensory foundation of the arts makes these subjects necessary for the education of everyone.

Chapman, Laura H. *Approaches to Art in Education.* New York: Harcourt Brace Jovanovich, 1978. Part I develops the topic of this chapter and includes many useful references for additional reading.

Eisner, Elliot W. *Educating Artistic Vision.* New York: Macmillan, 1972. The opening chapters review the history of art instruction in schools and are followed by the author's views on present and future needs.

Hardiman, George W. and **Theodore Zernich** (eds.) *Curricular Considerations for Visual Arts Education: Rationale, Development and Evaluation.* Champaign, IL: Stipes Publishing Company, 1974. The first thirteen chapters are relevant to this chapter.

Langer, Suzanne K. "Expressiveness," in *Concepts in Art and Education,* ed. George Pappas. New York: Macmillan, 1970. Develops the idea that art is non-discursive or non-sequential.

McFee, June King and **Rogena M. Degge.** *Art, Culture and Environment: A Catalyst for Teaching.* Belmont, CA.: Wadsworth, 1977. Relates art (drawing in particular) and cultural anthropology to the educational needs of all people.

Pappas, George (ed.) *Concepts in Art and Education: An Anthology of Current Issues.* New York: Macmillan, 1970. A collection of previously published articles on art education. Most are brief and easily readable.

Sagan, Carl. *The Dragons of Eden: Speculations on the Evolution of Human Intelligence.* New York: Random House, 1977. Chapter 7 summarizes the present level of knowledge about the functions of the two halves of the brain.

Saunders, Robert J. *Relating Art and Humanities to the Classrooms.* Dubuque, IA: Wm. C. Brown, 1977. Reviews varied points of view regarding the place of art in the schools.

Wilson, Colin. *New Pathways in Psychology: Maslow and the Post-Freudian Revolution.* New York: Taplinger, 1972. Explains Maslow's ideas in a very readable way.

r = readiness

how children's development
affects art teaching

6

The readiness of children to learn comes partly from their maturity and partly from the circumstances in which they live. Arguments continue on the question of whether the dominant force in a person's development is the environment or whether people develop primarily in response to the qualities that have been inherited. The position taken in this book is that both forces are at work and must be recognized. In addition, the task of teaching art is considered to be basically the same as teaching other school subjects; so your studies in the developmental psychology of children will also help you as you think of readiness for learning art. In sum, if you can establish the general readiness level of a child or a classroom full of children, you will have defined the range of art content that can most likely be learned at that time. Possession of such information removes the concern you may have had about including certain art content in your program. It enables you to spell out what can probably be taught and in so doing permits you to concentrate your attention on the creative opportunities open to teaching that content (see Chapter 8). Not least, as the school year advances, and as you become even more perceptive about the children's readiness levels, so the art program can be adjusted to suit their actual needs. But the initial decisions need to be as well founded as possible.

Art educators have given much thought to the art that children can do at certain ages or levels of development with little or no instruction. Very little has been written about the instruction that would need to be given to make the most of children's readiness to learn art. The first approach acknowledges the value of various kinds of art experiences at given levels of children's development, but gives little consideration to the instruction that could be given to make the most of the artistic potential that lies waiting to be developed. And yet elementary schools assume general responsibility for a program of instruction where the ideal is one of continually building toward more advanced performance to the point where each individual is able to reach the limits of his ability. The emphasis in this book is consistent with that ideal. The information in this chapter, therefore, provides guidelines to assist you in the best selection of the art that children can learn based on general levels of maturation. This information has been selected from the writings of researchers who have studied child development in general as well as those who have specialized in children's art development. Their work is listed for further reading at the end of this chapter.

CHILDREN'S DEVELOPMENT IN ART

Each child is unique, and so is every classroom of children; and yet as a group, children of similar ages share general developmental characteristics. Statements describing these shared qualities may not be applicable to children in all parts of the world, but they are useful for most of the children growing up in the United States and in countries possessing similar cultural characteristics. A child's age is not the only index of maturation, but it is useful; and rightly or wrongly most elementary schools are organized on the basis of age. For this reason, in what follows we will group children broadly by age into two categories: primary and intermediate.

PRIMARY: GRADES 1 TO 3 During the first three years of school and including kindergarten, children tend to be physically active; and yet their lack of physical and intellectual stamina requires frequent changes of pace and periods of rest. The activities they engage in best are those requiring large movements of arms, legs, and bodies, rather than small hand and finger movements. Eye development is usually incomplete until about age 8, and this accounts for books for primary children having large print. Frequent absences can also be expected as childhood illnesses take their toll. These absences may intrude on the continuity of instruction unless you anticipate them and make adequate provisions.

Children aged 6 through 9 are typically bubbling with enthusiasm, and you will have little difficulty in stimulating them to participate in classroom activities—especially in art. They tend not to be good listeners, however, and you may need to protect them from failure as a consequence of not listening. Nevertheless you exert considerable influence over children's attitudes during this period and many of them will worship you. This is an awesome responsibility because if your efforts fail the results can have a lasting impact. And thoughtless criticism of their art can have a crushing effect that can have a more lasting impact than criticism at later periods in their lives. Part of the teaching task during this period, in fact, is one of providing opportunities for children to experience success and earn approval. An important consequence is their sense of accomplishment and self-worth—where competition should be directed more toward competing with themselves than with other children. The creative development of children seems to advance fairly regularly until a child goes to school, and then it suffers a set-back. No doubt the conformity demands that school makes on children take their toll. Art, however, should be the one subject in the curriculum where children should be encouraged to invent unique solutions to problems and be rewarded for being different rather than the same.

Most learning at this time in children's lives is thus tied to direct experience with actual people and objects—all of which form part of their daily lives. During the first part of this period many children will still be behaving at an even earlier stage of development, where fantasy and reality are often so interwoven as to be one.

The artistic development of primary level children is dominated by the way they see the world around them, that is, by visual perception. Children show a natural urge to draw that is closely linked with their need to bring a sense of order to the environment. The drawings are rarely representational in any photographic sense, but they do convey what children think is right. Drawings are thus integral parts of healthy growing and help in identifying, describing, and classifying objects. Unfortunately, this natural predisposition for visual learning is not organized systematically in most schools. Elementary schools concentrate on academic tool skills; and the need for children to learn to read, write, and compute is indisputable. But by neglecting visual learning, the schools have not taken advantage of a positive force that affects all areas of the curriculum, as well as art.

Throughout their first year at school many children are still using art as a form of physical and personal involvement with their environment. Their art is more the result of an urge to express sensory feelings of kinesthetic pleasure than a concern for making pictures that other people will be able to understand (see Figure N). This "inner-world" focus makes art a matter of communicating with the self—of narrative fantasy—where the distinction between what is real and what unreal is not clearly distinguishable. In some cases, this state may continue into the second grade. At this time especially, a teacher should be cautious about trying to interpret meanings or even to identify images. Later, as children want to communicate more clearly, symbolic drawings evolve, and objects become more easily identified. But even then they are unlikely to be executed as adults perceive these objects (see Plates 9 and 10; Figures J and O).

During this period, children's pictures will usually show each object separate from the others around it. The bodies, limbs, and heads of people and animals will each be drawn as separate, simple shapes that join onto each other to make the whole object. Body parts will often be enlarged if they are considered to be important, while similar parts will receive slight attention if they are unimportant. Occasionally, people may be drawn like X-ray photographs to reveal their internal characteristics. And every detail of complex objects, such as trees and fields of flowers, will often be shown. All the windows of a building, for example, may be drawn (see Figure 77:cluster of 5).

FIGURE 77   Pictures by primary level children

Pictures by primary level children (cont.)

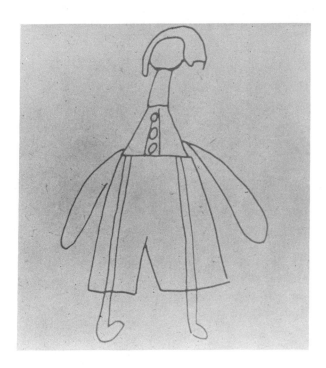

In many respects, children's drawings during this period are more a form of visual concept formation than art in the sense that adults understand art. Writers on child art, in fact, refer to these products as "schema" or symbols that carry visual information. Other art educators, notably June McFee, recognize the characteristics of children's drawings but declare that mature artists' drawings are also schematic and symbolic in that they are made on flat paper and include only what the artist wants to show (see Figure 78).

Teachers can assist children to advance their drawing ability in that differently designed objects can be introduced to increase a child's understanding and thus lead to modifications of schema. Visual memory can also be developed through drawing. Personal drawing styles can be encouraged. The main characteristics of childhood schema will remain, however. Subjects will be mainly of outdoor scenes, objects will be drawn singly, that is, not overlapping; and the best results are usually derived from objects that children like and know something about. These objects will usually be drawn on one or more "base" or "stand" lines, whose repeated use sometimes creates a sense of Oriental perspective, while the importance of whole objects or parts of objects is characterized by distortion of size and perhaps by the use of color and detail, much as in some ancient Egyptian art (see Figure 79:cluster of 4). Shapes appear to be tubular and do not include shadows. Whenever different objects are drawn for the first time the child tends to revert to an earlier style of drawing.

While drawing predominates among children, they are also capable of working three dimensionally. They generally enjoy working with clay, which

FIGURE 78   Rembrandt van Rijn, "Cottage near the Entrance of a Wood." Pen, wash and chalk. All rights reserved. The Metropolitan Museum of Art, Robert Lehman Collection, 1975.

is an extremely malleable medium and is well suited to developing such skills as pressing, squeezing, rolling, joining, and cutting. These skills encourage fine motor development and are basic to more advanced work with clay. The only way to develop an understanding of three dimensions, however, is to have direct experience with a solid, preferably malleable, medium like clay. And by no means least, clay is an excellent medium for building children's creative expression. Similar qualities and subject matter choices will tend to appear in clay products that are also noticeable in their drawings, namely that models are of single items rather than groups. Single viewpoints of particular objects will be shown as with drawings. And among younger children, symmetrical models will be more numerous than asymmetrical ones. Most children will move into this work easily, but some may experience difficulty at first in working directly in three dimensions. They may find the transition easier if they begin with a slab of clay into which they "draw" with a pointed instrument. Alternatively, they may make cookie-like cut-outs. A second stage is to dig out the background areas of a slab and model the important parts. They will then usually be able to move from this stage to full three-dimensional activity on their own (see Figure 80: cluster of 3).

138 CHAPTER 6

FIGURE 79   Primary level art showing base lines

FIGURE 80 Sculpture by primary level children

In the primary grades, teachers commonly think of art almost exclusively as an activity, but even at this level it is also much more than that. At every level art possesses subject matter that includes technical knowledge of skills and materials, information about art and artists, elementary art criticism, and a branch of philosophy known as aesthetics. While individual children's readiness determines in large part what can be included in an art curriculum, primary grade children can at least learn a basic art vocabulary that is comparable with what may be learned in any other subject. They can also learn to follow written and spoken instructions and learn about the materials, equipment, and techniques they encounter in their art activities. Abstract verbal information is generally inappropriate for children of this age, but they can become familiar with selected works of art and what they are about. They can also learn to recognize and express preferences for those works of art. But it is not important that they remember the titles or who the artists were. And preferences will rarely be associated with the aesthetic values typically enjoyed by better educated adults. Rather, the decisions will be influenced by such things as the association the child has with the object portrayed, and the excitement of the events that are shown. Beauty will often be associated with what is thought of as good, such as a good fairy. A villain or witch, by contrast, will tend to be viewed as ugly. The level of complexity of this verbal information must obviously be studied carefully, but no more so than in social studies or science. Perhaps the greatest obstacle to including these kinds of content lies in past art teaching practices, where little or no effort was made to require anything other than activity for its own sake from the children. The allegation that art, as a subject of study, lacks substance is clearly untrue when art content is fully represented in a curriculum in an organized way. And this may be achieved at any level in the elementary school curriculum.

INTERMEDIATE: GRADES 4 TO 6 No tidy transitions occur in children's development from year to year, much less from Grade 3 to Grade 4; but during the second half of their elementary school career certain general changes are normally observed that distinguish primary from intermediate level children. Girls usually show a pronounced growth spurt and advance in maturity compared with boys of the same age. Children's health generally improves and fewer absences are recorded compared with the primary years. Group behavior governed by peers outside school begins to assert itself in children's school behavior. Fine motor coordination makes considerable advances. Children's thinking begins to shift from the earlier exclusive focus on actual objects they have seen or touched and events they have witnessed or experienced to the abstract manipulation of words and ideas associated with adult intellectual behavior. The shift does not occur in any strict pattern and children can be expected to move to and fro from an earlier to a later style of behavior for some time before it stabilizes during the period between the fourth and eighth grades.

Children continue to advance in maturity throughout the intermediate grades. They frequently set unrealistically high standards for themselves in all kinds of activities that invite frustration and failure unless a teacher intercedes to help. The search for independence calls on teachers to provide support less obviously than formerly and also to help children learn how to persevere and to enjoy being industrious.

While these general changes are occurring, children's art behavior begins to change. Somewhere between ages 10 and 11, schematic drawing reaches a peak, after which the figures begin to become wooden-looking and robot like. The earlier popularity of drawing diminishes, partly out of a sense of frustration children at this age feel in not knowing how to advance beyond child-like schema toward culturally approved models of visual art. They are advancing intellectually to the point where the information value of drawing is being replaced by more satisfying methods of manipulative ideas and information that are verbal and abstract. They are also progressively better able to compare their drawings with the drawings of adults and become disillusioned about their artistic abilities (see Figure 81: cluster of 6).

Between the ages of 9 and 12, children start to lose interest in drawing people. They may restrict themselves to heads. Some will develop a caricature syle, which is an extension of their earlier schematic drawings in the direction of realism. A handful, however, will move almost effortlessly toward representational drawing. The mistake is to believe that mature artistic ability is necessarily bound up with what is commonly observed during this period of children's development in art. Artistic ability and interest will die as a result of neglect or continual negative reinforcement; but that need not occur. The insightful psychologist, Abraham Maslow, placed aesthetic pleasures at the pinnacle of human needs. Failure to overcome this crisis of later childhood can, therefore, inhibit or impair the further development of aesthetic pleasures. *Readiness in art instruction involves preparing for future educational challenges and oportunities, and this period must be looked on as one of the most important of all.*

(a)

FIGURE 81 Art by intermediate level children. (a) Courtesy, The International Collection of Child Art, Ewing Museum of Nations, Illinois State University.

(c)

(b)

144

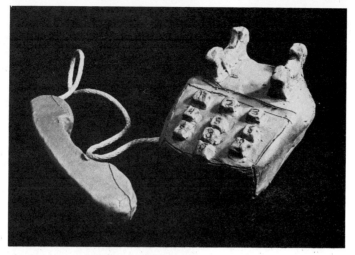

(d)

(e)

(f)

This crisis in children's drawing—formerly the mainstay of their art activity—is rarely anticipated by teachers in such a manner that they are prepared for the task of guiding children through it. The common outcome is that a small minority who, by good fortune, have developed the necessary skills may not realize that any crisis exists. The remainder—the vast majority—proceed through life believing that they are inartistic. Some may rediscover latent abilities in adulthood, but the proportion involved is very small. As a consequence, this pre-adolescent crisis is a major educational challenge. The irony is that the people who must attack it are predominantly classroom teachers who themselves probably lost confidence in their art abilities during this same crisis. Where special art teachers are employed in elementary schools the prospect may be somewhat better. On the other hand, these teachers are likely to be among those who in their own youth never realized that a crisis was occurring, and they may have difficulty in comprehending what most children of this age face as they approach adolescence.

In societies where photographic realism is not the measure of achievement for adult art, this transition period of later childhood is likely to be easier. Moslem children, for example, readily turn to decorative designs because their religion discourages renderings of the human figure. Tribal art forms in different parts of the world direct children's aspirations toward cultural symbolism (see Figure 82) rather than our kind of symbolism—we call ours "realism." Teachers in our own schools often find that children who neglect drawing will show a readiness to continue their art education in such areas as ceramics, weaving, and print making. The linear and creative requirements of these arts are demanding and yet none of them depend for success on drawing or painting in any conventionally realistic sense. The criteria for success are also more objective.

Those children who are able to continue deriving satisfaction from pictorial work will, of course, continue to need assistance. They, too, will tend to become scornful of their earlier work. They will often change in their uses of color, from bright colors toward the more subdued colors of the observable world, even to the point of working with single colors. This group emerges at various times throughout these three grades but increasingly so during the final year of elementary school. Some children are entirely self-sufficient in art; but of those showing ability in drawing, most will lose confidence in themselves unless a teacher satisfies their growing need for uniting skill with intellectual understanding. Areas of special concern for this group includes mastery of proportions, overcoming the base line to convey a sense of distance, placement of the horizon, ways of grouping objects to create a composition, shading to show form, and attention to details.

Most children develop verbally during this period to the point where, with sympathetic guidance, they are able to understand much more than before about artists and works of art. Reading and listening skills have usually reached a level where increasing amounts of information can be acquired

FIGURE 82 African woodcarving, female antelope. Wood, brass tacks, string, iron, quills, cowrie shells. Courtesy of The Art Institute of Chicago.

and put to use. Children become increasingly able to talk about art in terms of compositional elements and the messages contained in them, and so build both on earlier preferences and simple descriptions. A conscious awareness of the relationship between art and such areas as social studies and mathematics can also be built during this period—a relationship where each area is understood to complement the other. You may find it productive to subdivide a class into separate groups according to developmental need. Alternatively, you may prefer that all the children in your class experience substantially the same art program, because all of the content is important. In the latter case, you will want to assemble lessons that will satisfy as many of the different children's needs as possible at one time. But regardless of how you organize your classroom, the increasingly diverse personalities of the children will require recognition. At the same time, a corresponding conformity stemming from social pressures will also have to be allowed for. Most important of all, perhaps, is the growing need to develop effective working skills, whereby children are prepared for that time in the future when they are likely to want to show their needs and desires independently. All of these decisions will be reflected in the way you organize your instruction. Examples of these opportunities are introduced in Chapters 1 and 8, and in the data bank that appears at the end of this book.

EXCEPTIONALITY

The preceding information is an introduction to how the majority of children develop in their readiness for art during six years of elementary school. It does not begin to account for the innumerable individual differences that appear in every classroom, with which teachers must continually grapple. Two clearly identifiable groups of children can be described, however, who differ markedly from the others. Information about them should be useful, because they will be enrolled in your classes. The term *exceptionality* is a convenient way for referring to these children. Contrary to popular opinion, exceptionality includes the gifted as well as the retarded. Some authorities claim that as many as 20% of children are handicapped in some way, while others report half that number. Similarly, the gifted are reported to account for between 2% and 12% of the population. Traditional intellectual abilities are usually those referred to when determining exceptionality, but the definition can be—and should be—expanded to include art abilities. Notwithstanding the over-simplification, the two groups will be described here by the terms "gifted," and "handicapped." These terms are general, but they are familiar and adequate.

*GIFTED CHILDREN** Giftedness indicates the existence of superior performance or abilities as distinct from aptitudes which predict superior performance which has not yet shown itself. Giftedness in children may appear in any or all of the forms of human behavior, although it is subject to the normal limits of childhood. For example, physical exceptionality among children occurs but is still governed by the bodily and mental changes expected among children at a particular level. Likewise assessments of intellectual and emotional giftedness among children are also stated relative to normal expectations for children of a given age range. Extraordinary giftedness occasionally appears in the arts with prodigies, although historically music has been better represented than the visual arts. Nonetheless, uniquely gifted students in art do appear in elementary classrooms. The most noticeable kind of artistic giftedness shows itself through drawing and painting. Both forms of expression are popular among children during their early school years, so that superior performance is easily identified. Later the gifted child rapidly outpaces the typical student.

Gifted children in art may work more quickly, or they may have better ideas. They may demonstrate an outstanding sense of design. They may be able to concentrate for greater periods of time or remember detail more accurately than their peers. Their tool-handling skills are likely to be superior, so their art work looks especially good. They are likely to possess a richer visual imagination than is normally expected. Not least they will probably have advanced toward realism well ahead of their classmates (see Figure 83 and Figure M). A less expected kind of giftedness in art may show itself through superior verbal sensitivity toward works of art.

_____* A source for further study of art for gifted children appears at the end of this chapter.

FIGURE 83   Scene by a child gifted in drawing

However, *giftedness in any field will show itself only when the oppor-tunity arises to demonstrate the gift.* If a teacher is afraid to work with paint for fear of a mess, then a gift for painting may not be revealed. If no effort is made to work with clay or to make sculpture, then giftedness for three-dimensional problem solving may lie fallow. Evidences of giftedness in art depend in part, therefore, on the curriculum being such that they will have an opportunity to be revealed.

Giftedness tends not to be developed to its fullest extent, not merely because it goes unrecognized, but because teachers lack the preparation to develop it fully. This is likely to be particularly true in art, where many classroom teachers believe they lack the skills required to teach art, not to mention art for the gifted. In fact, the gifted student in art is often likely to be allowed by the teachers to follow his own interests. This practice is rarely satisfactory, however, because gifted children need guidance just as much as any other children if they are ever to develop their gifts fully. They continue to be children, regardless of their gifts, and teachers are present to help them. Without guidance, for example, a gifted child may prefer not to work with a new medium because the familiar medium leads to rewards without any risk of failure or the need for any additional effort. And yet, if ever there is a time when the opposite attitude should be nurtured, it is during the formative years of childhood. Children—especially gifted children—should be en-couraged continually to expand themselves through new experiences.

Perhaps the greatest tragedy of all is that gifted children of all kinds are frequently neglected because teachers are faced with classroom situations that demand attention in ways that cannot wait. A child who constantly requires the teacher's help or one who will create a discipline problem if not supervised is much more likely to receive attention than a gifted child who is also in need of assistance but is easily able to satisfy minimal classroom standards without help. The problem is a difficult one. Given the conventional self-contained classroom, all that a teacher can usually hope to do is make advance preparations of special lessons for gifted students to work at with minimal supervision. Teachers can also counsel the parents of such students to give them additional art experiences outside school to encourage their gifts to mature. Federal legislation* has been enacted to make money available to help the gifted and talented, and you may be able to take advantage of these resources to help any outstanding children you may have in your classes.

HANDICAPPED CHILDREN† This group includes the mentally retarded, the emotionally disturbed, and the physically impaired. One or more of these states may apply to any child. Until recently, most of these children would have been found in separate classrooms and separate schools. However, federal legislation‡ has been passed where all but those who must have institutionalized care are to be enrolled in regular classrooms wherever possible. Federal, state, and local funds are speeding up this process of mainstreaming, and it can soon be expected to be typical in most schools.

While some teachers may continue to disregard the needs of gifted children, no such treatment is possible when handicapped children are mainstreamed. They are too visible and too much in need of help. Handicapped children are not likely to be able to work on the instructional level or at the same speed as the majority of a class. And this is as true for art as it is for other subjects in the curriculum. For these reasons, teachers must have as clear an idea as possible of what these children can be expected to do in art in order to be able to prepare suitable art instruction for them.

THE EDUCABLE MENTALLY RETARDED The point where children fall into this category is when their intelligence quotient is reported to be between 50 and 75. Above that level they are considered "normal" and below that level they are in need of constant professional care.

While the above measures do not account for art as such, they do document behaviors that affect artistic performance such as general intellectual ability and physical coordination. And yet, some retarded children can be expected to produce surprisingly good art work. The reason for this is that while intelligence scores are useful, they do not account for all human abilities; and art is an integral manifestation of intellect. Retarded children—like anyone else—have areas where they are more capable than others.

_____* Gifted and Talented Children's Act of 1978 (Public Law: 95–561).

_____† A source for further study of art for handicapped children appears at the end of this chapter.

_____‡ Education for All Handicapped Children Act (Public Law: 94–142).

Generally, however, retarded children take longer to learn what normal children learn. They learn less than other children. And they function at an intellectual level that is below what is typically expected of children at a given age. Physically they appear much the same as other children of the same chronological age, although they are likely to be less well coordinated.

From these broad statements, a teacher can expect retarded children to respond best to art lessons that require relatively short periods of concentration on a very few, simple topics. Assignments should lead to completed products in each class period. Repetitive craft-like activities with limited creative expectations are likely to be most effective and to be most enjoyable for the child. Very gradually they should master coordination skills and can then be led to more expressive pictorial lessons. Depending on the ability of the child, crayons and brushes may be more serviceable than pencils. More abstract learning such as memorization, art history, and art criticism should be deferred until evidence is shown of readiness for this kind of work. Most of these children will have a history of frustration and failure in school, and their future educational progress largely depends on building positive experiences and minimizing negative ones.

These statements about retarded children are very general, but no more so than those made about the gifted. And yet what appears here does provide an introductory guide for what to expect when retarded children are present in elementary art classes. A twelve-year-old child may be reported to have a mental age of 8, in which case you might expect a general intellectual level corresponding with a typical eight-year-old. However, physically and to some extent socially, he may function at various points between eight and twelve. Moreover, after some contact with the child, his level of artistic performance may actually be closer to twelve than eight. When all available information is tallied, a teacher should prepare art instruction that seems to fit the child's needs. At its best, all teaching is based on a similar process of data gathering, out of which a teacher builds a hypothesis about what is best for the child. The lesson is then tested to determine its effectiveness. The same practice needs to be followed with each retarded child, because retardation is not a single phenomenon, but a complex state. Unfortunately, individual instruction cannot usually be given to the mass of children in a class but retarded children, because of their dependency, cannot be handled in any other way.

EMOTIONALLY DISTURBED CHILDREN While retarded children tend to be physically passive, the behavior of disturbed children is less predictable. By definition, retarded children function at a low intellectual level; but the intelligence of disturbed children may fall anywhere across a very wide range, from dull to brilliant. However, they are usually disorganized in their personal and work habits, and this often leads to extreme frustration among those who are more intelligent. When their work does not match their expectations, outbursts of temper can result which may be destructive to materials as well as to themselves and others. These children may withdraw into themselves or they may be irrepressible and disturb everyone in a class.

Others may be unable to remain seated for any length of time and consequently never complete any work.

Emotional disturbance is a very broad classification and consequently specific advice for teaching art to this group is difficult to make. The most practical susggestion is to find out from a professional source just what the nature of the problem is, and what kinds of remediation are recommended. Your task is then to translate instruction from your art program to serve those needs. In the absence of any guidance, you will have to assess a child's needs and plan a course of action yourself to help remediate the disability. Children who are fearful and withdrawn are likely to need continual praise and encouragement, for example. The more destructive kind of child is likely to work best in tightly structured situations. Group activities such as murals may be useful, not only to develop a sense of artistic achievement but also as part of a process of respecting others and collaborating with them. However, most disturbed children have short attention spans and one-period lessons usually offer the best starting places.

PHYSICALLY IMPAIRED Children in this category include those with hearing disorders, vision disabilities, speech defects, and those who are physically crippled. A number may suffer from multiple handicaps. Each of these categories includes numerous variations, moreover, so that a visually handicapped child may be partially sighted but unable to focus his eyes for more than a few minutes; or able to see only objects immediately in front of him; or may be completely blind. These children are likely to represent the normal range of intelligence, but they are likely to feel isolated from other children and to have become highly dependent on adults. Again, you should turn to a professional authority whenever possible. In the absence of such help, analyze the disability yourself, and plan art instruction that will either make the fullest use of what remains of a given sense or limb or compensate for what is lacking in one area with special attention to those where the child is fully functioning. Multiple-handicapped children present even more complex problems and yet in the absence of professional advice, the same approach as before must be used when assessing their readiness for particular art experiences.

A note of caution is worth including here, namely: a teacher has a responsibility to provide the best possible art program to *all* the children in a classroom. The majority of children you will teach will be normal. The few who are handicapped will need special attention and they should receive it—but not at the expense of the class as a whole. Moreover, gifted children deserve as much attention as those who are less fortunate; and yet, it is all too easy to neglect them.

ENVIRONMENTAL EFFECTS ON READINESS FOR ART

Abilities are distributed equally across all people in the world, but almost half of the world's population are taught to behave in ways that are proper for males rather than females. And what is proper for a Hindu girl living in a rural village in India is quite unlike the behavior expected of a Jewish girl living in Brooklyn. Behavior patterns are established in early childhood, and it is then that environmental influences make their greatest impression. They mold children to respond to people, places, and events in certain approved ways. While the strongest and most lasting influences on children occur before they first attend school, elementary teachers contribute significantly to this process—much more fundamentally than is possible at the upper levels of education. Older children have much they can learn; but their personalities by then are relatively fixed.

Art may form a part of a child's experience that is actively encouraged at home, although usually it will be treated casually at best. But just as the teaching of reading should not be left to chance, so the teaching of art should not be left to chance. The school art program is thus an instrument for influencing children's behavior in the directions that in our society are considered desirable. However, the art program will succeed only to the extent that the teacher takes into account the forces that affect children's art behavior. Readiness for art, in sum, is a complex web of factors involving biological maturation and environmental influences. Some of the more influential environmental forces are introduced here.

HOME AND COMMUNITY The development of highways, telephones, radio, and television has led to a reduction of the kind of control that communities used to exert over the behavior of its people. Nevertheless, certain attitudes regarding art are likely to exist in the home and the community, and abuses of these attitudes by teachers are likely to be condemned. For example, much great art includes nude figures. Wherever art and artists are suspected of having a morally corruptive influence, the display of nudity is likely to be a source of embarrassment to children who come from homes where nudity is considered unwholesome. A teacher should therefore select artistic images for children to study that accomplish the desired learning without creating social difficulties.

Not only will you find that children have been taught to react to works of art in certain ways, but that they have been taught certain things about doing art. For example, Indian girls from one Indian tribe in the southwest United States are not as good at art as the boys. This happens because these girls have been taught to believe that boys are better at art than they are. By contrast, some white boys have been taught to believe that art is girlish and are reluctant to excel at it. Others have been taught that art is not useful for earning a living. In contrast, some religious and ethnic groups may see art as playing a vitally important part in establishing a cultural identity after a period when these values have been neglected. Such people influence their children profoundly; and the leaders may even try to impose special points of view on a whole school, even though only a minority of that group are enrolled there.

YOU AND YOUR COLLEAGUES The art values of people outside school will have a profound effect on children's attitudes toward learning it.

During a school art lesson, however, it is your presence and your influence that will tend to dominate. Your art program can offer opportunities for learning that might otherwise never occur. And by neglect, it can prevent that learning from occurring. But even more important than the actual instruction is the point of view you, personally, communicate. As mentioned before, most people who became classroom teachers have had relatively little background in art. They are understandably apprehensive about the role they are expected to play in this part of the curriculum. They may even go so far as to decide that art is unimportant. Whatever position you take, it cannot help but be noticed by the children in your class. Apprehension and negativism show themselves when a teacher is unwilling to risk a mess in the classroom and deliberately restricts the art program to work on paper with pencils and crayons. Alternatively, art lessons may be allowed to degenerate into purposeless play periods on Friday afternoons. Children may not be able to translate what is happening into words, but they are sure to conclude that art is not an important part of education. They may have reached a level of readiness for certain art learning, but insofar as the teacher's attitude influences them, they are not likely to pursue it with much enthusiasm.

On the other hand, whatever else happens in an elementary classroom, children who demonstrate outstanding art abilities are likely to be singled out for special attention. Superior students should always receive the help and encouragement they need. In art, this often presents a special problem. One of the myths that we live by states that very few people are by nature highly talented in art and that the vast majority are not creative. We recognize talent in writing and mathematics, but that does not interfere with the efforts of teachers to help less able students grasp the basic skills. And yet, because of this attitude toward art, teachers are likely to accept—if not expect—only a handful of children ever to be outstanding in art and to expect that the majority will show little or no aptitude. This self-fulfilling but erroneous hypothesis plagues elementary art programs and does much to perpetuate the lack of support for art.

Sometimes highly talented children are encouraged to continue with their art at times when they should be engaging in other areas of study. When this happens, an educational disservice is rendered; and if this emphasis is maintained, a child may become so one-sided in her education as to have comparatively few career options open when she leaves school.

OTHER SCHOOL INFLUENCES The human influences affecting children's readiness for art instruction are very powerful. They modify the biological process of maturation in innumerable ways so that a teacher must consider both sets of forces when designing an art program. Program decisions are also affected by the physical environment of the school. Even as seemingly simple a thing as the presence or absence of a water supply in a classroom can affect the opportunities made available to children. And sloping desk tops may make painting such a hazard that both teachers and children would prefer not to continue with it. Of course, that kind of adversity can be turned to an advantage by having the children work on the floor; but the illustration does point to the influence of the physical environment of the school on children's artistic activities and their perceptions of success and worthwhileness.

The presence or absence of adequate storage is also likely to influence the kinds of three-dimensional assignments that are given. The quality of the ventilation or lighting can be of considerable importance in determining performance with the satisfaction derived from art—and the willingness to engage in art in the future.

Other factors that affect children's attitudes toward art also include the opportunities for the display of art work; the presence of needed supplies and equipment; and the use made of such instructional aids as films, slides, and prints. *In sum, the curriculum that you build, no less than your support and enthusiasm, is part of readiness, because all of these factors influence students' attitudes toward art.*

further reading

Anderson, Frances E. *Art for All the Children:* A Creative Sourcebook for the Impaired Child, Springfield, Illinois: Charles C. Thomas, 1978. A valuable source of information on handicapped children, including adaptions of conventional art lessons to meet the requirements of various forms of impairment.

Brittain, W. Lambert. *Creativity, Art and the Young Child.* New York: Macmillan, 1979. Focuses on art in nursery schools and kindergarten.

Gardner, Howard. *The Arts and Human Development.* New York: John Wiley and Sons, 1973. A scholarly study of the psychology of children's development in all the arts, including visual art.

Grove, Richard. *The Arts and the Gifted.* Reston, Va.: The Council on Exceptional Children, 1975. An introduction to the problems and opportunities in teaching all the arts to the gifted and talented.

Lark-Horovitz, Betty, Hilda Lewis, and **Mark Luca.** *Understanding Children's Art for Better Teaching,* 2nd ed. Columbus, Ohio: Charles E. Merrill, 1973. A thorough study of children's development in art for the serious student.

Lowenfeld, Viktor, and **W. Lambert Brittain.** *Creative and Mental Growth,* 6th ed. New York: Macmillan, 1975. Describes development in art from ages 2 through 17.

7

i=instructional objectives

the art that children can learn

A language lesson will understandably be directed at helping children learn how to spell better, perhaps to remember to add double consonants when writing "getting" from "get". A unit of science lessons may be designed to introduce a class to the regions of the earth where particular plant forms exist. The first lesson may be directed at identifying such regions as rain forest, evergreen forest, desert, and grassland. This will be followed by lessons where the class will learn more detailed information about each region. In much the same way, this chapter organizes the subject matter of art to make it easier to teach.

PREPARING CLEAR OBJECTIVES

In most school subjects, teachers select what they are going to teach from one or more basic textbooks, and then supplement it with kits, filmstrips, and books according to the needs of their class. But since basic texts for elementary art have only recently begun to appear, teachers do not usually have a firm foundation to turn to.

Imagine for a moment that you are observing an art lesson in grade four where the children are enjoying an exhilarating time painting pictures about Halloween. Would you expect to know what the children were learning from the painting lesson by watching them? Would you think of asking the teacher exactly what art the children were learning? Would you expect the children to be able to tell you what they were learning? None of these questions would be unreasonable to ask if you were observing a Social Studies lesson. You may believe that Art is different from other subjects and that you should not expect answers to these kinds of questions for individual art lessons. But why not? A bubble of mystery often surrounds art lessons, but when it occurs it is usually because the reasons for teaching the lessons were never clear in the teacher's mind. Art has a very real mystery to it, but the preparation of art instruction is not one of them. That is a craft that can be learned.

This chapter shows that most art objectives can be written down just as easily as objectives for any other subject in the curriculum. Some art objectives are easy to state in words but difficult to evaluate; but that problem occurs just as frequently in other subjects whenever human feelings are involved. This difficulty does not prevent teachers having children express personal feelings in writing or having them interpret stories orally—and also grading their work. When faced with these kinds of tasks, teachers recognize that they cannot be sure that the learning they hoped will occur has been achieved. And the same situation is true for certain kinds of art objectives.

If you can accept the idea that art instruction can and should include clearly stated objectives, the next step is to write them. Instructional objectives are really small subdivisions of the whole subject matter of art, and each class period should include at least one of them—but usually not more than four. In fact, the presence of objectives is the only reason for having an art lesson; and the objectives in each lesson should all build together toward the achievement of the art education purposes you developed in Chapter 5. If you are able to write down clearly what a class is to learn, you are almost certain to know it well enough yourself to help children learn it. Moreover, instructional objectives are most useful when the children can also read them for themselves.

The following objective is written for a teacher to use, and it is clearly stated: "Have children explain that artists make drawings of objects to help in remembering how they look." In contrast, the next objective is unclear and should be re-written: "Establish a basis for understanding non-objective painting." Here is the same objective but this time written in two parts so children whose reading level is approximately Grade 4 could understand what was intended: (a) Explain the word "non-objective" to mean the kind of art that does not look like anything, and (b) Paint a non-objective picture to go with the title, "The Smell of Peanut Butter."

Once you have developed skill in writing clear objectives, you will have confidence in yourself and control over the art program. A word of caution is in order here, however. Beginners are inclined to go to extremes in their efforts at being exact, with the result that they often choose objectives that are easy to write and to teach but are trivial compared with other art objectives that a class of children could be working toward. Skills such as pasting with the least possible paste, or cutting neatly with scissors have their place in an art program; but they should not be allowed to become more important than objectives that stress creative ideas and human emotions.

Art objectives include everything you believe the children in a class are able to learn in the time available for an art lesson. The list will include the meanings of words such as "design," "assymetry," and "paint." The contents of the list of objectives will also be directed toward the development of memory and imagination. For example, a class might make clay models showing the human figure to develop their visual memory of human proportions. Another objective might be to model a person who is very hungry. Achievement of the objectives about proportion can easily be checked. We say these objectives are *explicit*. Achievement of an objective that involves the expression of hunger, however, would be difficult if not impossible to assess accurately by anyone other than the person who experiences the feeling. That objective is *tacit*, and the result has to be taken largely on faith. Both objectives may nonetheless be clearly stated, and both are important in the study of art.

While the content of learning in all subjects ranges from explicit to tacit, few if any tacit objectives are found in elementary mathematics and science. More are found in social studies and language arts. The greatest number occur in the creative and performing arts. And yet a large proportion of elementary school art objectives can be expected to be closer to the explicit end of the scale than the tacit end because of the need for children to establish basic skills and concepts. Moreover the progress of intellectual development in children limits the abstract learning that can be observed. Secondary school and college art studies focus progressively more on subjective, tacit objectives; and again, this is equally true for all subjects of study.

Your best guide in preparing for a career in an elementary classroom is to try and write objectives that have results that both you and the children can see. Where this is not possible, make the objectives clearly understandable to the children. And remember the limitations of these objectives when you come to evaluate children's achievement.

A SIMPLE STRUCTURE
FOR ORGANIZING ART OBJECTIVES

Many more art objectives exist than can ever be taught in one year. By the time you have worked your way through this book you will know more art than you can use; and you will have to be selective. In order to make the best possible choices and to avoid unnecessary duplications and unwanted omissions, objectives need to be organized. For this reason, the remainder of this chapter introduces a way of organizing art instructional objectives; first through a simple basic structure, and then through an expansion of that structure. The introductory statement may satisfy all your needs. However, the expanded structure provides a more complete understanding of the forms that art objectives can take.

The subject matter of art falls into three categories: Seeing, Knowing, and Doing. First of all, objectives that lead toward the improvement of seeing are central to art. They range from recognizing the color green to identifying works of art done by the same artist. They become very personal as children learn to express personal aesthetic judgments about the things they see. Second, an art program requires special words to be known, as well as information on such topics as how pottery is made and why Egyptian art looks the way it does. Children also need to know some important works of art in detail and to know what the artist was trying to tell us. The final category, Doing, includes the skills that children learn, such as how to mix paint to a proper thickness, or to attach pieces of clay so they will not come apart when the clay dries. This category also includes the making of art, where children use their skills and their understanding of art to make pottery and to paint pictures that express strong personal feelings.

The categories of Seeing, Knowing, and Doing provide you with a simple checklist to use for selecting art objectives. Moreover, each part is linked to the others. For example, a class may learn (Knowing) what overlapping means and that artists use it to create a sense of distance in pictures. This knowledge can be shown visually (Seeing), and a child can be asked to point out examples of overlapping when they occur. A drawing may then be required (Doing) in which objects are made to overlap. These three related objectives could become the foundation for a lesson on painting a picture about camping in the summer. If the lesson is successful, the child's art education will have been advanced in ways that were simple to state and easy to understand.

Unless some kind of organization of art objectives is used, your art program is likely to concentrate almost exclusively on the Doing category. Making things is appealing to children of all ages and should be an important part of every child's art education, but activitiy in itself can only lead to a program that lacks substance. The subject matter of art for an elementary school program properly includes a range of art content selected from each of the three categories, not from just one of them.

The structure of art content is a useful framework. The content to be learned now needs to be identified. Children can paint, or model in clay, or carve plaster. Some forms of art, such as drawing, are universal in elementary schools. Others, such as batik, are taught less frequently. The selection of suitable forms of art will be governed by what you know. It is also governed by what you believe your children are capable of handling and by the materials that are available in the school. You will recall from Chapters 2 and 3 that the two main types of art are two dimensional (flat) and three dimensional (solid). Flat art activities tend to predominate in school because of a lack of storage in classrooms and also because flat work tends to be cleaner than three-dimensional work. However, three-dimensional art belongs in an art program just as much as two-dimensional art.

For a given grade level, you may decide that the art for that year should include work in drawing and painting, pottery making, and weaving. The organization for your objectives is now better described as a *matrix* because it consists of two sets of coordinates, as shown in Figure 84. As you become experienced in using the matrix, you may see the need to move objectives from one area of art to another or to repeat objectives in different art areas. At all times, however, you will know what objectives are included in your art program. You will be in control!

	SEEING	KNOWING	DOING
Drawing and Painting	Point out examples of objects in the classroom that are overlapping.	Learn that artists show distance in pictures by making more distant objects smaller and by overlapping.	Draw a scene showing a place you know, using overlapping and objects that look smaller because they are more distant.
Pottery Making	Distinguish pottery made in Greece and Rome from pottery made in China and Japan.	Learn that clay is changed into pottery by baking it in an oven called a kiln.	Wedge clay properly and use slip to bond pieces of clay together.
Weaving	Pick out weaving done in class that looks different from the others.	Define a loom as a framework that stretches warp threads for weaving.	Weave cloth on a cardboard loom, using a design made of contrasting colors.

FIGURE 84   Basic matrix and simple entries

Practice Assignment   Study the objectives listed in Part III, Appendix B (p. 250) and pick out all those that could be learned through clay modelling. Place these art instructional objectives in their proper categories in the basic matrix.

AN EXPANDED STRUCTURE FOR ORGANIZING ART OBJECTIVES

With practice, the basic matrix can become a useful tool for designing art instruction. And yet it can give even better service if each of the categories is subdivided. You are then able to check whether the content of your program is properly balanced in the best interest of the children. (If you do not feel the need to go into such depth, the basic matrix is perfectly adequate.) In this expanded structure, the *Seeing* (perceptual) objectives have been elaborated; the *Knowing* (information) objectives are divided into definition, knowledge about art, and art criticism; and the *Doing* (performance) objectives are separated into skills and art production. Each of these categories will be discussed in turn.

A. SEEING OR PERCEPTUAL OBJECTIVES   Three kinds of perceptual objectives occur in art: (1) observation and memory development, (2) imaginative perceptions, and (3) aesthetic judgments.

Observation and Memory Development. These perceptual skills have to do with the way things look to us, the most important being the ability to see shapes and objects against backgrounds. If you cannot see an object against its surroundings, it is not there so far as you are concerned. Military camouflage is a deliberate effort to make objects difficult to see, whereas highway signs are made to stand out clearly against buildings and trees. All art depends for its existence on the relationships that occur between what is called the *figure* (the things our eyes focus on) and the *ground* (the things our eyes see but do not focus on). In George Bellows' painting (see Figure C), the first thing you see are the two boxers. Only later do you begin to study the other people in the crowded room.

Another type of everyday perceiving that is important in art has to do with knowing what we see. The more we look at something, the more details and subtle differences we can see. People who train themselves to see become sensitive to details and differences and learn to search for them.

Children can be helped to broaden their knowledge of things that can be seen and to remember how things look. These perceptual skills are useful both for daily living and also for the improvement of their art work. Through such learning, children are able to tell when some paint they have mixed matches another color perfectly. And they are able to draw a table top showing the thickness of the wood, because they have learned to look for it. The ability to distinguish details and subtle differences is a mark of an educated eye. It matures with experience and is clearly evident among competent professionals in all walks of life. It happens intentionally, not by chance. This information is collected and becomes part of a visual memory that is in as much need of educating as our memory for facts, sounds, or movements when swimming.

People learn, compare, and remember shapes, colors, lines, and textures as they exist in the world around them. The same kind of learning goes on when these visual qualities are organized by an artist into a work of art. And children can be helped to expand their familiarity with art objects if suitable lesson objectives are included.

Lastly, children can learn how people see things. This information belongs properly under Knowledge (objectives), but children's understanding is much more complete if they observe what happens as well as learn about it. For example, a clump of trees will often be easier to see as one big shape than as separate trees. This kind of organization is by *proximity*. Brightly dressed people in an otherwise drab-looking football crowd will seem linked together by the *similarity* of their bright clothing. Our eyes search for *continuity*, and when seeing a regular pattern they will expect it to repeat itself as before. Our eyes and brain also fill in what we cannot see, so that if we can see only the head and shoulders of someone and their legs, our minds fill in the rest of the body. With a well developed ability for *closure* people quickly recognize an error in a picture where the legs and head of a figure are too close together. The pictures by Thomas Hart Benton (see Plate 1), Henry Moore (see Figure 107) and the sculpture by Louise Nevelson (see Figure 85) all show examples of these kinds of organization. Try to identify them.

Understanding and seeing what happens as we look at three-dimensional space is also important in an art program. The guidelines for the simple perspective that children can learn include overlapping, changes in visible detail, size and color changes, and position in a picture. Each was explained in Chapter 2. Showing distance in art is not so simple, however,

FIGURE 85 Louise Nevelson, *Sky Cathedral* (1958). Assemblage: wood construction painted black, 11′3½″ X 10′¼″ X 18″. Collection, The Museum of Modern Art, New York. Gift of Mr. and Mrs. Ben Mildwoff.

because our brains alter what our eyes see. This is called *constancy*. An elephant will still look big, for example, even though it is a long way away. This is because we know elephants are big. Another kind of constancy shows itself when children draw a window in a house as a rectangle although what they can actually see is a trapezoid (see Figure 86). And colors often seem as bright in the distance as they do up close just because we know the color is bright.

Everyday perception is partly inherited and partly learned. Insofar as it is learned, it needs to be included among the objectives in the elementary art program.

Imaginative Perception. Imaginative perception calls for creative objectives where children learn to associate things that are seen with those that are remembered. A flickering shadow might make a child think of an image of a little goblin or a snake poised to strike. A chance view of a stunted tree might conjure up a strange image of a hand and a foot (see Figure 87). Painters often include such shifting colors and images in their pictures with a kind of "first you see it, now you don't" experience for the observer (see the color picture by Joseph Stella, Plate 2). Fluffy white clouds or ominous thunder heads may each suggest smiling angels or angry giants. The same thing can

FIGURE 86 Rectangles distorted to appear as trapezoids.

happen by looking at the pattern of wood grain on a board, —or better still, making a rubbing when the grain has been raised as a result of being weathered or burned. This kind of objective can also be developed by dropping a blot of watery paint in the center of a sheet of paper and then folding it in half. When the paper is opened out, a class can talk about what the blot makes them think of. The children may even go one step further and make an entirely new picture from the idea stimulated by the blot.

Artists, poets, and composers all use this kind of perception and through it one idea is often transformed into another and eventually lead their ideas from the world of real objects to one filled with visions, dreams and fantasies.

Aesthetic Judgments. The third kind of perceptual objective involves enjoying visual qualities for their own sake. The purple and orange colors in a sunset can be enjoyed not because they are part of a beautiful sunset and not because they remind you of something, but because these purples and oranges when seen together are beautiful. This level of perceiving is often referred to as "consummation." It is enough that what you see is there to be seen; it does not need to be there for any useful reason. You may want to look at the art works in this book and ask yourself if you feel this way about any of them. Abraham Maslow, a psychologist who has been concerned with human excellence—a quality he describes as "self-actualizing"—thinks of aesthetic perception as a part of that quality. It involves "savoring, enjoying, appreciating, caring, in a non-interfering, non-instructive, non-controlling way."* It is the opposite of detailed, logical analyzing; but is every bit as important for human development. The full achievement of this state of mind is unlikely to occur with children, and yet full realization will never occur unless it is continually nurtured from earliest childhood.

In order to learn to perceive in this way, a person must be able to abandon past ideas about the way things look or should look and permit themselves to look at an object with the same sense of wonder that a very young child might who has never seen anything like that object before. It is a kind of perceiving that is both innocent and sophisticated at the same time. If the objectives for imaginative perception are less explicit than those for image development, the ones for aesthetic judgment are essentially personal and tacit. You will have to accept a child's recognition of them without reference to more objective means of measurement.

FIGURE 87 Pavel Tchelitchew, *Tree into Hand and Foot* (1939). Watercolor and ink, 14 X 9 3/4″. Collection, The Museum of Modern Art, New York, Mrs. Simon Guggenheim Fund.

_____* Abraham H. Maslow, *The Farther Reaches of Human Nature.* New York: Viking Press, 1971, p. 69.

Here are three perceptual objectives—one for each category—written for a teacher to read: "(1) Have the class pick out all the right angles that are visible in the classroom. (2) Each child is to say what the shadows you have arranged in the corner of the room remind him of. (3) Each child is to look through picture magazines and draw circles around the colors he likes best."

B. DEFINITIONS Adults use words so often for the things they see that the process becomes habitual. School studies concentrate on verbal communication to the extent that the objects in the real world that led to the invention of words in the first place are often forgotten. This tendency should be reversed in the elementary art program. Direct experiences with objects, materials, and techniques should predominate, while words should fulfill a service function. During the earlier years of elementary school, children use both words and drawings to communicate ideas. Only at the upper grade levels does verbal expression and artistic activity become clearly separate. Doing art and talking about it are inseparable for young children. In Grade 1, for example, a word might be linked more effectively with a picture of an object than with a verbal definition. By the end of their elementary school career, children are usually ready to handle generalizations and more abstract expression. The choice of words selected for them to learn will reflect these needs.

In Appendix B, definitions are given for words that elementary children can learn at each grade level. Your choice of them is conditioned by the readiness of a given class of children, while the actual wording of the definitions you use will be determined by the level of verbal comprehension a class has achieved. Here, for example, is a definition objective for a primary child to hear or read: "*Texture* means the way things feel."

C. KNOWLEDGE ABOUT ART Art knowledge objectives fall into three sub-categories: (1) information about art and artists; (2) media and techniques; and (3) art history.

Information about Art. Children—and many adults—have only a very limited idea of the different kinds of art that exist. To many people, art is restricted to painting, drawing, and sculpture; whereas it also includes architecture, jewelry, ceramics, printed and woven textiles, printmaking, clothing design, advertising design, industrial design, and others. An elementary art program needs to include information about the kinds of art that exist. This information is also needed to dispel popular misconceptions about art, where people believe that it makes little contribution to our way of life. Useful information about the different kinds of art and the artists who create it appears in Part III and throughout the book.

Media and Techniques. Children need to learn about the various art media and the techniques of using them, regardless of whether they are actually able to work with all of them in school. For example, they can learn how clay should be prepared so that it is in good working condition. At the same time or later they can actually prepare clay. They may not have the opportunity to cast a clay model in plaster, but they can learn about how it is done. They will probably never in their lives be able to cast clay models in bronze, although they could visit a foundry where bronze casting is done. And they can learn the basic information about this traditional process for transforming water soluble clay sculpture into permanent metal.

These examples illustrate something of the range of information that can be learned about art media and techniques. Chapters 2 and 3 include numbers of other kinds that are suited to elementary art programs when modified to an appropriate readiness level.

Art History. People have made art for as long as human beings have existed. In fact, works of art are among the most important historical records we have. Becoming familiar with what certain historical works of art look like is a perceptual task; however, information about these works and about the artists who created them is art history. Children can learn facts about African art (p. 238) that will help them understand it better when they see it. They can learn about the lives of Leonardo da Vinci and Rembrandt (p. 282). Objectives can also be written so children can learn about such contrasting painting styles as imitation and fantasy (pp. 263-268).

Three information objectives written for children at different maturity levels to read are: (a) Explain that two pieces of clay can be stuck together with a mixture of water and clay called *slip.* (b) Learn that architecture is a kind of art. (c) Learn that some of the earliest art was painted on the walls of caves.

D. ART CRITICISM The best time for children to begin learning how to make critical judgments about art works is when they are young. It then becomes a natural part of living rather than something tacked on to an education in high school or college. And since most people eventually spend more of their time responding to art done by other people than doing it themselves, this category of objectives deserves to be well represented in the elementary art program.

Instructional objectives for criticism are made about individual works of art—including children's art. Children can learn to recognize various drawings, paintings, prints, sculptures, and architectural structures when they see them. And they can learn to make personal aesthetic judgments about works of art. These are all perceptual objectives. Art criticism differs in that it involves analyzing works of art so that everything about them is known, regardless of whether a person happens to like the art or not. A way of doing this has been developed by Edmund Feldman* of the University of Georgia and has been successfully applied to elementary classrooms by Gene Mittler† of Indiana University. A set of four steps enables a child to move toward the goal of becoming an intelligent critic: (1) literal description, (2) visual analysis, (3) expressive interpretation, and (4) judgment.

_____* Edmund B. Feldman, *Varieties of Visual Experience,* 2nd ed. Englewood Cliffs, N.J.: Prentice-Hall, 1971.

_____† Gene Mittler, "Experiences in Critical Inquiry: Approaches for Use in the Art Methods Class," *Art Education,* V. 26, No. 2, 1973.

Literal Description. The first step toward making a critical judgment is to become familiar with everything that is included in an art work. Children can be helped to describe all the objects to be seen in a particular drawing or painting. A descriptive objective for a class of intermediate level children might read like this: "Be able to name all the things you can see in the picture, *After the Hunt* by William Harnett" (see Plate 6). For the teacher, the same objective would read like this: "Have the class list all of the objects in Harnett's *After the Hunt,* including the four dead birds and the rabbit that the hunter shot; the shot gun and pistol; the powder flask; the hunter's hat and shoulder bag; his staff with its metal point; the saber; the deer antlers; and his drinking flask." This list could easily be extended to include the items on the door—including the door, itself. It could also include more detailed descriptions of each of the items. These decisions rest with the teacher. The advantage of itemizing them, however, ensures that nothing is unconsciously omitted.

Visual Analysis. Works of art often include images taken from the world around us. But instead of naming what is shown, we can use the language of art to explain what we see. A picture of a house among some trees will then be described as an arrangement of light and dark shapes. A sculpture of a fat man riding a skinny mule may be described as a bulbous form that contrasts with an irregular, jagged form. Visual analysis, then, consists of identifying the lines, colors, shapes, and textures present in a work of art and explaining how they are organized.

Harnett's, *After the Hunt* will now be looked at differently. A teacher might want a class to notice the following things: (a) Most of the objects are painted in warm golds and browns that contrast with the cool green of the door; (b) many of the shapes cross underneath the hat to make a design that radiates from that point; (c) while the staff and saber do not cross, they parallel the rifle barrel and the saber; (d) the circular shape of the hunting horn is similar but larger than the brim of the hat. The analysis could be extended to include the balance between the vertical shapes of the dead animals and the horizontals of the door hinges. And as before, the internal qualities of each object could be analyzed.

On completion of the analysis, a child would know the picture much better than if he had looked at it without guidance.

Expressive Interpretation. The task here is to explain the meaning of a work of art. With younger children a teacher may simply want to encourage them to talk freely about what the artist intended. Later they will need to build on the preceding steps and eventually arrive at a well-reasoned conclusion about the artist's intention. In order to do this, however, objectives from the verbal information category C may need to be included to provide background to a work. For example, portraits painted at different times in history were done to make exact records, to flatter powerful people, and to show qualities such as holiness or great wisdom. No one could be expected to interpret the artist's intention in a particular portrait adequately without first understanding something of the intent underlying that particular portrait.

On some occasions artists have written about the meaning of their work; but artists are not always the best interpreters of their work. Eventually, a person makes his own interpretation: it is a hypothesis!

Objectives for critical interpretations consist of probable explanations that children can learn. If several possibilities exist, then individuals might be given the choice of the one they prefer. Harnett's picture tells a story about a man's successful day hunting. The battered hat and the walking staff suggest that he is not a young man. The hunting horn and antlers tell about past enjoyment hunting, while the saber carries a more ominous message about the hunter as a young man. Overall, however, one senses a feeling of great unpretentious satisfaction. And every bit as important as the meaning of the objects is the clear desire of the artist to paint as realistically as possible.

Judgments. A person who is well educated in art criticism will withhold judgment about a work of art until all the other information has been gathered. But to do this calls for a level of artistic knowledge and an ability for abstract reasoning that cannot be expected of elementary children—or of most adults. A more practical goal for your elementary art program is to help children be at ease with the first three steps of this system. Children will still make judgments, of course, and they should be encouraged to pass intellectual judgments about works of art, but these judgments cannot be expected to be complete. (This category is not included in Part III.)

For your information, perhaps more than to help with your teaching, judgments are of three kinds. In the first, the critic compares a work of art with similar works from other historical periods and styles and with the functions performed by those works, then and now. "In making a critical evaluation," writes Feldman, "it is important that the work under scrutiny be related to the widest possible range of comparable works."* The Harnett picture, for example, belongs to a tradition of realistic still-life pictures that dates back to a group of American artists who worked in Philadelphia; and before that to the realistic Dutch still-life paintings of the seventeenth century.

The second kind of judgment is an examination of a work for originality. Where an art object cannot be related to a comparable work from the history of art, it can be judged relative to the artistic problem it is attacking. Harnett was a capable artist but was not noted for his originality. By contrast, the British artist Henry Moore viewed the world in a most original way, like no one else before him (see Figure 107).

The third kind of judgment relates to craftsmanship. The critic studies an art work to determine whether an artist used his materials properly. Uncraftsmanlike work is evident in pottery when a piece has cracks because it was dried or fired carelessly. Harnett was a skilled craftsman in oil paint and his work has retained its brilliance and has not cracked with age. Craftsmanship refers to the choice of materials and techniques as well as to their usage. For example, glass would be a poor choice of material for an object that must withstand frequent jarring shocks.

_____* Feldman, *Varieties,* p. 651.

A note of caution is due here. Experiencing pleasure from works of art is important (see Aesthetic Judgments, p. 164), and one result of children's being able to analyze art critically may be to stimulate enjoyment. But objectives about critical judgments as described here do not involve personal feelings of pleasure, preference, and emotion.

E. SKILLS Learning the necessary skills for making art is quite different from what has to be done when producing an art work. The two need to be treated separately. Skill is required to shade with a pen or pencil in such a way that the change from dark to light is gradual (see Figure 94). The word that artists use is *gradation* (see p. 268). Skill is also required when weaving strips of paper over and under a paper loom (see p. 260). An advanced, upper level elementary school child may be ready to master the first skill. Typical second graders are usually ready to master the second. Other art skills include preparing clay for use, tearing paper in half accurately, mixing paint together to produce a special color, tying macramé knots neatly and evenly, and using paste correctly. Appendix B provides a list of the most common art skills for each grade level. Choices of skill objectives are determined by the availability of art materials, the readiness levels of children, and your own knowledge of art. As with most skills, mastery comes with practice, so you should expect skill objectives to reappear periodically in lessons throughout the school year.

Here is a skill objective written for a child to read: "Mix five different colors of green, using different amounts of yellow and blue."

F. ART PRODUCTION An effective art program requires work in both understanding and producing art, and yet for most children the production of art will lie at the heart of their interest. The key to writing good product objectives is to be sure that the class is perfectly clear about what you want done. If you just ask them to paint a landscape when you really want them to paint a landscape in tempera, showing farmland and trees, where the picture is to fill all of a sheet of paper, then both you and the children will end by being dissatisfied. Moreover, the best product objectives will be deliberately correlated with objectives from other categories, for example, checking to be sure that the horses are properly proportioned (Observation); knowing that tempera paint should be thick and creamy (Knowledge: Media); or showing an ability to mix tempera thickly (Skills).

USING YOUR MATRIX OF OBJECTIVES

The categories of art objectives discussed in this chapter require you to be clear about the art you want children to learn; and the matrix makes the task manageable. Any organization of this kind, however, will always be in the process of being improved. You will be continually adding, deleting, and modifying objectives in keeping with your experience as a student and a teacher.

The matrix permits you to insert objectives in the appropriate categories. It also enables you to check through the other categories of the matrix to determine whether any related objectives need to be included. The categories and subcategories give you a checklist to assist in setting up sets of interlocking objectives that can eventually go together to form the basis for lessons.

Figure 88 illustrates the process of building a set of objectives. You might begin by writing under the Skills category (E) the objective of mixing paints together to make variations of brown. This skill objective would be proper if a class of children had already learned how to prepare paints and to wash brushes before changing to a new color. This task relates directly to the everyday perceptual task (A) of being able to make subtle distinctions, in this case among different kinds of brown. The information category (C) then might include an objective where the children learn which colors can be mixed together to make brown, and also what browns can be expected from using different proportions of those colors. An objective for the art production category (F) might then be proposed, whereby a landscape was to be painted but with the color restricted to different browns. This decision might cause you to insert the word "landscape" and its definition under (B). You might also want to include the word "monochrome," if you felt your class was ready for it.

As demonstrated, you would now have a set of painting objectives for five out of the six categories. A set of painting objectives for a sequence of lessons or even a full year of instruction can be built in the same way. When a collection of objectives seems complete, you should evaluate it to determine whether anything important has been omitted and whether any of the

FIGURE 88   Using the expanded matrix for planning instructional objectives

	SEEING (Perceptual (Objectives) (A)	KNOWING (Information Objectives)			DOING (Performance Objectives)	
		Definitions (B)	Knowledge about Art (C)	Art Criticism (D)	Skills (E)	Art Production (F)
Painting	Distinguish different kinds of brown	"Landscape": a picture of the outdoors showing a view. "Monochrome": a picture painted in variations of one color.	Red and green make brown. Red, yellow, and black make brown.	None on this lesson.	Mix different kinds of brown.	Paint a fall or winter landscape with the colors restricted to different kinds of brown.

objectives are inappropriate and should be deleted or modified. The same procedure is followed with all of the areas of art you wish to cover in the art program. Appendix B will be useful to you as you build a matrix of objectives of your own.

further reading

Baker, Robert L. and **Richard E. Schutz** (eds.). *Instructional Product Development,* New York: Van Nostrand Reinhold, 1971. A technical introduction to instructional development for the serious student.

Davies, Ivor K. *Objectives in Curriculum Design.* Maidenhead, England: McGraw-Hill Book Co. (UK) Ltd., 1976. A readable guide to the various points of view about objectives in education and the problems faced by educators as they plan to make use of them.

Hardiman, George W. and **Theodore Zernich,** (eds.). *Curricular Considerations for Visual Arts Education:* Rationale, Development, and Evaluation. Champaign, Illinois: Stipes Publishing Co., 1974. The articles from the one by Walker through to the one by Duchastel and Merrill are most useful relative to objectives in art teaching.

Rouse, Mary J. and **Guy Hubbard,** "Structured Curriculum in Art for the Classroom Teacher: Giving Order to Disorder," *Studies in Art Education,* Winter, 1970. Presents an organization for objectives in art education based on research.

8

S = strategies for teaching

the design of imaginative art experiences

Teachers need a clear understanding of the kinds of art children are capable of learning. By themselves objectives give little or no indication of how that learning might be accomplished. Successful art teaching requires that lesson experiences encourage the achievement of objectives in every possible way.

An important first step is to understand clearly the difference between what objectives are and what needs to be done so children accomplish them. An objective is something you want children to learn. The strategy is your plan for getting them to learn it. For example, an art lesson may involve visiting a zoo and drawing an elephant. The class has an exciting trip and all the children draw an elephant in the way you asked. You asked them to draw the elephant so its legs, body, head, and trunk were all the proper size and thickness. You also asked them to draw in the shading to make the elephant very solid-looking. But the visit to the zoo, in itself, was not included among the objectives of the lesson. The visit was a strategy designed to interest the children to such a degree that the actual objectives—learning the proportions of an elephant and using shading on simple rounded shapes—would be achieved. *A strategy, then, is a plan for accomplishing an instructional objective; it is a means of achieving an end.* Means and ends both belong in the design of art lessons, but do not confuse them. If you do confuse them, you may find yourself measuring a child's achievement of a strategy and neglecting the achievement of an objective. This is easily done and is a disservice to the child.

When you feel clear about this distinction, you are ready to start searching for possible solutions—strategies—to questions such as: What are the more effective ways of helping children learn how to mix the color brown? Does art history always have to be taught from books or slide-lectures? Are some other ways of teaching hand-built pottery better than the one you use? To elaborate on this last question, you might ask whether it is best to give a demonstration or to have the class work through the process with you, step by step. Might it be a good idea to set up a mirror over your head so the children can watch your hands from the same position they see their own?

Since art is essentially visual and manipulative, it is natural to expect art teaching strategies to include those kinds of activities. But since the content of art also includes learning verbal information and critical skills, so opportunities for the development and practice of these competencies need to be considered. However, art is above all individual, exploratory, and expressive; so strategies of art instruction need to stimulate those qualities especially.

The characteristics of the children who are to do the learning were discussed in Chapter 6, but what may not have been emphasized is the irrepressible urge shown by children to draw, paint, and model. Not until they reach pre-adolescence during the upper intermediate grades does this desire diminish. In effect, a natural force supports your art teaching. If a difficulty exists, it lies in teachers not feeling the need to put undue energy into preparing art lessons compared, say, with reading. And yet, if instruction is not planned sensitively, this natural artistic urge will diminish or will not reach the heights that otherwise would have been possible. Both in school and out it often appears that where anything is particularly enjoyed it is judged to be unimportant and may be neglected in favor of other activities which are not enjoyed as much or where students are less successful. It is entirely too human to become overly involved with obvious educational obstacles at the expense of experiences through which children might learn what it means to excel in something. This is one of the dilemmas of elementary art teaching.

Instructional resources for elementary art are typically very modest. The level of art skills most classroom teachers possess also tends to be modest, because of a lack of experience. On the other hand, teachers soon come to know their children very well; and as indicated above, individuality is the essense of art. In effect, classroom teachers are well informed in all that is needed in a good art program—except for personal expertise in art. And since it is the children who do the art and not the teacher, even that obstacle ceases to be critical. The important quality to be developed is imagination.

You are a designer of events. Up to this point, you have had to explain your beliefs and to learn about how children's development influences art teaching. The culmination of that process was the preparation of clearly stated objectives. This chapter differs in that you now need to apply your creative imagination so that children will learn as effectively as possible.

No one correct way exists for successfully organizing art instruction, although some school districts may require teachers to follow a particular approach. However, good art instruction tends to have certain things in common. One of them is that effective lessons are those that have been thought through carefully and completely before they were taught. While that may seem obvious, lack of clarity and completeness is the most common pitfall for the beginning teacher. Part of the problem is quite understandable. A college student or new teacher has yet to learn what the basic needs of an art lesson are, or what opportunities or obstacles need to be anticipated. This chapter is directed at helping you prepare yourself so that with the addition of some practical experience, you will be able to assemble lessons satisfactorily. Putting lessons together involves judgments about whether all the parts are present, whether each part is clearly stated, and whether the parts are arranged in the best way possible. These judgments will also include decisions about communicating the lesson material to children. The model used in this book, for example, departs from traditional art teaching practice in that children are given access to the contents of the lesson in the form of material written specially for them—in much the same way that occurs in academic subjects (see Chapter 1 and Appendix A of the data bank). The reason for this approach is that children as well as teachers are likely to perform better if they have clearly prepared information in their hands that can be used as needed. The strong emphasis on specific visual supports for art lessons in this book (Chapter 4) accounts for another communication decision, this time arising from the uniqueness of art as a subject of study: Words are rarely adequate for carrying the predominantly visual information and ideas that are part of art study. While neither of these decisions is highly original, a surprising amount of art teaching is carried on without children having anything to read or to look at that might help them learn the lesson objectives.

A solution to the problem of how to stimulate individuality in classrooms of 25 children when class periods are 40 to 50 minutes has also been proposed. In Chapter 1 a plan for sequencing instruction that embodies choices for children to make offers a solution (see p. 11). This one works well in practice, but perhaps you have an idea that surpasses it; in which case, try it. See whether it works and if so, use it. But your belief that the support of individuality in the art class will encourage the achievement of art objectives comes before your decision to try out any strategy of individualization. And should you conclude that children in some future class were very immature and would find such freedom of choice frustrating, then you might adopt a different strategy—regardless of what you thought was ideal.

You will also need to repeat objectives, for the simple reason that few people ever learn anything fully the first time they are exposed to it. An instructional objective may remain exactly the same, but you will need to design a different art experience for the children to do. At this point, you begin to look beyond individual lessons to strategies that extend over a period of time and allow for objectives to be periodically reinforced so that by the end of the year, a class will know them thoroughly. Skills improve with practice, but not by repeating the exact same lesson. That would lead to boredom. Information about art has to be built up systematically over time. In sum, the design of art instruction consists of manipulating lessons and lesson parts so that children are aided in their learning as fully as possible; here this means using the raw materials outlined in Appendix B of the data bank.

So far, the discussion has only referred to planning, and careful planning is essential. But a plan has value only when put to the test. People always want their good ideas to succeed, and one of the difficult tasks facing a teacher is to withhold judgment on an idea until at least the first trial is over. Even then, people tend to defend what they did, unless it was an obvious failure. The best approach is the opposite, and that is to believe in your ideas and yet also be on the constant lookout for imperfections when those ideas are tried out. You are likely to resent criticism from another person; but if you can be critical of yourself, you will continually be refining good ideas and discarding those that are less good.

The remainder of the chapter is about techniques you can use when designing your art program. By way of introduction, you may want to keep the following ideas in mind. Art instructional strategies exist for the sole purpose of transmitting one or more of the three kinds of objectives discussed in the previous chapter: Seeing, Knowing, and Doing.

A Christmas card lesson could be used to teach lettering design, or printing skills, or designing shapes to fill a space—or all three. Similarly, bringing a pet to school to draw may be done to help make objects look solid, to understand animal proportions, to draw surface textures, or all three. More creative strategies will occur as you practice thinking of unusual ideas, such as having a class model in clay when blindfolded, or draw with the opposite hand from the one they normally use.

Since some art objectives are more intellectual than physical, you will also want to consider how best to incorporate them into your program without disappointing a class of children who have been looking forward to the physical involvement of more conventional art lessons. For example, were a portrait photographer to visit a class to talk about his art, and to take some pictures, the children would learn about photography as an art and would probably be so enraptured by what was happening that they would not give a thought to the loss of an opportunity to paint or draw.

While strategies function to serve objectives, you may often find yourself starting with a particular strategy and selecting objectives to fit that strategy simply because good ideas do not happen as often as you would like. Since no one part of a lesson is more or less important than another, it probably doesn't matter much which comes first—just as long as you fully understand the different functions that are being performed by each.

Finally, as you assemble lesson material for a school year, you will want the program to have character. Special experiences scattered through the year will add spice, something to look forward to with anticipation and something to look back on with pleasure. Novel experiences that do not require excessive preparations contribute greatly to maintaining a high level of interest in art. Other experiences, by contrast, should be quieter and less dramatic in order that other kinds of learning can be accomplished. Moreover, a constantly high level of excitement is likely to be more than most children can tolerate. The design of art instruction, at its best, is an art—but not one that is reserved just for a specialist.

TECHNIQUES FOR TRANSMITTING OBJECTIVES

Some of the more useful techniques through which art instructional objectives may be transmitted are listed here. Examples appear in each category to explain how they may be used in an elementary art program. But you should see these examples as points of departure for your own imaginative ideas rather than as statements describing the limits of what is possible. As you study this material, keep clear in your mind what elementary children are like. Success in selecting strategies depends as much on the readiness of a class to respond positively to the experience as it does to the accurate matching of experiences with the objectives to be learned.

STORIES, MUSIC, AND MOVEMENT Stimulation for visual art lessons often arises from other arts that children enjoy. You only have to watch children's faces as they listen to a teacher reading a thrilling story to appreciate the impact it is having on their imaginations. Some adults—perhaps you—have an aptitude for inventing stories. And children themselves are often willing to engage in their own story telling.

Stories have a wide range of applications in art teaching, from drawing objects and events that were described to trying to capture the feelings expressed. Poetry can provide a similar kind of assistance, with perhaps even greater opportunities for suggesting visual images than prose. Poetry rhymes, and children can read poems to help them better understand rhythm in pictorial design. Poetry is linked with music through singing, and most children like to sing. Songs can be used both to support a happy classroom atmosphere and to help children learn to draw and paint different types of lines to correspond with the moods of different songs. The addition of melody will often increase the effectiveness of words in a song to give children a better opportunity for making expressive designs and pictures. The range of songs from choral to western to country to popular will be limited only by what is available and seems suitable for helping a particular class learn.

The range of instrumental music is every bit as great as the range of songs. Music moves through time like lines move across paper. It can be colorful or plain, busy or quiet. Harmonies can be rich and complicated or bold and simple. Music possesses qualities that describe people and places; it conveys human emotions; and music makes appealing sounds that only have meaning as music. It is a natural teaching strategy to use when communicating art skills and concepts, undoubtedly because its purposes are similar to those of art but through sound.

Dance is another related art that can be used effectively to help in your teaching. Children soon begin to move rhythmically when you play music that has a beat to it. Hands and feet start first, followed by the whole body. Dancing captures bodily feelings that can be translated into pictures and clay models, and it opens the door to talking about how artists like Edgar Degas have captured dance movements in their work (see Figure 89). You can expect spirited results from a class that is asked to paint a picture of dancing waves on a sunny afternoon after they, themselves, have imagined themselves to be dancing waves.

DRAMA AND GAMES Drama can mean charades, puppet plays, parades, and dressing up, just to name a few examples. Halloween and Valentine's Day celebrations need not degenerate into the all too familiar mass production of stereotyped pumpkins and hearts if the teacher recognizes the creative opportunity these festivals offer. Children may enjoy creating valentines and also learn to block print greeting cards. Thanksgiving can be a time for making collages of turkeys where each one is quite unlike any other turkey they have ever seen and yet still looks like a turkey. Children may also find out what a real turkey actually looks like and not take their information from the cartoon stereotypes that bombard them every November.

FIGURE 89 Edgar Degas, Bronze statuette of a dancer. All rights reserved, The Metropolitan Museum of Art, Bequest of Mrs. H. O. Havemeyer, 1929, The H. O. Havemeyer Collection.

Ideas for Halloween masks can lead to studying masks from other parts of the world, such as Africa, the South Seas, and Far East. The class might act out the characters portrayed by masks they like and then make their own versions, thus learning about customs in different parts of the world (see Figures 90 and 91). From the same task, they can learn techniques for attaching materials securely. From mask-making, it is only a step to creating costumes to go with the masks, culminating in lessons in criticism where the class talks about their masks and costumes.

FIGURE 90 Mexican dance mask

FIGURE 91 Indonesian theater mask. Courtesy of the Indiana University Art Museum.

Puppet plays also offer rich opportunities for uniting art with role-playing. At the same time, children can learn about correct proportions of the face and also distortions that convey certain emotions. Construction techniques with clay and papier-mâché offer additional learning opportunities with puppetry. All of this information and skill could be acquired by some other kind of activity; but this is just one method of conveying important skills and concepts to a class of children.

Games in art fulfill related functions to dramatic play in that the activities make use of knowledge or require that it be learned. One visual memory game is to have each child complete a small part of a large picture. Blindfold guessing games can lead them to heightened awareness of how objects feel to the touch; this will help with sculpture as well as drawing. Remembering artistic reproductions can become a speed competition. Or it may be used as a detective problem, in which only a small piece of a picture is visible and the children have to identify the whole work. These kinds of activities may begin as little more than guessing games, but they can mature to the point where individuals are able to reach sophisticated conclusions about works of art and also to compare the quality of each other's ideas.

USING THE ENVIRONMENT   Classrooms can be dull, lifeless places or they can be constantly changing, vibrant supplements to teaching. Children's art lends itself naturally to be displayed, but displays enhance learning only if they are well planned. The work from a given lesson, for example, may be put on the wall, together with a brief written statement announcing what was learned from that lesson. The display then becomes a continuation of the lesson, which reinforces the objectives in ways that would not happen were the works to be filed away immediately on completion or sent home to be shown to parents. Displays of art from other rooms in the school and items from local secondary schools can also contribute significantly to the art instruction in your class. Local artists may also be only too happy to display their work in your room. The presence of original works can have a profound effect on the attitudes of children toward art.

Pictures include various parts of our environment, such as clouds, bridges, grassy banks, and boats. But pictures are flat, while real environments consist of solid objects surrounded by space. Pictures are the results of interpreting an environment; but younger children are not likely to comprehend abstract pictorial relationships, although they are beginning to understand the positioning of one object next to another in the real world. They can move around in the classroom environment, touching the parts, and in doing so learning much more than is possible by viewing a scene from only the one position shown in the picture.

Special events during the year, such as birthdays and Christmas, can provide opportunities both for transforming a classroom and providing instruction in art at the same time. A room is a three-dimensional volume, and decorating it effectively is a design problem where the task is to organize objects in space so they enhance the overall appearance of the room when seen from any and all positions.

Schools are often so bound up with working on the flat surfaces of books that it is easy to overlook the fact that children—and you, too—are enveloped in a world made up of solid objects and that people need to be as well educated to work in that solid world as in more bookish ways. To decorate a classroom for Christmas thus fulfills an educationally more profound function when seen in this light. Rather than being a pleasant but superficial experience, it becomes an important educational experience into which you may introduce instruction in academic subjects.

Perhaps the most striking environmental value comparable with it is to build enclosed spaces within the room-space of a classroom. You may have the construction skills yourself, or you may have to recruit willing parents to help you. But children delight in small environments that suggest tree houses, jungle dens, space ships, or simply quiet corners. With your help they can learn how to organize themselves in space and how to embellish their surroundings. A classroom so modified becomes a daily adventure in the lives of children that expands their understanding and attitudes toward the imaginative use of space in ways that are not possible in rooms furnished only with stark conventional school room furniture.

VISITS AND VISITORS   Do you remember going on field trips when you were a child? Such visits often have a lasting impact on attitudes both then and later in life. Perhaps you went to a circus, a baseball game, or a rodeo; or maybe the first time you saw a ballet was through a school outing (see Plate 11 and Figure J). Visits that enhance the art program can be most effective and where visits are not possible, individuals may be invited to your room and have considerable impact on your class.

A visit to an art museum will probably require the granting of parental permission, the scheduling of a school bus, the presence of chaperones, and other arrangements. If the visit is properly organized for instruction, you or one of the museum staff should talk to the class about the museum some time before the visit. Some museums send out sound filmstrips to enable teachers to prepare their classes for what they will see. The educational staffs of museums are usually more than happy to help with the particular instructional needs of classes. Long before the visit, you should go to the museum to plan what should happen. For example, if you think that a certain Greek pottery statuette (see Figure 92) is important to see because your class will soon be making some of their own models, then inform the staff. A collection of African art (see Figure 93) may be important for your black children to see, because it represents the artistic values of the land where their families came from. The possibilities for useful integration of museum visits with your art program are almost limitless. But good results will occur only as a result of thoughtful planning.

Art teaching objectives are as appropriate in natural history museums and aquariums as social studies objectives are appropriate in art museums. Visits need not be confined to museums, however. Children will not fully comprehend the streets they live in until required to look at them. A walk

FIGURE 92 Greek statuette of a workman cooking, 5th century B.C. Courtesy, Museum of Fine Arts, Boston, Catherine Page Perkins Fund.

FIGURE 93 African wood-carving from the Camaroons. Courtesy of the Indiana University Art Museum.

through the neighborhood surrounding the school may thus be a revelation if it is thoughtfully planned and is directly related to in-class work. Such a lesson could be to make a picture that shows the things to be seen in the neighborhood (see Plate 10 and Figures K and M). Even a lesson that takes the class into the school grounds and directs their attention at what may be observed there can sharpen the perceptions of what is to be seen in ways that will never occur as long as they see it solely as a place for play. Wherever you take them, your goal is to open their eyes—or rather their whole beings—to places and events in ways that will enlarge their experience and their ability to express themselves. Younger children, especially, are voracious learners, but they need to be fed with real life experiences not ones that are abstract or remote from their experience. Drawing, rather than language, is perhaps the most forceful way for many of them to demonstrate their growing understanding of these places and events. In this sense, then, your art is as much a basic school subject as any of the more familiar basic subjects—if not more so.

Going outside the classroom is always a special treat. However, the presence of visitors is another way of stimulating the desire to learn. Most prospective visitors are as close to you as the end of the nearest telephone. Numbers of parents, you will discover, are either employed as artists or are engaged in art-related occupations. Others will have art expertise either because of their past education or because of a vocational interest that has developed during adulthood. One child's father may be a competent metal sculptor while the mother of another child is an accomplished potter. The parents of another child may have an absorbing interest in the art of Japan as a consequence of military service overseas. All of these people possess abilities that can be very helpful for teaching art objectives. Your task is to identify them and then invite them to your class.

Professional artists and designers may also be invited to come and talk about their work. Architects may bring slides or models. Illustrators may make sketches of some of the children. Photographers may be willing to set up their studio lights and take pictures. Experiences such as these leave indelible images in the minds of children about art and artists that richly enhance their understanding and are likely to help modify the unfortunate cultural stereotype of the artist as a grubby and impractical person. If you explain in advance your course objectives with these visitors, you will find them to be invaluable resource people for reinforcing your art teaching goals—and the children may not even realize what they have learned until they begin using it in later lessons you have designed.

INDIVIDUAL REWARD AS THE KEY TO SUCCESS

This chapter discusses art teaching as a design process where content is organized so children can learn it. The task involves class-sized groups, but the results appear as individual solutions to problems—all of which can be correct. No special sequence of learning is necessary in art instruction as in mathematics, for example. And children are drawn to art in ways that are not typical of other subjects. Moreover, professional artists are present in all communities and follow a variety of careers. Large buildings are erected to house historical and contemporary works of art of which no duplicates exist anywhere. And no day goes by without children being exposed to art and design. A person may choose not to read, but he cannot disregard the visual arts. In effect, art is quite unlike other subjects in the school curriculum, and at best an art class will differ from what goes on in mathematics and physical education.

Children solve artistic problems in their own unique ways, and as long as solutions meet the objectives all of the children in a class who succeed deserve to be recognized. Moreover, since single correct solutions are unlikely in art, everyone can be a winner in a different way. The task of evaluating success in art is often difficult simply because of the uniqueness of the subject, and that topic will be addressed at length in the next chapter. The point to be made here is that evaluations are more than assessments of performance or indicators of the need for remediation. Evaluation at its best is a force to stimulate learning. A warm, encouraging smile may dispel fears about the possible failure of an art product. Direct references to the parts of a child's art work that are successful can be a powerful motivational force in the effort given to adding to that success. You may permit children to re-do a part of their work that was unsuccessful to give them an opportunity to improve it. The evidence of improvement is then present to be observed and give pleasure. Such an outcome can lead to the willingness to exert the extra effort needed to achieve the next objective.

Some children may seem to be unsuccessful in spite of every effort. However, if you can find something good to comment on in what the child has done, then the crushing sense of defeat that is likely to lead to reduced effort in future lessons can be alleviated. All subjects should probably be taught in this manner, but art presents a special need for it, especially among pre-adolescent children in the upper levels of the elementary school. As you read in Chapter 6, children of this age are beginning to realize the ambivalent cultural attitudes toward art and artists. Most of them are becoming aware of their inability to draw and paint in the generally approved representational style. They are likely to be aware of the popular myth—and it is a myth—that in art, unlike other areas of study, people succeed because of native talent; and those without talent cannot be successful at all. Teachers of children in this upper level of elementary school, therefore, need to take every measure they can to minimize failure and to maximize success. For many if not most children, the upper elementary years mark the decline of confidence in themselves artistically. Armed with the knowledge of the problem, however, a thoughtful teacher can do much to prevent the kind of total eclipse that occurs so often in the art of adolescents.

Knowing what success feels like is vital to healthy growth, and for most children art provides this experience. For some it may be the only occasion in school where this occurs; and it is specially important for the art of these children to be taught well.

Your own success when teaching art is as important as that of your children, for the reason that if you do not enjoy it then the quality of your teaching will suffer; and however hard you try not to let it interfere with your teaching, it cannot help but have a negative influence. For you, personally, the enjoyment may be in trying your hand at making art the children are to do or reading about art and artists they will learn about. You may alternatively—and ideally—find your pleasures in designing innovative lessons. But whatever else may be neglected in your art teaching, your own rewards must be protected.

All of the experiences described in this chapter are natural vehicles for helping the visual art program. Moreover, imagination and fantasy are among the qualities that distinguish healthy individuals of all ages—including you. And people solve problems creatively because of a highly developed sense of playfulness, where they do not feel bound by a sense that only one correct answer to a problem is possible. Ideas for creative teaching are much the same. The issue is not that any single way of teaching exists, but that a teacher—often with the help of a class of children—continually plays with ideas for alternative methods of teaching. Unlocking these talents is one of the most valuable services that educators can perform.

further reading

Fraser, Kathleen. *Stilts, Somersaults, and Headstands:* Game Poems Based on a Painting by Peter Bruegel. New York: Atheneum, 1968. An unusual approach to art lesson ideas.

Hurwitz, Al and **Stanley S. Madeja.** *The Joyous Vision:* A Source Book for Elementary Art Appreciation, Englewood Cliffs, N.J. Prentice-Hall, 1977. Extends the topic of the chapter and reports on numbers of successful art appreciation programs that have been developed.

Mattil, Edward L. *Meaning in Crafts.* Third edition. Englewood Cliffs, N.J.: Prentice-Hall, 1971. A rich assortment of crafts experiences suitable for regular elementary classrooms.

Shissler, Barbara. *Sports and Games in Art.* Minneapolis, MN. Lerner, 1966. More ideas for art lessons.

Wachowiak, Frank. *Emphasis Art.* Third edition. New York: Thomas Y. Crowell, 1977. Contains many ideas for art lesson strategies and is profusely illustrated with examples of children's work.

The two monthly magazines, *School Arts* and *Arts and Activities* contain a wealth of art lesson strategies. Study of back issues can be particularly useful.

9

m = MEASURING ACHIEVEMENT

the art that children have learned

Most people who have been students for a long time think of the process of evaluating achievement as a special event—often a threatening one—that comes at the end of a course of study. The results of examinations are expected to reveal how well a person has learned the content included in that course. However, teachers need to look at this stage of educating more broadly. Education is really a continuous process, so the end of one task is at the same time the beginning of the next one. Measuring achievement is better thought of as part of a cycle of events, therefore, than as a conclusion. If anything, a child's elementary education marks only the beginning of learning, never the termination.

Because art is often thought to be lacking in valuable subject matter, considerable attention has been given throughout this book to the tasks involved in preparing instructional objectives. And yet, the importance of knowing whether those objectives have been achieved is every bit as great as having defined them clearly in the first place.

In order to help you understand what is involved in this part of teaching art, the chapter is divided into several sections. The first introduces you to what is meant by measurement in art. This is followed by an explanation of how to reach decisions about children's success and failure and the methods to use for assessing each of the outcomes of the different categories of objectives. The chapter continues with suggestions for a program of art evaluation and how to report the results. A final statement directs your attention to analyzing the effectiveness of your own teaching efforts. Achieving objectives is what children should do; but they will be helped or hindered by the decisions and actions of teachers. The entire process of educating is a joint enterprise that involves both children and their teachers, and the efforts of both need to be evaluated.

ACHIEVEMENT IN ART
CANNOT BE TAKEN FOR GRANTED

As a result of a unique history, art education has been allowed to develop in elementary schools with little or no attention given to what children are actually achieving. The resistance to measuring achievement in art is partly the result of a tradition where people believe that art cannot be treated like other kinds of learning. Those holding this point of view believe that if children work enthusiastically in an art class, then their education in art will unfold naturally and adults should not interfere. That claim would never be made about other subjects in the school curriculum, however, and rightly so. Teachers are employed to steer children toward achieving desirable knowledge and skills. These actions are deliberate efforts to achieve certain results. Education is too important to be left to chance; and this is as true for art as for any other subject.

This does not mean that art can be evaluated easily. Art possesses its own unique peculiarities. But it does mean that every effort should be made to report what has been learned as fully as you can. Success in art, therefore, cannot be taken for granted.

In the absence of any planned system of evaluation, you will have to rely on personal feelings, which may or may not relate to worthwhile instructional objectives. Some of the more intelligent children in a class will rapidly realize when instructional objectives are irrelevant and the actual objective for art is actually to please the teacher. It is never possible to separate your feelings entirely from any part of what goes on in the classroom, but every effort should be made to use valid evaluation procedures, that is, to measure achievement only against the objectives selected for given instruction. This approach does not guarantee your professional success, but it does make your efforts honest. The more you can adopt a rational, objective way of judging what children have done, the better able you will be to propose enrichment and remedial experiences—and the more you will earn the respect of the children in your class.

Another difficulty with art teaching is the unwillingness of teachers to pass negative judgments on children's art works. This is sometimes the result of classroom teachers not knowing very much about art and consequently feeling themselves to be unqualified to express judgments. Some teachers are of the opinion that children should all believe themselves to be successful in art and that it is harmful to say otherwise. However, no one does this in other school subjects, regardless of their personal background. This is partly due to the fact that objectives in other subjects are usually stated fairly explicitly. Moreover, principals and parents would not permit such disregard for achievement. Those who lose most of all when art assessment is disorganized, of course, are the children.

The word measurement is usually used in connection with standardized tests where fairly precise assessments can be made. It is used more broadly here to encourage you to make every effort toward being precise. The words "assessment" and "evaluation" are used interchangeably throughout this chapter for the same kind of activity, but "measurement" is emphasized, for the reason that it is necessary to take a stand about what children have learned.

At the risk of over-reacting to what has often happened in the past, this chapter has been written to encourage you to adopt a strong position in measuring achievement in art. This situation in art teaching is not any different from what it has always been: some kinds of achievement can be assessed more easily than others. But instead of adopting the negative position of declining to commit yourself at all, you are encouraged to look at the situation positively. Many, if not most, objectives in elementary school art *can be evaluated* with reasonable certainty, and you owe it to the children you teach to report their achievement as fully and as accurately as you can. Difficulties are inevitable; but measuring achievement in every subject presents special problems. If you do take a firm stand, however, you will discover that as your experience increases, you will be progressively better able to resolve the difficulties arising from the more individual and abstract kinds of achievement that occur in art.

GUIDELINES FOR MEASURING ACHIEVEMENT

When you write an instructional objective for art, the intent is to state what you want the class to learn. It is something to aim for in your teaching. When the time comes to decide whether a class (with your help) has achieved an objective, the task changes. You then have to decide what the children need to do to show you that they have learned the objective. You also need to decide on the best method to use for measuring the achievement of the various objectives you have chosen. These decisions, moreover, have to be made in advance of the time when you will actually do the evaluating.

If an objective is clearly written and is well fitted to the readiness of a given group of children, sufficient information will be present about what a child should be able to say or do that some form of assessment can occur. You might require children to learn the meaning of a word that is an important addition to their vocabulary. Your evaluation of success might range all the way from acceptance of a word-perfect definition to recognizing that a seeming jumble of words captures the essential meaning of the word. On the other hand, you would reach a point where a child would respond in a wholly unacceptable way. He would then have failed to achieve the objective.

In contrast, an objective that calls for skill in shading with pencil to show gradations from dark to light calls for measurement techniques that are visual rather than verbal. You could try and use words to explain success as shading that had no uneven parts to it, but it would be much easier to show an example of a gradation done with pencil and use it as the standard or criterion. A child would then be judged against the quality of the example

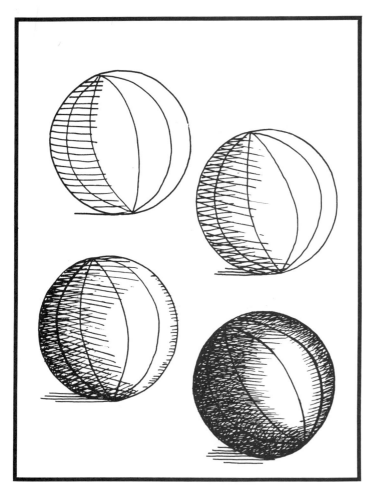

FIGURE 94 Gradations

rather than against a descriptive verbal statement. In order to test yourself, look at the pen & ink gradations in Figure 94 and decide which one you think is satisfactory for a typical child in Grade 4. Then pick out the gradation where the quality of work is only just satisfactory for a child in Grade 4. You will probably experience considerable difficulty at first making these kinds of decisions; and yet with practice the task becomes easier.

While these two examples are both relatively simple, they illustrate the two principal ways in which learning in art shows itself and can be evaluated. And as your skill improves in the verbal and visual measures of achievement, both you and the children you teach will know when success has occurred. Evaluation of learning in art will then cease being a mystery.

Preparing criteria for acceptance becomes a problem when personal feelings are involved. For example, an objective might require that an ink blot be used as a stimulus for imaginative perceiving. The objective might read like this: "Describe an idea for a picture after looking at an ink blot." The objective is stated satisfactorily, but the only criterion for judging a child's achievement is that she should describe an idea—her own idea. You would have to accept whatever she said for this kind of imaginative objective, just as you would where a child made a personal aesthetic judgment about a piece of sculpture. On the other hand, as children continually make statements of these kinds, they can be steered toward ever-increasing depths of feeling and given reasons for those feelings.

The work of developing personal ideas and feelings is a most important part of an art education, but the results cannot be evaluated with much precision. The best you can do is make as honest an appraisal as you can of what children say and do.

The results of these efforts inform you of the success children are experiencing. They can also tell you when your expectations are too simple or too difficult. If in a class composed of children of mixed abilities all succeed superlatively in a given set of objectives, you will want to ask yourself whether the success level was high enough, or whether they had previously mastered these objectives and the lesson was unnecessary—or whether your teaching was so good that all the children learned the content in the lesson. Any one reason or any combination of reasons might be correct; but you need to be alert to these possibilities and take action based on your conclusions. Similarly, action is appropriate when all the children in a class experience difficulty.

ACHIEVEMENT IN SEEING Perceptual achievements refer to images that can be seen, remembered, imagined, or valued. For example, if children are expected to identify the medium of watercolor when used in painting, they must first be instructed on what a watercolor painting looks like (see Plate 13 and Figures H and N). Later, they can be tested. Each child might be asked to check numbers or letters assigned to a series of pictures, where one or more were watercolor paintings. The result would identify those children who could recognize a watercolor and those who could not. Alternatively, children could be questioned individually and respond by pointing to a watercolor painting—or failing to do so. This evaluation process is a relatively simple one to manage, and yet most perceptual objectives that involve identifying, recognizing, and comparing visual images can be treated in much the same way, that is, with written or spoken reference to things that are visible to both you and the children.

A less immediate but no less valid evaluation can be made when you observe the use of an image of something or a visual technique—overlapping, for example—appearing in a child's pictures some time following instruction that had asked for overlapping to be used (see Figure 95). Were you then to praise the pupil for using overlapping, it might become more firmly established and appear regularly in his art work from then on.

FIGURE 95   A beginning use of overlapping

Visual progress shows itself in the same way when children study art objects like paintings and sculpture. Children can be tested for their ability to identify paintings done by Ben Shahn (see Figure F) or to distinguish between designs from an early and a late period in the career of the American architect Frank Lloyd Wright (see Figure 116).

Assessing achievement of all these objectives requires careful thought, but it is not particularly difficult to do. The gains for children are immense, however, since through such work they amass a reservoir of visual images that may be called upon at any time to help solve artistic problems.

As mentioned earlier, the more personal kinds of perceptual objectives cannot be evaluated with the same certainty as the above forms. You can question children about the visual ideas they have imagined, and you can encourage them to expand upon the feelings they have about works of art. You can also take note of the imaginative forms appearing in their art work that have their origins in images they have learned earlier. These objectives are most important and children should be taught to develop all these aptitudes to their fullest; but when the time comes to evaluate achievement, no clear way exists for doing it. You need to record what you judge has been achieved; and yet you also need to acknowledge the limitations of your efforts. You cannot see inside people. As you mature as a teacher, however, you can expect to develop a sixth sense about these kinds of achievement.

Your insights will be invaluable, and they belong in the evaluation record; but they need to be clearly identified as personal, subjective judgments.

Perceptual Assignment	Select three pictures from this book, one of which clearly shows the use of distortion. Then explain how you would use these three pictures to find out who in a class of 25 Grade 2 children had learned to recognize visual distortion when they saw it.

ACHIEVEMENT IN KNOWING These objectives are similar to those that predominate in academic subjects, consequently you are likely to find them less of a problem when evaluations are required. As described earlier, a child can be asked to define a word he has learned. He can be tested for his ability to use it correctly in language. In a less formal way, a teacher may engage a child in conversation where given words need to be used properly. The same approach may be used for determining whether children have learned certain information about art. They can be questioned orally; short essays may be written; multiple choice, true-false, sentence completion, and any of the other forms of objective testing can be used. This kind of evaluation is not any more accurate just because it is more familiar. The results are important, but they do not deserve special consideration when you are assembling records on children's progress in art.

The results of the literal and visual steps of critical analysis can be assessed in much the same way as other kinds of art knowledge. The only difference lies in the task to be performed. On the assumption that children have had every opportunity to learn the objectives, you need only ask them to tell you what they know. For example, you could instruct a class to be aware of three particular objects in a sculptural relief. Or you could instruct them to be aware of certain contrasting light and dark areas in a picture which together created a composition that was asymmetrical. In both instances, you could ask the children to name all or most of the parts.

The most difficult decision in all areas of knowledge testing is determining just how many items have to be included for an answer to be considered satisfactory. For example, where a class has studied a particular work of art and has been instructed by you how to make a literal analysis of it, then the questions will be primarily tests of memory. And you may want to demand a set of fairly complete and accurate answers. Where a class has not studied a particular work of art previously, the results will be more a measure of the children's ability to apply what they have learned about the process of visual analysis. Assessment is likely, then, to focus on the thoroughness of the amount of analyzing that has gone on rather than a conclusion that conforms to what you might think is correct.

Interpretations and judgments can also be asked for based on the objectives used during the instructional phase of a lesson; or they can be applied to unfamiliar works of art in much the same way as described in the preceding paragraph.

Knowledge Assignments

1. Chapter 3 includes a description under plaster of Paris (p. 78) of how to make a sand casting. Given that information, what would you accept as evidence that a Grade 5 child understood how to make a sand casting; and how would you find out about her knowledge.

2. On the assumption that your class of Grade 3 children have never seen the painting *Gulf Stream* by Winslow Homer (see Figure A) write down the questions you would ask to enable them to interpret the meaning the artist intended.

ACHIEVEMENT IN DOING   Skill objectives are among the easiest to evaluate. If a child were tested for his ability to mix dark green paint from yellow and blue, you would only need to see some dark green made without the assistance of black to be satisfied that the objective had been achieved. In the same way, you can check whether a child can mix green paint to match the green of a leaf by comparing the two. You can watch children's behavior to determine whether safety instructions for using linoleum tools or scissors are being followed. Proficiency in a particular skill may also be observed. You can watch a child as she tears a sheet of paper in half. You can watch how she holds a brush as she applies paint exactly up to a line.

The major difficulty encountered when measuring skills arises when you have to decide what "satisfactory" means for a given skill. What kind of care with scissors is safe enough? How ragged a torn edge of paper is skillful enough in Grade 4? If you expect perfection, very few children will ever succeed. If you ask for particular improvements each time a child works for a given skill, then you will probably find them. A carefully written statement of what is expected is necessary, therefore, and so is presence of visual criteria —as shown earlier in the examples on gradation.

As you evaluate skill performance, remember that only skill is to be evaluated. A child who also tells you how the skill is performed is combining knowledge with skill. Each deserves to be recognized, but each is a different kind of learning.

Actual art products are a problem to evaluate when an objective is not written carefully. If, for example, an objective required children to paint a picture of an interior of a building, then as long as that is done, you would have to accept every painting equally. If, of the other hand, you described what you had really wanted in the picture, the assignment might read like this: "Paint an indoor picture with all the light coming from one place. The colors you use should also look quite different from anyone else's in the class."

Such a statement would let the children know what was expected of them. Above all, it would be relatively simple to evaluate. As a result, you would not be tempted to judge the work against objectives that had never been asked for.

The conditions governing product objectives can include content that has been learned in the other two main categories of objectives, including skills. Knowledge about what is meant by movement in art and how it can contribute to pictorial composition may be learned in advance. However, exactly the reverse is also possible: An attempt may be made at painting a picture in which bold action is important. The results could then be assessed with a view to instructing children about how action is used by artists. It could also lead to making children familiar with works by artists, such as Bellows (see Plate 3), and Benton (see Plate 4), who regularly used violent action in their work.

Finally, an important word of caution needs to be reemphasized as you prepare to evaluate children's art work. *Unless you discipline yourself, a very real tendency exists to favor art work that appeals to you personally and not to evaluate it against the actual achievement it demonstrates.* If children sense that the real test for success is to please you, they will quickly abandon any effort to achieve objectives drawn from the subject of art, and your program will be a failure.

| Doing Assignment | Choose any one of the color pictures of children's art at the beginning of Chapter 5. List all the objectives you think show themselves in that picture. |

GUIDELINES FOR A PROGRAM OF ASSESSMENT

So far, you have been introduced to ways of measuring children's achievement with single objectives. These are the building blocks of long-term plans for art assessment. The following guidelines present a working plan for the assessment task that will face you during an extended period like a semester or a school year. Ideally, the school where you teach will already have an operating evaluational plan for measuring achievement in art that you can fit into comfortably. But if such a plan does not exist, you should be able to practice your own system effectively.

The following material falls under three main topics, followed by two briefer but no less important ones. *Diagnosis* is the task of discovering what children already know. *Formative evaluation* occurs throughout the art program. *Summative evaluation* occurs at the end of a period of instruction. These three main topics do not necessarily account for unexpected or unmeasurable objectives, or account for the recording of results. The last two topics discuss these issues.

DIAGNOSIS You may have prepared an excellent art program for a given level in school, but it may fail miserably if the children have already learned much of what you hoped to teach. They will rapidly become disenchanted and you may discover your error only after much valuable time has been lost. For this reason, a sampling of the kinds of learning you plan on including is necessary. A study should also be made of the prerequisite kinds of knowledge that children need for success in the program—learning that should have occurred already. Your plan for instruction in paper sculpture may, for example, assume that the children already know how to cut paper with scissors, fold it, and perhaps score it. If these skills have not been mastered beforehand to a sufficient degree, then they must be included as part of your plan for instruction in paper sculpture. The only way to resolve this problem is to prepare a set of questions or tasks that will reveal the knowledge and skills they possess—or do not possess—that relate to objectives present in your art program.

This kind of investigation should also occur each time a different kind of art experience is introduced, because it is not possible for diagnostic sessions at the beginning of the year to reveal everything you need to know. If you have access to a written art program the children experienced the year before, or if you can talk to the teacher they had, you may gather information even more efficiently. Nothing should be taken for granted, however. A class may have worked at weaving the year before but have forgotten much of what they knew. When they reach you, you may carry on with weaving from where they left off, but first of all you need to discover exactly what they remember. Further, you should try and find out what strategy was used previously to teach weaving and consider approaching the topic differently. If children feel that the experience is something they have done before, they are not likely to put as much effort into what is to be learned this time as they might do otherwise. Much learning occurs as a result of repeated experiences; but if that repetition is perceived as tedious, then little learning will occur. Your diagnostic inquiries, therefore, need to include gathering information about strategies for teaching just as much as discovering what children know.

FORMATIVE EVALUATION Each lesson marks a time period, at the end of which one or more objectives are expected to have been learned. The same is true for a sequence of related lessons. Throughout a school year, in fact, there are numbers of natural breaks when children's progress in art can be assessed. The results may confirm that the desired learning has indeed occurred; or it may reveal weaknesses that call for remedial instruction and consequently cause you to modify your original teaching plans.

Assessments of achievement during a lesson need only take a few minutes of your time and they rapidly grow into an invaluable cumulative record. Moreover, when more ambitious sessions are planned, such as at the end of a lesson sequence or just before a holiday break, it will be possible to assess how much of the course content has been remembered and how much needs to be repeated to make up for what has been forgotten.

This process is handled best when it does not intrude into the on-going life of the art program. Formal tests have their place from time to time; but your main effort should be directed at assessing the children's typical behavior. Low-key evaluation is most important when you want to report on the less explicit kinds of achievement that will occur. Individual objectives, for example, do not account for changes taking place over a period of time; and yet you will be looking for such changes as an improvement in a child's visual memory or an improving ability to show details in drawing. Each calls for personal judgments that you will want to be as objective and as professional as possible. The only way that this can even begin to occur is for you to avoid being influenced by anyone else as much as possible. These conclusions, together with those arising from more clear-cut results, govern the future course of your art program.

In addition to assessing expected achievements, you need to be prepared for results you did not expect. A primary school child might show an ability in perspective drawing that does not normally occur with so young a child and was not part of your art program. Another child might have seen pictures by Abraham Rattner which led to his work reflecting the same kind of ghostly fantasy to be found in Rattner's art (see Plate 5). Results like these may easily be missed if you study the actions and products of your children only with reference to objectives that were declared in advance. The most striking instances of unexpected achievement are naturally noticed first, but some teachers can become so sensitized to the presence of individual abilities that non-programmed achievement plays a substantial part in assessing children's total growth in art.

SUMMATIVE EVALUATION For better or worse, tests are a part of school life. At best, they report student achievement at the termination of a course of study. And, insofar as another art course is to follow the one that is ending, the results serve as diagnostic information. If the results are never used to advance a child's education further, then the effort is a waste of time. In the elementary school, all studies—art included—should be cumulative and continuous, in that each year of work should build on what was done in the preceding year. Only when a child is about to graduate and move on to middle school or junior high school does the task approach being described as summative. And even then it is only summative insofar as the elementary school is concerned: the children continue living and learning.

Year end assessments are nevertheless important. This is the time when achievement is measured for the period during which you have been responsible for the art education of your class. Achievements from the entire year need to be assessed by whatever means open to you; and in anticipation, you may want to review what was learned in the early part of the year. This kind of evaluation obviously only permits part of what was included during the year to be judged, so you should select a representative sample of objectives from your program.

This is also the time when you should be able to view the art achievements of the children in perspective. You have observed them for ten months and have accumulated formative records that have a place in the summative statement. Your periodic judgments about trends in the art both of the class as a whole and of individuals in it, should all be synthesized at this time into one final statement.

COMMUNICATING RESULTS

Much education is carried on in an atmosphere of competition. Students receive grades that are arrived at through placement of scores on a curve. Some kinds of achievement in art, such as information, can be applied to a normal curve but not enough to warrant thinking of a curve as generally useful. When a child satisfies the requirements for success with an art objective, she will often do so in a way that is different from the way other children have demonstrated their grasp of the same objective. All those who succeed with any objectives deserve to have their success acknowledged; but because of the individuality of many solutions, norms are generally not appropriate.

Scores may be assigned for the achievement of art objectives. Objectives that in your judgment are more complex or more important can be given higher scores than others as long as this weighting is not kept secret from the children. Performance that is demonstrably superior may also receive higher scores as long as the criteria separating what is typical from what is superior performance has been adequately defined in advance. Moreover, if you find yourself in a school where you are required to grade art, you may do so with a clear conscience. First, you need to find the sum of the accumulated scores. You also have to decide on the point separating one level from the next—especially pass from fail. If you can do this much and are prepared to make it known publicly, you will be as honest as it is possible to be. In addition, you may want to hold back a block of scores to report achievement for which no accounting is normally made. A girl, for example, may have made remarkable progress in her ability to make mixtures of colors during a particular grading period. She should receive credit for her accomplishment. Not least, you should be ready to face criticism by people who believe that it is only legitimate to assign a few As, more Bs, and still more Cs. When you measure the achievement of your class in art, you may well find that all the children satisfy the criteria you established for an A or a B, and that you actually report more As than Bs.

If you object to using numerical scores and grades for art, you can prepare a chart that names all the objectives in your program. For easier reporting, you might want to cluster similar objectives together. You would then place a check-mark beside all the objectives where achievement was satisfactory. Individual comments could be added either beside the check marks or at the end of the report.

Parents have a right to information about the progress of their children so your reports should be prepared in such a way that parents can read and understand what you have to communicate. The teacher in the grade the children will go to next needs this information in order to build on what was achieved in your art program. Principals, art supervisors, and others may also need your reports; although these people tend to be further removed from the daily life of educating children.

While adults need achievement information, children need it even more. And they should be continually informed of their level of success and where improvement is needed. In Chapter 8, this process of feedback was described as a motivational strategy directed toward additional learning; and it is. It is also a way of reinforcing in children's minds what they have learned so that it will be less likely to be forgotten. Reports of achievement at best, therefore, are part of the fabric of instruction and not something tacked on to a teacher's duties to satisfy parents and public officials that school taxes are being spent wisely.

ASSESSING YOUR OWN EFFORTS

The success of children in art is your success. Their failure is your failure. And every teacher hopes that children will progress because of the effort she puts into teaching and not in spite of it. For this reason, a chapter on measuring achievement should direct the attention of a reader to the quality of the teaching efforts as well as the efforts of the children doing the learning. The classroom is your laboratory, but only rarely will anyone visit your room and systematically evaluate the quality of your performance and help you improve it. Such a practice could be extremely beneficial, but the realities of school life are such that you will have to do it yourself if it is to happen at all.

The place to begin is with what happens during a lesson. Your preparations are hypothetical until tested in the classroom with children. While it is often difficult to be critical about your own actions, the process of self-evaluation requires that you should study each part of a lesson during and after it has been taught to determine how it can be improved. You also need to be continually asking yourself whether the order in which the subject matter is presented is right for your students. Nothing exists that cannot be improved, so this task is never ending. The discovery of a more imaginative method of teaching; or a more effective organization of instructional objectives; or the introduction of pictures that are more appealing to children than those you already have are all part of the reward for teaching art well.

further reading

Hardiman, George W. and **Theodore Zernich** (eds.). *Curricular Considerations for Visual Arts Education:* Champaign, Illinois: Stipes Publishing Co., 1974. The articles by Scriven and Wilson are relevant to evaluating student success in art.

Hubbard, Guy. *Art in High School.* Belmont, California: Wadsworth Publishing Co., Inc., 1967. While the book is intended for future art teachers, Chapter Seven is relevant to the evaluation of art instruction at all levels.

Stake, Robert (ed.), *Evaluating the Arts in Education:* A Responsive Approach. Columbus, Ohio: Charles E. Merrill, 1975. An innovative treatment of evaluation for the more serious student.

part
Three
your
art teaching
data bank

The final part of this book contains information that can be put to immediate use in the classroom. Appendix A consists of a collection of art lessons suitable for children on the primary (Lessons 1-10) and intermediate (Lessons 11-20) levels. Several of these lessons have deliberately been left incomplete so you can practice your lesson-writing skills.

Appendix B consists of the raw material of art teaching from which lessons and year-long art programs are developed. The most important section is a grade-by-grade list of art objectives. This is followed by a list of the forms of art and related art materials likely to be appropriate for elementary classrooms. A set of lesson topic ideas is given at the end.

Part One of this book introduced the practical foundations of art. You need to have had experience in making art, yourself, in order to teach it satisfactorily. Part Two introduced the theoretical foundations that underlie effective art instruction. Part Three, in conjunction with the instructional guidelines to be found in Chapter One, provides all the information you need to build an art program you can be proud of.

FIGURE C George Wesley Bellows, "Stag at Sharkey's." Oil on canvas.
Courtesy, The Cleveland Museum of Art, Hinman B. Hurlbut Collection.

FIGURE D Albert Bierstadt, "In the Mountains." Courtesy, Wadsworth Atheneum, Hartford,
Connecticut. Gift of John J. Morgan in memory of his mother, Juliet Pierpoint Morgan.

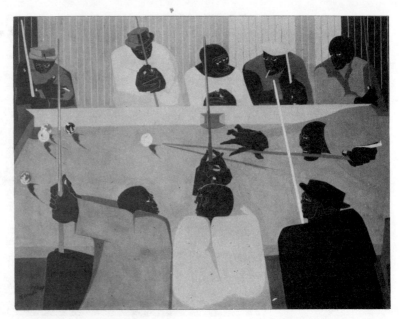

FIGURE E Jacob Lawrence, "The Pool Game." Gouache (tempera). Courtesy, Museum of Fine Arts, Boston, Emily L. Ainsley Fund.

FIGURE F Ben Shahn, "Miner's Wives." Courtesy, Philadelphia Museum of Art. Given by Wright S. Ludington.

FIGURE G Andrew Wyeth, "The Hunter, 1943." Tempera on panel. Courtesy, The Toledo Museum of Art, Elizabeth C. Mau Bequest Fund.

FIGURE H Charles Burchfield, "Noontime in Late May, 1917." Watercolor and gouache (tempera). 21 5/8 x 17 1/2 inches. Collection of the Whitney Museum of American Art.

FIGURE I   Mary Cassatt, "The Boating Party (1758)." Oil. Courtesy, National Gallery of Art, Washington, Chester Dale Collection.

FIGURE J   Primary girl, Indianapolis, Indiana. Chalk, "Circus."

FIGURE K Intermediate boy, Thailand. Oil pastel. "My School."

FIGURE L Primary boy, Brazil. Felt marker. "Space Rocket."

FIGURE M Intermediate boy, Japan. Tempera. "City." Courtesy, International Collection of Child Art, Ewing Museum of Nations, Illinois State University.

FIGURE N Primary boy, Cincinatti, Ohio. Watercolor. "Tall Buildings."

FIGURE O   Primary girl, Indianapolis, Indiana. Collage. ''Bird Family.''

FIGURE P   Intermediate girl, Cincinatti, Ohio. Collage. ''City.''

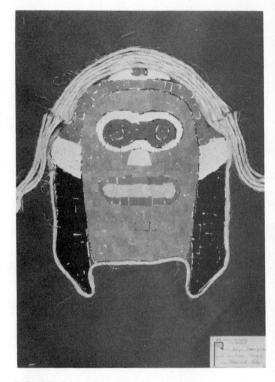

FIGURE R Intermediate boy, Indianapolis, Indiana. Mosaic. "Mask."

FIGURE Q Intermediate girl, Canada. Montage. "Mixture." Courtesy, International Collection of Child Art, Ewing Museum of Nations, Illinois State University.

FIGURE S Intermediate girl, Indianapolis, Indiana. Stitchery. "Bear."

FIGURE T Primary boy, Wapakoneta, Ohio. Yarn painting. "Clown."

FIGURE U Intermediate girl, Bloomington, Indiana. Appliqué. "Mountain View."

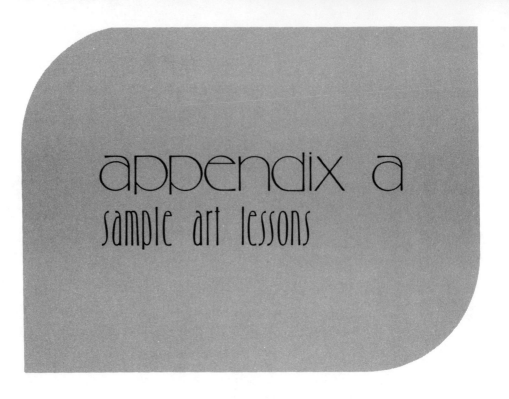

appendix a
sample art lessons

EXAMPLES OF ART LESSONS FOR THE PRIMARY GRADES

lesson 1

ME

 Purpose   (The reasons for believing that children should learn the objectives in this lesson):
A child's world is self-centered and an individual normally benefits from experiences that enhance self-knowledge.

 Readiness   (The reasons for believing that children of this age can succeed in this lesson):
The assignment is basically one of filling in the parts of a tracing and is not likely to present problems for normal primary level children.

Instructional objectives * (Some or all of these things are what the children should be able to do):

A Seeing: Point to heads, arms, feet, bodies, faces, and the clothes they are wearing.

E Skill: Draw round the edges of a person lying on the floor (unless done by the teacher).

F Product: Color themselves to show how they look and what they are wearing.

 Strategies for teaching (The things you can do to help children achieve the above objectives):

Preparations: Roll out paper on the floor or in a corridor. Move furniture as needed. Have large shears ready so you can cut out the figure drawings.

Delivery: Have the class divide into pairs. Demonstrate the process of having one child lie down on the paper and the other member of the team draw around him to make a silhouette. With young children it may be necessary to make all the outline drawings yourself. Cut the paper out roughly so that each child is working on his own sheet. The figures can be cut out more carefully as the work is closer to being finished.

The finished work should be displayed either by taping to the wall or pasting to a large sheet of paper to make a mural. The class members can fill in the spaces and write their names beside their drawings.

Motivational Support: Color your own silhouette. You can have your outline made beforehand or it can be done by the children. In this way, the class can see more clearly what is expected of them.

Subject Correlation: Dancing and rhythmic movement can make children more aware of their body parts. Beginning readers might pratice the words *head, legs, jeans, dress, crayons, paper,* etc., when used in stories.

Measurement (Ways of finding out whether children have learned the objectives):

A Seeing: When they point to the appropriate parts of bodies that are named.

E Skill: The drawn shape is to approximate the figure of the model.

F Product: The body parts are to be present and the colors used are to approximate those of the model.

_____* The six-part organization (types A–F) introduced in Chapter 7 is used throughout.

ME

I WILL:

1. Draw all of me.
2. Color my picture.
3. Put my picture on the wall.
4. See how I look.

Who is biggest?
Who is smallest?
Who is tallest?
Who is shortest?
Who has brown hair?
Who is wearing jeans?
Who has black hair?
Who is wearing a dress?

FIGURE 96 Section of a mural by primary level children

FIGURE 97 Crayons

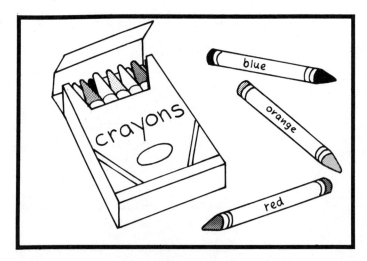

MY PET

P **Purpose** The art program should assist children to explore their visual environment more thoroughly than will happen without guidance by focusing attention on objects with which they are likely to have a close affiliation.

r **Readiness** To adults the works of young children may not look like the objects they have chosen to represent: but children use drawing as a means of giving meaning to objects and they continually refine these ideas when given the opportunity.

i **Instructional objectives** (Some or all of these objectives):

A Seeing: Identify the kinds of animals that other members of the class have modelled. Describe the large and small parts of their own pets. Describe the textures (or the "feel") of their pets.

B Define: "Modelling" as art that is solid.

D Criticism: Describe the body parts of their model of a pet.

E Skill: Make either oil based or water based clay ready to use.

F Product: Make a model of a pet that shows the main forms and when possible, any details of heads, feet, and surface textures.

S **Strategies for teaching** (The things you can do to help children achieve the above objectives):

Preparations: Arrange with several children to bring their pets to school. Be certain that the animals will be under proper control by confirming all arrangements with the parents. Make whatever formal arrangements are required by the school principal and any other authorities.

Make sure you have enough clay and newspaper and that the clay is soft. Have old shirts available for the children to wear.

Delivery: Have the owners tell the class about their pet, such as: name, species and/or breed, identifying the various parts of the body; and any other information that might interest the class.

Motivational Support: (*Be certain of safety for pet and for child*): gently stroke the pet. Have children who couldn't bring their pets bring slides to show the class.

Subject Correlation: Read stories or look at movies about pets who were special in some way (e.g., who did brave things). Listen to music about different animals and try to identify the music or instrument that represents each (e.g., Prokofiev, "Peter and the Wolf"; Saint-Saëns, "Carnival of the Animals").

Measurement

A Identification and description of details is confirmed by the children's answers to questions.

B The child should link the word "modelling" with "solid art".

D Any statement is acceptable as long as it includes mention of the main body, limbs, head, and surface of the model.

E Observe that clay is being prepared properly.

F Any kind of model is to be accepted that a child will acknowledge as an animal.

lesson 2

(Child's Copy)

MY PET

I WILL:

1. Make a model of my pet.
2. Talk about my pet.
3. Talk about other models of pets.
4. Make clay ready to use.

FIGURE 98 A dog

FIGURE 99   A cat

lesson 3

MY BIRTHDAY CAKE

P **Purpose**   Festivals are important in all cultures, and birthdays are the occasions when individual children feel the impact of festivals most of all, because they are the centers of attention. The birthday cake is one of the primary symbols of these festivals, and it offers an opportunity for creative design.

r **Readiness**   Crayons and paintbrushes are natural tools for communication among young children.

i **Instructional objectives**

B   Define "decorate" as adding to shapes and objects to make them look better.

F   Draw a large picture of a decorated birthday cake. Paint a drawing of a birthday cake, using a variety of colors.

S **Strategies for teaching**

Preparations: Have enough paint mixed in juice cans for each child to have several colors. Brushes should be placed in the cans and used only for those colors. The best situation is one where paper is on easels and the cans of paint are in special troughs that hold the paint cans upright. Have smocks or old shirts available.

Delivery: Show pictures of decorated birthday cakes. Talk with the class about the kind of decoration individuals would like on their cakes. Ask them to make their cakes fill the paper. Have them draw their cakes before painting them.

Motivational Support: Invite a local confectioner to visit the class and demonstrate the decorating of a birthday cake. Have a birthday party for one of the children and arrange for a nicely decorated cake to be brought in.

Subject Correlation: Play birthday games. Sing birthday songs. Write verses for birthday greetings.

lesson 3

(Child's Copy)

MY BIRTHDAY CAKE

I WILL:

1. Say that decorating is making things look pretty.
2. Draw a big picture of a birthday cake.
3. Paint my drawing of a birthday cake in different colors.

FIGURE 100   A birthday cake

lesson 4

DRAW TO MUSIC

P **Purpose** Rhythm comes easily to children but will not advance without help. Rhythm shows itself in dance (body movement), music, and art.

r **Readiness** Young children find the kind of large movements asked for in this lesson to be comfortable for them, while rhythmic requirements usually happen naturally.

i **Instructional objectives**

A Point to designs made with lines that match the rhythm of a piece of music.

B Define a "line" as a mark that goes somewhere.

F Make a line design about a piece of music.

S **Strategies for teaching**

Preparations: Bring records to school of different kinds of music—ethnic emphasis depending on the school population. Prepare a sample line product to a piece of music.

Delivery: Explain that lines take time to draw and paint. Every line has its own character (stiff, wavy, skinny, fat, furry, smooth, etc). Making a line in time with music tells about the music.
Have the children read their copy of the lesson aloud into an audio tape recorder, and then play it back to the class. Look at the pictures that go with the text. Demonstrate a line made to music. Play short musical passages as the class paints. Beat or sing out the time to help those who may have difficulty. Do as many designs as time permits. Pin the art works on the wall as they are done. Pin a label with each group describing the piece of music that was played.

Motivational Support: Have the class stand up and close their eyes. Have them move their arms and bodies in response to different kinds of music.

Subject Correlation: Dance to music. Sing to music. Pick out class line pictures to dance to. Fit line pictures to pieces of music.

m **Measurement**

A Match the line art correctly with music when it is re-played.

B Talk about lines having to do with directional movement.

F Any brushwork line designs done to the music.

lesson 4

DRAW TO MUSIC

I WILL:

1. Say that a line is a mark that goes somewhere.
2. Make lines that tell about music.
3. Find line pictures that look most like some music.

Figure 101: These lines are about noisy, crashing music. Figure 102: These lines are about smooth, flowing music.

FIGURE 101 Primary child's crayon drawing to music: "Rah, Rah, Rah!"

FIGURE 102 Primary child's crayon drawing to music: "Skater's Waltz"

lesson 5

FROGS, BATS, AND SPIDERS

P **Purpose** Art is a visual language and through it people express their feelings and emotions. Like all languages, it requires continual practice. Healthy people enjoy rich fantasy lives which mature only if regularly encouraged in lessons such as this one.

r **Readiness** Young children have a natural disposition for make-believe that lends itself to expressive art activities. They regularly enjoy subjects that are mildly frightening.

i ## Instructional objectives

A Pick out all the pictures they think are most frightening.

C Learn that artists are always striving to communicate messages or ideas through their work.

Good art can show frightening and ugly objects as well as pretty ones.

D Describe all the feelings the other children meant their pictures to have.

F Make a horror picture using colored chalk or oil pastels on black paper. The picture is to fill most of the paper.

S ## Strategies for teaching

Preparations: Find a story or poem about animals and insects that children might find mildly frightening. Halloween themes might be good.

Delivery: Have several children draw on the chalkboard to demonstrate the effects of working with light on dark. Read the story or poem to the class—with plenty of expression.

Motivational Support: If the time is late October, have older children from another class visit in Halloween costumes.

Subject Correlation: Play charades or guessing the identity of scary animals. Music about ghostly events could be introduced.

m ## Measurement

A Any statements about pieces of class art that individuals declare to be most frightening.

C Statements must include references to art as a way of communicating and that both pretty and ugly objects can be good art.

D   Any statement of feeling about particular pieces of class art they thought was intended.

F   Any picture that fills the paper.
Any picture that has horror images in it.

lesson 5

FROGS, BATS, AND SPIDERS

Read This: Some things look pretty. Some things look scary. Frogs, bats, and spiders look scary. Can you make a picture about a scary story? Put frogs or bats or spiders in a scary picture. Make your picture fill all the paper.

I WILL:

1. Learn that artists make scary as well as pretty pictures.
2. Learn that pictures tell stories.
3. Make a picture that tells a scary story.
4. Pick out the scariest pictures.
5. Say why a picture is scary.
6. Fill my paper with my picture.

Art materials: Chalk and black paper. Look at the picture called "Place of Darkness" (Plate 5) and the picture by someone your own age (Figure 103).

FIGURE 103   Primary child's picture using colored chalk: "Halloween"

224

lesson 6

FUNNY FACE

 Purpose Dramatic play incorporates both dramatic and visual art and should be encouraged continuously throughout a person's school career as explorations of expressive behavior. Children should also learn the parts of a person's face.

 Readiness Children are able to execute the cutting and pasting tasks, and they are normally enthusiastic about engaging in make-believe.

 Instructional objectives

B Define "mosaic" as a design made with paper squares.
Define "mask" as a picture of a face that people wear.
C Learn that people wear masks when they want to pretend that they are someone different.
E Stick paper squares on to a piece of paper securely.
F Make a paper mosaic mask showing a funny face.

 Strategies for teaching

Preparations: Cut up enough 1/2" squares of colored construction paper for each child's needs. Cut out face-sized pieces of cardboard with holes for eyes. Also staple elastic on so the masks can be worn.

Delivery: Talk to the children about the lesson and show them the pictures. Be sure to include reference to all the objectives. Write the main information on the board. Question the class for comprehension. Tell them that they can stick small boxes on the masks to make noses before they begin to stick mosaic pieces on. Suggest that they pencil or crayon in some of the spaces between the paper squares to make their work look better.

Motivational Support: Visit a circus and if possible meet one of the clowns; or have a clown come to the school. Visit a museum to see mosaics and masks (from Africa or Japan). Teach children to act out the part characterized by a mask.

Subject Correlation: Social Studies: people in different parts of the world decorate their faces and wear masks on special occasions.

Measurement

B Mosaic: they must talk about pictures made of small squares. Mask: they must talk about wearing a face on top of their own.

C Statements must include reference to pretending.

E Paper squares do not come off and no excess of glue present.

F Any paper mosaic mask.

Art materials: 1/2″ squares of colored construction paper Face-sized pieces of cardboard Paste Newspaper Small boxes for noses

Picture to go with this lesson: *see* Figure R.

lesson 7

SURPRISE COLLAGE

P **Purpose** Everyone has potential for being creative, and when it is encouraged it leads to higher levels of performance and satisfaction. One kind of creativity occurs when images and materials are combined in unusual ways. A common reaction to such recombinations is surprise and laughter, and as such it establishes the connection between creativity and pleasure.

r **Readiness** The cutting and pasting requirements fall within the typical performance levels of most Grade 2 and almost all Grade 3 children. They will also tend to respond spontaneously to the novelty of recombination.

i **Instructional objectives**

A Describe the parts of class collages they think are funny.

B Define "collage" as picture making made by sticking paper and other flat materials down flat.

C Learn that one type of creativity happens when artists arrange ideas and materials in unusual ways.

E Cut out magazine pictures carefully.
Paste down pieces of cut paper with just enough adhesive.

F Make a pictorial collage using magazine pictures showing combinations that are funny.

S **Strategies for teaching**

Preparations: Collect pictorial magazines of all kinds. Prepare text for the lesson on a large sheet of paper for everyone in the class to read. If it is done carefully it can be re-used the next time you give the lesson.

Delivery: Tape the prepared text on the board. Have the children read it aloud and answer questions to be sure they understand what they are to do. Then have the class perform the activity.

Motivational Support: Have the children try on some non-stereo-typed Halloween masks, perhaps made by you. Also, have them wear old clothes in combinations that were obviously never intended.

Subject Correlations: Excerpts from stories like "Alice in Wonder-land" and "Pinocchio" include unusual characters that extend the theme of this lesson.

 Measurement

A Any statements, laughter, pointing, etc. indicating that children believe certain collages to be funny.

Problem: Write down what would show achievement of the other objectives

Art materials: *Problem:* List what you would need for this lesson.

Picture to go with this lesson: see Figure Q.

lesson 8

(Teacher's Copy)

OUR TOWN

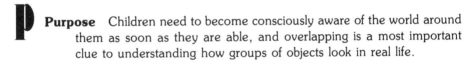

P **Purpose** Children need to become consciously aware of the world around them as soon as they are able, and overlapping is a most important clue to understanding how groups of objects look in real life.

r **Readiness** At the upper primary levels children are normally ready for simple problems that show distance in pictures. Overlapping is one of the simplest ways of introducing this topic.

i **Instructional objectives**

A Identify examples of overlapping in photographs and paintings.
B Define "overlapping" as one thing covering up part of another.
C Learn that city buildings overlap each other.
F Make a picture of overlapping buildings by cutting them out of cloth or paper.

S **Strategies for teaching**

Preparations: Have additional large pictures of buildings from the community the children live in pinned up all around the room for them to refer to in this lesson. (The local newspaper will usually have photographs on file).

Delivery: Have the children describe their community. Draw out from them the different shapes and colors of buildings. Draw out the presence of overlapping. Have the class repeat to you how scissors should be used and how paste should be used. Ask them to cut out each building in different light colored paper. Ask them to draw in windows, doors, etc. and color the buildings. The cut out buildings are then to be pasted to dark colored paper. The buildings are to fill most of the picture and overlap each other.

Motivational Support: Go for a walk through local streets and stop periodically to point out examples of buildings that overlap. Alternatively, show slides of views showing overlapping of buildings.

Subject Correlations: *Social Studies:* How communities look in different parts of the U.S.A. and/or world. *Literature:* Descriptive passages about different communities, especially references to those like the one in which the children live.

 Measurement   *Problem:* Write down exactly what you would expect Grade 3 children to do to show they had achieved the objectives.

Art materials: Different colored cloth or construction paper   Newspapers   Scissors   Paste   Pencils and erasers   Water supply   Paper towels

Pictures to go with this lesson: see Figures 63 and 16 and Figure P.

lesson 9

ADVENTURE ON THE HIGH SEAS

Purpose   An important part of any art education is to become familiar with works of art. Teachers should, therefore, guard against an exclusive emphasis on making art by including lessons and parts of lessons that focus on learning about works of art.

Readiness   Children in the primary grades are capable of beginning their education in art appreciation and art criticism as long as the task is not permitted to become abstract.

i Instructional objectives

A   Pick out parts of the picture they like more than others.
Say how the picture makes them feel inside (i.e., lonely, warm, windy, excited, etc.)

C   Learn that this picture is by an American artist, named Winslow Homer.

D   Describe the things to be seen in this picture: a boat that has lost its mast, a sailor lying on the deck, sharks in the water, a sailing boat in the distance, a waterspout also in the distance (like a tornado at sea).
Explain what the artist was trying to tell us: that the sailor had no hope of surviving; or that the sailing ship was probably going to rescue him before the sharks got him or the storm sank the boat.

s Strategies for teaching

Preparations: Make sure that each child will be able to have a good colored reproduction of "The Gulf Stream" by Winslow Homer to look at or that a large reproduction is available for everyone to see at once. A slide is perfectly satisfactory; and if additional slides of details of the picture are also available, that would be better still.

Delivery: Ask the children questions related to the objectives and (if a large reproduction or slide is used) have them come up to the front of the room and point out the parts they like, feel strongly about, etc. Be sure to allow for differences of opinion to be heard so that individual ideas are encouraged. You may want to write the different ideas that are expressed on the board for review later.

Motivational Support: Have a local person who has been a castaway in to talk about how it feels. Read excerpts from stories that tell about drifting helplessly at sea to get at how the sailor is probably feeling.

Subject Correlation: For language study they might complete the adventure by saying what happened next to the sailor. Play music about ocean waves or sea chanties about being shipwrecked.

m Measurement

A   The only requirement is that each child identifies one or more parts that are liked specially and also says how he feels about the picture.

C   They need to name the artist and say that he was an American.

D   The items listed above as important are to be named: and some kind of interpretation is to be attempted.

Picture to go with this lesson: see Figure A.

lesson 10

VALENTINE ART

Purpose   *Problem:* Explain why this lesson should be taught.

Readiness   *Problem:* Explain why this lesson is suitable for primary level children.

Instructional objectives

A   Choose the best looking valentine card of three they made.

B   Define "print" as making a mark by pressing a painted shape on to paper.

C   Learn that greeting cards are a special kind of art that people use on important occasions.

E   Make clear prints.

F   Print at least three Valentine cards and add suitable words.

Strategies for teaching

Preparations: To save time and to produce better work, fold pieces of paper in advance to make greeting cards.

Collect scrap objects for printing, such as: bottle caps, toothbrushes, keys, popsicle sticks, broken toys, pieces of sponge, cookie cutters.

Delivery: Show the class printed Valentine cards made by children. Tell them that this is what they are going to do, but that they must invent their own designs. Refer to the objectives very explicitly.

Have them practice making good finger-prints before making scrap prints.

Motivational Support: Ask a salesman representing a company that has a reputation for having good quality greeting cards to bring in his sample book of Valentine cards and talk about the designers who create them.

Subject Correlation: *Social Studies:* The importance of the invention of printing. Also the history of St. Valentine's Day.

Measurement

A   Any choice is acceptable.

B   Link the word *print* with a stamping action on paper (not lettering).

C   Statements must include mention of greeting cards being art and that they are printed.

E   Observe the prints to be clear.

F   Check that three cards have been printed.

Art materials: Scrap materials   White or colored paper for practice and the cards   Paints   Water   Paper towels   Brushes and mixing trays

Picture to go with this lesson: see Figure 104.

FIGURE 104   Primary child's Valentine prints

EXAMPLES OF ART LESSONS FOR THE INTERMEDIATE GRADES

lesson 11

HAPPY SCRAPS

P

Purposes The decision about what is useful and what is useless has to do with creativity. The creative person sees applications for materials that are not usual or obvious. The development of this kind of intelligence requires practice and art helps do this. In addition, children need to be educated to think creatively in three dimensions as a normal part of their education.

r

Readiness Manual dexterity has usually developed well enough by this time that children can attach objects securely to surfaces. They are also becoming ready for more abstract thinking.

Instructional objectives

A Choose objects and parts of objects that go well together. Decide which items of classwork—or parts of them—are most interesting to look at; and from which directions.

B Define "three dimensional" to mean all things that are solid (i.e., have depth as well as length and breadth).

C Learn that the art of every individual is best when it is different from the work of everyone else.

D Explain what their sculpture is supposed to be about.

E Attach objects together securely.

F Make a piece of sculpture that is to be looked at from several different positions.

 Strategies for teaching

Preparation: Collect items for children to use in this lesson. You might want to take time and collect items over several weeks by having the class bring things to class. Alternatively, you might go to a nearby dump and load the trunk of your car with clean items for the lesson.

Delivery: Have children read all the parts of their text aloud. Question them for comprehension. Pay special attention to the five objectives written in their text.

Motivational Support: Direct the attention of the class toward the artists' pictures to help overcome the rigid attitude of thinking of discarded material as useless.

Subject Correlation: Music: A theme and variation shows how the same sounds are used in different ways to create new sounds.

Literature: When several individuals report on the same event from their personal point of view each report will seem different from all the others.

Measurement

A Any selections are acceptable just as long as some declaration is made.

B Definitions must refer to solidness or depth.

C Statements must refer to the idea that individually different work is good.

D Any coherent explanation of their work is acceptable.

E Secure attachment will be adequate if the pieces hold together for at least a week.

F Any sculptural product made with scrap material will be acceptable.

lesson 11

HAPPY SCRAPS

How To Do This Lesson

Read This: What can you do with a wheel from a broken toy, or an old shoe, or the saddle from a bicycle, or the insides from a coffee pot? Most people just throw these kinds of things away. But artists have different ideas. An old shoe and some pieces of broken toys can be turned into the body of a scary looking insect. Old cookie cutters might be turned into a sleek spaceship. The insides of an old typewriter might be joined with parts from an old car to make a robot spider.

This lesson is to help you do things in your own special way. If you don't know what to make just begin by putting things together. Good ideas often come just by playing around with things to see what will happen.

Make sure that all the pieces you use are held together strongly. Be sure that the finished sculpture looks interesting from all views—back; front; sides; and top.

Objectives

YOU WILL:

1. Join scrap objects and pieces of objects together strongly to make a piece of sculpture that is not like any one else's.

2. Make your sculpture look good from different positions.

3. Learn that the name for things that are solid is *three dimensional.*

4. Explain what the shapes of your sculpture are meant to be about.

5. Pick out class sculptures that are the most different to look at.

Art materials: Scissors   A collection of man-made objects that are usually thown away: old shoes, broken toys, small pieces of machinery and household appliances.   Glue and applicators   String   Adhesive tape   Thin wire   Pliers

Look at this picture: see Figure 105.

FIGURE 105   Intermediate child's scrap sculpture

lesson 12

SHOW WHAT YOU CAN'T SEE

p **Purpose**   People invent visual symbols to communicate ideas, and children should begin this process as soon as they are able; with words, mathematical symbols, and also with a wide range of visual symbols.

r **Readiness**   Older children are usually more mature and are ready to begin working with abstract ideas.

i **Instructional objectives**

A   Select examples of class work—or parts of them—that are comparatively unique (to the children).

B   Define "invisible" as a condition where something cannot be seen.

C   Learn that people invent images for ideas and experiences whether they are visible or not.

E   Mix colors together to make new ones.

F   Paint a picture that shows something that is normally invisible. Write in its name.

Strategies for teaching

Preparations: Have samples to smell (peanut butter, etc.) and "hear" (bells, etc.)

Delivery: Have the class read their text to themselves. Have them suggest other, similar experiences to those listed and shown to them.

Motivational Support: Show a television program with the sound track turned down, then replay it with both video and sound. Have the class talk about the experience. For a humerous experience, tune in a radio station and show just the video on the television.

Alternatively, construct a "texture tunnel" by taping large cardboard cartons together to make them light proof. Fill the tunnel with objects that have varied surface characteristics. Have the class crawl through it one at a time and then tell about what they felt around them while inside.

Subject Correlation: Literature/Drama (including movies and TV): myths and fantasies that present invisible phenomena, such as poltergeists.

Science: Studies in electricity, magnetism, gases, sounds, wind tunnels, etc.

 Measurement

A Individually or as a group, the class is to point to work that they judge to be unlike what the rest of the class has done (artistic quality is *not* to be judged).

B The class—either individually or as a group—must link the word invisible with the idea of not being seen.

C The class—either individually or as a group—must report the information about images for ideas and experiences.

E During class, observe that all children do mix colors together to make new ones.

F Check that each child has painted a picture and named the invisible thing it is about.

lesson 12

(Child's Copy)

SHOW WHAT YOU CAN'T SEE

How To Do This Lesson:

Read This: You cannot see the wind. Yet it is there. And you can feel it. Sugar tastes sweet, but you cannot see the sweetness.

You can see peanut butter, but you cannot see the peanut butter smell. There are many things we cannot see. We call them invisible.

Artists have always made shapes for the things they cannot see. Sometimes these things are made to look like people or mixture of people and animals. A gentle breeze may be made to look like a graceful dancer. Silence may be a grouchy old man hunched up so he will not be noticed.

Think of something that is invisible. It could be something like being hungry, the scent of a rose, the taste of lemon juice. How does it sound, or smell, or taste, or feel? Put all that you know together to show how you think it would look—if you could really see it. Mix your colors especially to get the colors that look just right.

Objectives:

YOU WILL:

1. Name things you cannot see as *invisible*.
2. Make a picture of something that is invisible.
3. Pick out the class pictures that are different from the others.
4. Mix colors together to make new ones.

Art materials: Pencils and erasers   Paints, brushes, mixing trays
Drawing paper   Water, paper towels, mop   Smocks or old shirts

Look at this picture: see Plate 7.

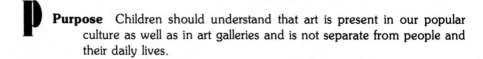

lesson 13

WHAAM!

P **Purpose** Children should understand that art is present in our popular culture as well as in art galleries and is not separate from people and their daily lives.

r **Readiness** These children are at an age when they are responding to the popular arts and they will normally possess the intellectual maturity to link pictures with elaborate verbal expressions.

i **Instructional objectives**

A   Select those class products that are unique (this is not to be a judgment of art quality but of differentness).

C   Learn that some words sound like the actual sounds in real life.

F   Make a drawing showing objects with words added that help describe the sound that would be heard.

 Strategies for teaching

Preparations: Have the children bring in comic books so they can pick out the content in the lesson from this kind of popular art. Video tape one of the better Saturday morning children's TV cartoons.

Delivery: Have the children read their text aloud. Have them practice saying the words and then saying what pictures might go with the words.

Motivational Support: Play charades using simple sounds to help the class guess at the meaning—or an opposite meaning.

Subject Correlations: Language arts: an introduction to onomatopoeia in poetry (probably without using the technical expression).

 Measurement

A   Make the selections described above.

C   Give examples of words that are like the sounds.

F   Produce a picture as described. (This evaluation is not to be a judgment of art quality.)

lesson 13

(Child's Copy)

WHAAM!

How To Do This Lesson:

Read This: The comics are full of words that are not real. The words come out like noises if you try to say them. The sounds on television cartoons are like the noises you read in the comics.

Make your very own drawing—not a copy—that would fit a "sound word." You can use more than one sound word if you like. Here are some extra words you can use. Invent your own words, too. Be sure the words and pictures fit together nicely. See how different you can be in thinking up pictures. Color your picture if you want to.

Objectives:

YOU WILL:

1. Pick out class art work that is quite different from all the others.

2. Learn that words can look like sounds.

3. Make a drawing that uses words to help make the picture have a stronger meaning.

Sound words: Garumphh! Zoom! Pow! Zzzzz. . . . Yeeow! Wump! Ugh! Whee . . . Oooof! Prrr. . . .Meeoww! Brm, Brm, Brm. Glug! Wuff, Yap, Grr. Pinggg!!! Kerplunk! Pssst! BooHoo Tweet Baa . . . Baa . . . Baa Squawwk!

Art materials: Drawing paper   Pencils, erasers, and crayons

Look at this picture: see Figure 106.

FIGURE 106 Intermediate child's crayon drawing: "Hee Hee Hee!"

lesson 14

AFRICAN ART

P **Purpose** Children should become familiar with the art from their own cultural origins and also the origins of other people who live in their community.

R **Readiness** While elementary children expect art lessons to consist of activities, they are usually mature enough in the upper grades to accept an occasional art lesson that is limited to reading and discussion.

Instructional objectives

A Describe the general appearance of art from Black Africa.
Describe the general feeling conveyed by art from Black Africa.

B Define "symbolism" in art as the inventing of shapes to represent important ideas.

C Learn that Black Africa begins on the south side of the Sahara Desert and extends southwards from there over the rest of the continent.
Learn that African art is tribal and changes from tribe to tribe.
Learn that all pieces of African art have their own symbolic meaning.
Learn that African artists are more concerned about what their work means than with trying to make it look realistic.
Learn that during the 20th Century artists in Europe and America have used ideas from African art in their own work.

Strategies for teaching

Preparations: Be sure that the students will all be easily able to see the examples of African art and also a map.

Delivery: Have the students read the text about art from Black Africa. Have them identify those images and parts of images that relate to parts of the text. Once this introductory period is over, have the class attend to tribal differences among the art works, and some of the names of the tribes, and also where in Africa those people live. Focus attention on the meanings present in the works (see captions to pictures) and emphasize the symbolism in this art—as distinct from that realism they are accustomed to seeing in Western art.

Motivational Support: Invite a docent from an art museum or a local person who has a collection of African art and knows the symbolic meaning underlying the pieces to visit the class and explain the work. A motion picture or film strip might be an acceptable alternative.

Subject Correlation: Social Studies: Religions and life styles of people in different parts of the world; the effects of other cultures on our own.

Music and Dance: Films and records and even actual performances that expand on the visual culture of Black Africa.

Measurement

A Any descriptive reactions that relate to African art in general.

B Definitions must refer to a symbol as a visual idea.

C Mention the area in Africa; tribal organization; art is symbolic and not realistic; and that Europeans and Americans have been influenced by it.

lesson 14

AFRICAN ART

How To Do This Lesson:

Read This: The Black African artists who live south of the Sahara Desert are respected by their people. Their art works are used in every part of the daily life of the tribe.

Artists make carved poles, called staffs, which chiefs use to show how important they are. They carve stools, cups, and pipes that help show the importance of people. They carve and decorate weapons that are used by warriors for fighting and for decoration. Artists make masks for use in their religion and in their secret clubs that are an important part of people's lives. Masks have special powers that can protect the tribe and bring good luck. Small figures are also carved to protect people from evil spirits. These shapes stand for important ideas. They are called *symbols.*

Although many African artists are carvers, some weave cloth and baskets. All of them spend many years learning their art. They learn how to use carving tools, and how to show old designs that have been handed down to them. They learn their art from older people in their own tribe, so art works from the same tribe are usually similar. But the work of each artist usually looks a little different from the others.

All African art shows things which the artist saw in nature and in people. But he also uses his own ideas. He does not just imitate nature. The parts of the body are usually changed. Because legs hold people up, they are often shown as very short, round and strong. Because heads are important, they are often made bigger.

Modern artists in America often use the same ideas in their work as African artists. It has taken us many years to learn what African artists discovered long ago.

Objectives:

YOU WILL:

1. Distinguish Black African art from art made in other parts of the world.

2. Say how African art makes you feel.

3. Explain that the word, *symbol,* means a picture or object that stands for an idea.

4. Talk about the things in this lesson that explain African art.

Art materials: None

Look at these pictures: see Figures 82 and 93.

MODELING WITH UNITS

P **Purpose** The need for developing creative people begins in school when children's imaginations are most receptive.

r **Readiness** Organizing identical forms into different combinations requires a level of intellectual maturity of a kind that can be expected in the upper elementary grades. The units should be kept simple, however.

i **Instructional objectives**

B Define "module" to mean any simple three-dimensional unit used repeatedly to make a larger structure.

C Learn that the art of every individual should be as unique as possible.

D Describe all the shapes and shadows to be seen in the sculpture.

F Build a piece of sculpture from a collection of similar objects.

S **Strategies for teaching**

Preparations: Be certain that enough modular items have been collected for each student to have at least ten.

Delivery: Have one or two students read the text aloud. Give particular attention to the objectives and question the class to ensure they understand what is expected. Study the pictures that show modular construction.

Motivational Support: Invite a parent or friend who is able to build tall structures with playing cards or dominoes to make a spectacular, flimsy structure. See a movie clip of gymnasts making a pyramid or similar structure by standing on each other's shoulders.

Subject Correlation: Science: Modular cell structures of living organisms, also models of atomic structures.

m **Measurement**

B Definitions to include reference to the phrases: *three dimensional; object;* and *used repeatedly.*

C Any statement about the importance of individuality in art.

D Point to parts that are dark and light and shaded. Describe the shape of the module and the over-all shape of the sculpture.

F Any modular structure is acceptable.

lesson 15

MODELING WITH UNITS

How To Do This Lesson:

Read This: Machines do their work in exactly the same way over and over again. They can print thousands of books very quickly. They can weave thousands of yards of cloth. Solid things, like bricks and plastic cups are also made by machines. But people use bricks to build all kinds of different shaped buildings. A brick is a simple object, but when it is put together with other bricks, we can make many different shapes. Any object that is used over and over again like this is called a *module.*

Make a piece of sculpture using only one kind of object. Use it over and over again, until you have a piece of sculpture that you think is interesting to look at. Try and make your work different from everyone else's in the class. See how many interesting ways you can discover for attaching your modules together. Also study the shapes and shadows in your sculpture.

Objectives:
YOU WILL:

1. Explain the word *module* as a simple solid object that can be used over and over again in sculpture and buildings.

2. Remember that it is important in art to try and do work that is different from everyone else.

3. Build some sculpture from simple objects.

4. Describe the shadows you can see in your sculpture and also the shape of the modules you used.

Art materials: A collection of simple, solid objects that are all the same (paper/plastic cups, paper plates, plastic spoons, etc.). String, thread, adhesive tape, glue and applicators   Scissors   Newspapers

Look at these pictures: *Problem:* Make your own example of sculpture composed of modules.

lesson 16

POETRY COLLAGES

 Purpose   Students need to realize that all the arts are related in that they all express human feelings. This lesson links art with music and literature.

r   **Readiness**   Children in the upper elementary grades are usually ready to begin thinking about abstract relationships and they need practice in doing this in order for the ability to develop.

i   **Instructional objectives**

A   Individually pick out the class art work that shows the feeling of a particular song or poem most strongly.

B   Define "collage" as a way of making pictures in which small pieces of paper, cloth, and leaves are stuck on to a sheet of paper or cardboard.

F   Arrange natural materials on a sheet of paper to make a collage that expresses the feeling present in a particular song, poem, or piece of music.

s   **Strategies for teaching**

Problem: Design the preparation, delivery, motivational support, and subject correlation for this lesson.

m   **Measurement**

A   Individual selections must be made. Any reasons are to be accepted. The task is to have practice making public these kinds of choices.

B   The definition must refer to flat materials being stuck to a flat base to make a picture or design.

F   Any collage is acceptable as long as it is made of natural materials. The child's word is to be taken at face value for the expression of feeling.

Art materials: A collection of natural materials: leaves, grasses, feathers, flowers, seeds, flat shells, dry seaweed, pieces of bark, etc.   Glue and applicators   Strong paper or cardboard for bases   Newspaper

Picture to go with this lesson: see Figure 13.

lesson 17

LOOK AT LITTLE THINGS

p   **Purpose**   *Problem:* Explain why this lesson should be taught.

r   **Readiness**   *Problem:* Explain why this lesson is suitable for intermediate level children.

Instructional objectives

D Describe every part of the visuals used to illustrate this lesson. Describe every part of a work by another child.

E Draw part or all of a natural object showing every possible detail that can be shown with lines.

Strategies for teaching

Preparations: Make sure that your class picture file is ready to be used (see Chapter 4). Collect suitable objects for the children to draw, such as bird feathers, flowers, pieces of bark, etc.

Delivery: Have each child in the class pick out a picture from a class picture file and study it carefully in preparation for describing it. You might give a demonstration, description and/or have the class as a whole do a descriptive analysis of some art work.

Motivational Supports: Have children study objects through magnifying glasses. Some nature movies show excellent and beautiful close-ups of animal and plant life. Video-tapes from network television are also excellent.

Subject Correlations: *Science:* Recording all data is fundamental to science and scientific illustration.

Measurement *Problem:* Write down exactly what you would expect children to do to show they had achieved the objectives.

Art materials: Pencils and erasers   White paper   Magnifying glasses

Pictures to go with this lesson: see Plate 6 and Figure G.

lesson 18

(Teacher's Copy)

INTERNAL AND EXTERNAL FORMS
(sculpture by Henry Moore)

Purpose It is as important to learn how to think critically about works of art as it is to be able to make art.

Readiness: As students reach the end of their elementary school years, they become increasingly able to think more abstractly about works of art and the meanings that underlie them.

Instructional objectives

> *D* Describe all the parts as rounded on the inside and on the outside, a heavy outer shell surrounds a thin, twisting upright shape inside; the open front of the outside form is broken by a curving diagonal that is similar in character to the internal form; the inside of the external form emphasizes some of the curves found on the outside by repeating them; and the empty spaces between the carved wooden parts possess a roundedness that is similar to the solid parts.
>
> Interpret the artist's meaning from among the following or from some combination of them: the idea of upward growing young life that is surrounded by a shell or a similar protective covering while it is young; the feeling of a mother's instinct to protect a young child; or the roundedness of the forms suggesting branches, roots, and hollow trees to give the viewer a sense of silent growth in nature that continues night and day.

Strategies for teaching

> *Preparations:* Collect photographs of the sculpture "Internal and External Forms" by Henry Moore (and other pieces by Moore) viewed from several positions, including close-ups of areas of special interest. If a three-dimensional model is available, bring it to class.
>
> *Delivery:* Explain that the work was made by carving pieces of wood and then assembling them. Show examples of Moore's art, including this piece. Have them withhold any statement about liking it or disliking it and engage them in a descriptive analyses of the formal visual qualities present. Steer the students to respond to the qualities listed in the first set of objectives.
>
> When the formal analysis is complete, have the students explain what they thought the artist was trying to say to us through his art. While all ideas may be accepted initially, interpretations present in the second set of objectives are those most likely to predominate; and they should be encouraged.
>
> *Motivational Support:* Visit the Albright-Knox Art Gallery in Buffalo, N.Y. to see the original sculpture or visit a nearby art museum where sculpture by Henry Moore or other artists who work in a similar style are on display.
>
> *Subject Correlation: Science:* Close-up photographs of plants to show similarities—and possible sources of inspiration.

 Measurement Spoken statements from the students that correspond with the analysis and interpretive objectives while also allowing for well-thought-out alternatives to be accepted.

Art materials: None

Picture to go with this lesson: see Figure 107.

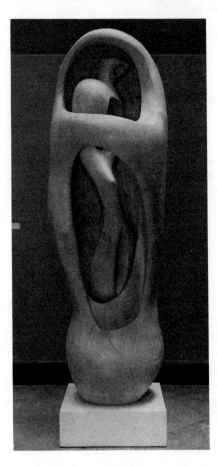

FIGURE 107 Henry Moore, ''Internal and External Forms'' (1953–54). Elm, 8′7″ high, 109″ wide, 36″ deep. Albright-Knox Art Gallery, Buffalo, New York, General Purchase Funds, 1955.

lesson 19

PARTY HATS

P **Purpose**   The observance of festivals contributes to the sense of personal and group identification; and visual imagery fulfills an important function in these events.

r **Readiness**   All children enjoy parties. By the upper elementary grades they are likely to possess the necessary skills for working three dimensionally with paper and cardboard.

Instructional objectives

> *A* Identify whole hats and parts of hats from those made in class that are distinctly different from the rest.
> Select party hats that are liked best from those made in class.
> *C* Learn that the kinds of hats people wear often tell us about who they are and how they feel.
> *E* Curl and bend paper.
> Attach pieces of paper securely with adhesive.
> *F* Make a party hat from cardboard, paper, foil, and plastic.

 Strategies for teaching

> *Preparations:* Find out which children have birthdays soon and arrange for a class party.
> *Delivery:* *Problem:* Devise an original way for delivering this lesson.
> *Motivational Support:* Bring music and plan some games.
> *Subject Correlations:* *Social Studies:* Seasonal religious and political festivals in the United States and other countries. *Literature:* Writers' accounts of well-known festivals. *Music:* Festival music of various kinds. *Physical Education:* Dances for festivals.

Measurement *Problem:* Write down exactly what you would expect children to do to show they had achieved the objectives you chose.

Art materials: *Problem:* Select materials that are best suited for the objectives you want the children to achieve.

Picture to go with this lesson: see Figure 108.

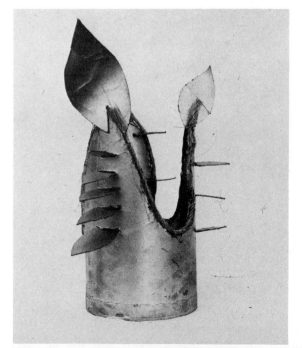

FIGURE 108   A party hat

KITES

Complete all the parts of this lesson based on the following Instructional Objectives:

Instructional objectives

A Say what a kite is imagined to look like as it flies in the sky (bird, ghost, umbrella, spaceship, etc.)

C Learn that the tail of a kite maintains its balance in the air.
Learn that designs are good only if they work properly as well as being attractive to look at.

E Attach lightweight strips together to make a frame.
Stretch paper over a frame to make a strong, flat surface.

F Make a decorated kite that flies well.

Picture to go with this lesson: see Figure 109.

FIGURE 109 A kite design

1. Complete the lessons that are incomplete by responding to the problem statements.

2. Re-write any lesson to fit the other category, that is; change primary lessons so they become intermediate lessons; and vice versa.

3. Re-write any lesson for a class composed of children from a particular ethnic minority: Black, Hispanic-American, American-Indian, Pacific-Asian.

4. Re-write any lesson to make the most of a local setting such as New Orleans, Louisiana; Juneau, Alaska; Great Falls, Montana; Laredo, Texas; or New York City.

5. Re-write any lesson to make it suitable for either primary or intermediate grade children who are gifted in some way. State the nature of their giftedness.

6. Re-write any lesson to make it suitable for children who are handicapped. One lesson could be re-written several times for each of the following groups: educable mentally retarded; emotionally disturbed; visually impaired; palsied, or any other group that interests you.

7. Re-write and expand any lesson to make it suitable for all the children in a class that has been mainstreamed. The class consists of children who are gifted, normal, retarded, and disturbed—all in the same room.

8. Construct a sequence of three related lessons using one of the methods described in Chapter 1. Modify any of the lessons as necessary to make a good sequence. State whether the sequence is to be for primary or intermediate level students.

9. Prepare a strand as described in Chapter 1.

10. Match as many pictures in the entire book as possible with the 20 lessons in this appendix. Use a picture more than once if it fits the objectives of a lesson.

appendix b
parts of lessons
and how to assemble them

INSTRUCTIONAL OBJECTIVES FOR GRADES 1 THROUGH 6

The following list of objectives will help you as you design an art program. The items are organized according to the expanded matrix presented in Chapter 7, and serve to keep your art program balanced. Children will not usually learn objectives the first time they are introduced, so you can expect to repeat them. Each objective is listed once only, however, so if a child in Grade 4 has not yet learned an objective listed for Grade 2, you will need to reintroduce it. The vocabulary used throughout is suited to the children's understanding for the grade level.

This list includes more objectives than a class will actually have time for during the school year, which means that you will have to establish priorities. In some situations you may have to redistribute objectives differently across the grades from the way they are listed here so they will better suit the needs of particular groups of students. But whatever your decisions, clearly stated objectives should be the foundation for all your art lessons.

Illustrations for many of the following objectives can be found throughout the book, but it is not possible to show a visual image of everything listed here. That is especially true for the art history objectives listed in Grades 5 and 6. Good books on art history and the practice of art, containing an abundance of suitable illustrations, may be found in most libraries.

GRADE ONE

A. SEEING

Identify and Remember:

Scissors and the word *scissors.*
Crayons and the word *crayon.*
Paste and the word *paste.*
Pencils and the word *pencil.*
Paper and the word *paper.*
Red and the word *red.*
Blue and the word *blue.*
Yellow and the word *yellow.*
Green and the word *green.*
Orange and the word *orange.*
Violet and the word *violet.*
Darkened forms of primary (red, blue, and yellow) and secondary colors (green, orange, and violet).
Lightened forms of primary and secondary colors.
Warm colors (red, yellow, and orange).
Cool colors (blue, green, and violet).
Tops and bottoms of objects.
Right and left sides of objects.
Flat surfaces of objects.
Rounded surfaces of objects.
Rough surfaces of objects.
Smooth surfaces of objects.
Dark grey, light grey, middle greys.
Basic geometric shapes: circles, squares (and rectangles), triangles.
The parts of faces (ears, eyes, nose, mouth, chin) and name them.
The parts of people (arms, legs, bodies, hands, feet, neck, head) and name them.

Compare/distinguish between:

The darkest and the lightest colors in a selection (such as in one or more pictures)
The roughest textures and the smoothest in a selection.
The biggest shapes and the smallest in a selection.

The thinnest lines and the thickest lines in a selection.

Real textures and pictures of textures.

Lines that are the same or nearly the same in a selection.

Shapes that are the same or nearly the same in a selection.

Textures that are the same or nearly the same in a selection.

Colors that are the same or nearly the same in a selection.

Visualize:

Shapes that fit musical or other sounds/rhythms.

Lines that fit musical or other sounds/rhythms.

Colors that fit musical or other sounds/rhythms.

Textures that fit smells.

Colors that fit smells.

Select:

Art works that make you feel good (the works are to be selected either from artists' pictures in the color section of this book or from similar works of art).

Color(s) that is/are favorite(s).

Kind(s) of line(s) that are favorite(s).

Kind(s) of texture(s) that are favorite(s).

Kind(s) of shape(s) that is/are favorite(s).

Kind(s) of art lesson(s) that is/are favorite(s).

Kind(s) of art work(s) (class/artist) from the color section that is/are favorite(s).

B. KNOWING

Definitions:

Art: pictures and models made by people.

Art Show: art work that is put on the wall to look at.

Black: paint that makes colors darker.

Blue: the color of the sky.

Colors: red, blue, yellow, orange, green, violet.

Decorate: make things look pretty.

Frame: a border around a picture.

Green: the color of grass.

Grey: a mixture of black and white.

Line: a mark that goes somewhere.

Mask: a shape of a face that people wear at parties and Halloween.

Mural: a picture painted on a wall.

Orange: the color of an orange.

Red: the color of ripe tomatoes.

Rubbing: showing a surface by rubbing with pencil or crayon through paper.

Shape: the space inside a line when a line loops around to join itself.

Texture: the way that something feels—like smooth, bumpy, rough.

Violet: the color of dark colored grapes.

White: paint that makes colors lighter.

Information (about art, about artists):

Warm colors are those like yellow, orange, red.

Cool colors are those like green, blue, violet.

It is good to do things in art that are different from what other people do.

Art can tell stories.

Art can tell about feelings.

Some art is made from what people see in front of them.

Some art is made from what people remember.

Colors are used on signs to say things, like red and green in traffic lights.

Shapes are used to say things, like road signs.

Picture making is a kind of art that fills all the paper.

Media and techniques (about tools and materials):

Crayons are used in art.

Pencils are used in art.

Scissors are used in art.

Paints are used in art.

Clay is used in art.

Brushes must be washed before using with a new color.

Brushes must be washed carefully before they are put away.

Clay can be rolled flat with a rolling pin.

Pictures can be stuck on to big pieces of paper to look better.

Art History:

None

CRITICISM:

1. WINSLOW HOMER, "GULF STREAM," (Figure A.)

Literal Description:

A sailor is lying on the deck of a sailboat that has lost its mast in a storm.

Hungry sharks are swimming round the boat hoping for a meal.

Most of the picture is filled with big waves.

There is a big sailing ship in the distance.

Visual Analysis:

Most of the shapes are tipped over to make you feel that everything is moving.

The only smooth curves in the picture are on the boat and this contrasts with the choppy shapes of the water to make it look even more dangerous.

Expressive Interpretations:

The artist tried to make people understand what it is like to be all alone on the ocean.

We know that the sailor is probably going to be rescued by the sailing ship. The sailor doesn't know this yet because he is looking the other way.

2. BLACKBEAR BOSIN, "PRAIRIE FIRE," (Plate 3.)

Literal Description:

Two indians riding horses are galloping away from the fire.

Deer are leaping in the same direction as the Indians to escape the fire.

Three coyotes are running away from the fire.

The ground is sandy and the grass looks very dry.

Flames and smoke fill most of the top part of the picture.

Visual Analysis:

The shapes of the animals and Indians are all curved as they run and try to escape the fire.

The flames and smoke look like fingers that fill the whole sky and seem to be reaching out to trap the Indians and the animals.

Expressive Interpretations:

The artist knows that prairie fires move very quickly and is telling us that the only way to escape is to be quick.

We see that hunters, deer and coyotes all forget that they are enemies when things like prairie fires happen.

3. GUTZON BORGLUM, MOUNT RUSHMORE NATIONAL MONUMENT, Figure 110.

Literal Description:

The heads of four presidents (George Washington, Thomas Jefferson, Theodore Roosevelt, and Abraham Lincoln) have been carved out of a mountainside

Visual Analysis:

Each head fits the shape of the mountain and tells you that the artist picked a place which already looked like people's faces.

The shapes of the faces are very simple so people can see them easily from far away.

Expressive Interpretation:

The sculpture was done so people would remember forever four great American presidents.

C. DOING

Safety (of children, clothing and equipment):

Hold scissors point down and away from people.

Hold pencil points away from people, especially faces.

Keep paint and clay off clothes (wear a smock).

FIGURE 110 Mount Rushmore National Monument. Artist: Gutzon Borglum, U.S. Department of the Interior.

Keep water cans only half full.

Proficiency (care and use of materials):

Sharpen a pencil.

Clean brushes gently and thoroughly.

Wash brushes before changing colors.

Imitate real textures with pencil.

Imitate real textures with crayon.

Cut out neat squares, circles, and triangles following lines.

Cut out squares, circles, and triangles without lines drawn in.

Stick pieces of paper without too much or too little paste.

Clean up thoroughly after using paste.

Frame a picture by sticking it on to a bigger sheet of paper.

Roll clay into slabs.

Clean up thoroughly after using clay.

Make clear texture rubbings.

Store brushes flat when not in use.

Art Production:
Flat Art:

Decorate shapes with crayons.

Decorate shapes with paint.

Print a blot to make a mirror image.

Make a picture or design in warm colors.

Make a picture or design in cool colors.

Make a picture or design using several kinds of lines.

Make a picture or design using several kinds of shapes.

Make a picture or design using several kinds of colors.

Make a picture or design using several kinds of textures.

Make a collage from texture rubbings.

Solid Art:
Make Paper Sack Masks:

Make an impressed clay mosaic.

Arrange an art show.

GRADE TWO

A. SEEING

Identify and Remember:

Objects and events that are colored in primary and secondary colors.

An oval shape.

How the neck joins the head.

Basic geometric shapes (triangles, squares (including rectangles) and circles) in pictures and photographs.

Lines that seem to move or point in one direction.

Shapes that seem to move or point in one direction.

Foreground in a picture.

Background in a picture.

A drawing.

A painting.

A piece of sculpture.

A collage.

A weaving.

An angle made by two straight lines.

Different kinds of lines: broken, straight, scribble, curved, wavy, jagged.

Christmas shapes (symbols): trees, Santa Claus, stockings.

Halloween shapes (symbols): pumpkins, witches on broomsticks, black cats.

Valentine shapes (symbols): hearts.

Places to be seen on the way to school.

Things to be seen at home.

Things to be seen in school.

Deliberate distortion of the way things usually look (i.e., *not* optical distortion).

Smaller parts of large objects.

Compare/Distinguish between:

Lighter colors and darker ones.

Smoother textures and rougher ones.

Art works and things that are not art.

Art works by artists and art by children.

Art that looks different from anyone else's in a classroom.

Impressions in clay and the objects that made them.

Shapes and parts of shapes with the correct words: triangle, square, rectangle, circle, top, bottom, side.

Parts of people with the correct words: head (eyes, mouth, nose, ears, chin), neck, body, arms, hands, legs, feet.

Different kinds of lines with descriptions: skinny, lumpy, tender, stiff, wooly, strong, weak, droopy, lonely.

Different kinds of textures with descriptions: scratchy, shiny, lumpy, prickly, furry.

Visualize:

Geometric shapes that look like cows, cats, hippos, turtles, giraffes.

Lines that look like objects and animals, such as worms, grass, fences, jungle gyms, trees.

Lines that look like moods and feelings such as: angry-sad, happy-miserable, brave-frightened, ghostly.

Shapes that look like moods and feelings, such as: angry-sad, happy-miserable, brave-frightened, ghostly.

Curved lines that look like: animals, waves, clouds.

Select:

Artist's work that is liked (the works are to be selected either from artists' pictures in the color section or from similar works of art).

Art materials that are preferred.

Subjects in art that are preferred.

Class art that should be in an art show.

B. KNOWING

Definitions:

Arrange: move things so they look right.

Background: parts of a picture that are farther away.

Circle: a round ring.

Clay: powdered-earth mixed with water.

Collage: a picture made by sticking down pieces of paper.

Collect: bring things together.

Foreground: parts of a picture that are closer.

Mosaic: art made with small squares of paper.

Original: being different.

Oval: egg shaped.

Papier mâché: a mixture of pieces of paper and paste used for modelling.

Pattern: repeating a design over and over.

Primary colors: red, blue, yellow.

Print: when a painted shape is pressed onto paper to make a design.

Rectangle: a shape that has two short sides and two long sides, and each corner is square.

Sculpture: art that is solid.

Secondary colors: orange, green, violet.

Square: a shape that has four equal sides and each corner is square.

Tile: a flat decorated clay square.

Title: a name for art work.

Triangle: a shape that has three straight sides.

Information (about art, about artists):

Artists all work in their own ways—like careful, splashy.

There is no single right answer in art.

Artists tell us what they think through their art.

Sculpture is seen from all positions.

Weaving is a kind of art.

Greeting cards are a kind of art.

Media and techniques (about tools and materials):

Crayon can be used in different ways: points (sharpened – blunt); side (wrapper removed); overlapping; pressing heavily; pressing lightly.

Pencils can be used in different ways: points (sharpened – blunt); side; short lines; long lines; pressing heavily; pressing lightly.

Artists often mix materials (paint, crayons, collage, etc.).

Art History:

None

CRITICISM:

1. THOMAS HART BENTON, "ARTS OF THE WEST" Plate 1.

Literal Description:

On the right are two cowboys breaking in horses.

In the center two men are playing cards.

Above the cardplayers are two hunters.

On the left is a three-man band playing for the people who are dancing.

At the top between the hunters and the dancers are some people playing horseshoes in the street.

Visual Analysis:

The picture is made up of four separate groups of people.

The groups of people are linked together except for the cowboys in the corral. They fill in an empty circular space.

The people, horses, and the tree are all made of lines and shapes that seem to be turning and twisting. This is very different from the straight lines of the building, the boardwalk, and the corral fence. Warm oranges, reds, and browns contrast with cool blues and greens in all parts of the painting.

Expressive Interpretation:

The artist uses shapes and lines as well as people doing things to help us understand the action-loving people who live on the prairie farms and ranches.

2. ANDREW WYETH, "THE HUNTER," Figure G.

Literal Description:

We are looking down from high in a big tree that fills most of the picture.

It is fall and most of the leaves have fallen. The wheat has been harvested and the grass has turned brown.

A hunter walks by underneath the tree.

Visual Analysis:

The thick, twisting, shapes of the tree branches stand out against the detail of the grass and the simple curves of the hills.

The same kinds of brownish and greyish colors are all over the picture and help to hold it together.

Expressive Interpretation

Andrew Wyeth helps us feel what it is like to be an animal when it hides in a tree from a hunter. All the leaves have fallen, so the only thing to do is to sit very, very still and hope that the hunter will not look up.

3. EERO SAARINEN, "GATEWAY TO THE WEST," Figure 63.

Literal Description:

The shape is a flattened circle. It is taller than the distance across. It is made of stainless steel.

Visual Analysis:

The arch becomes thinner toward the top, and this makes it seem higher and even more delicate than it really is.

Expressive Interpretation:

Saarinen wanted people to know that most of the people who pioneered the Western United States left from here.

He wanted to give the feeling of hope for success that the pioneers took with them across the prairies. He could easily have designed a decorated arch but instead he decided that he could give a better feeling for his idea with a very simple, elegant shape.

C. DOING

Safety (of children, clothing, equipment):

No new ones.

Proficiency (care and use of materials):

Make crayon lines by pressing heavily.

Make crayon lines by pressing lightly.

Fill spaces with crayons using dots.

Fill spaces with crayons using the sides.

Mix crayon colors using dots.

Mix crayon colors rubbing one layer over another.

Make pencil lines by pressing heavily.

Make pencil lines by pressing lightly.

Roll a clay slab of even thickness.

Mix different kinds of orange with red and yellow.

Mix different kinds of violet with red and blue.

Mix different kinds of green with yellow and blue.

Draw lines using sticks and sponges.

Rub powdered chalk to make a design.

Fold paper in half accurately.

Cut small shapes with scissors.

Cut squares of paper into strips.

Tear paper into squares, triangles, and circles.

Weave paper over and under accurately.

Prepare pulp papier mâché.

Make clear impressions in clay with objects.

Attach objects to each other securely.

Mix secondary colors (orange, green and violet) from two primary colors (red, blue, yellow).

Art Production:

Flat Art:

Draw or paint simple things from memory.

Make a big picture from a small drawing.

Make art that tells a story.

Make art that is different from anyone else's.

Make a design or a picture that fills all the spaces on a sheet of paper.

Make art that conveys a mood: sad, angry, etc.

Make a picture using rubbed chalk dust.

Make a design or picture using only a brush and paint (no pencil).

Make a design by blowing watery paint.

Make a design with string between two sheets of paper.

Make a picture using light colors on dark paper.

Make a collage with materials collected from home.

Weave a design with paper strips.

Print a design with a block.

Show angles in art work.

Solid Art:

Make tiles from clay.

Build sculpture with boxes and cartons.

Decorate boxes.

Decorate a classroom.

Make papier mâché jewelry (strips over forms).

GRADE THREE

A. SEEING

Identify and Remember:

Parallel lines.

An ellipse.

Solid geometric shapes and the words that represent them: cube, cylinder, pyramid, sphere.

Objects in pictures and photographs that appear near to and far away.

Contrasts of color, shape, line and texture when observed.

Optical distortion in photographs and pictures (windows and doors mainly)

Hair that is wavy, straight, frizzy: and also blond, black, brown, red.

Edges of shapes in photographs and pictures that do not have outlines around them.

Parts of buildings: steps, doorways, windows, balconies, chimneys, fire-escapes, window boxes, roof gardens, swimming pools, air conditioners.

The eye-level in pictures or photographs (horizon).

The eye-level in the classroom.

The very smallest parts of objects.

All the art works by artists shown during the year.

The colors that symbolize Christmas – red/green.

The colors that symbolize Halloween – orange/black.

The colors that symbolize Valentines – red and white.

The colors that symbolize Spring and Fall – (bright) green and (golden) brown.

An angle made by two planes.

Compare/Distinguish between:

Relief and free-standing sculpture.

Realistic and unrealistic colors in pictures.

Art having outlines around shapes and art whose shapes are separated only by edges.

Kinds of colors with descriptions: heavy, light, friendly, empty.

Kinds of shapes with descriptions: heavy, light, friendly, empty.

Class art work with real places that can be seen.

Visualize:

Shapes that have special meanings (stars, moons, suns, hearts, crosses).

What a watery blot of paint/ink might mean or look like.

Natural and man-made phenomena (waves, mountains, crowds, etc.) from abstract rhythms.

Select:

Children's work in the color section that is liked.

The colors in a picture that are preferred and rank them.

How the sculpture pieces make you feel.

Which sculpture you like.

Which sculpture you do not like.

B. KNOWING

Definitions:

Architect: an artist who designs buildings.

Block: an object used to print with.

Carve: to cut away.

Center of interest: the most important part of a piece of art.

Contrast: showing a big difference in art.

Diagonal: slanting.

Distort: change a shape to make it look less realistic.

Design: an arrangement of shapes or the plan for something

Gradation: a slow change of color or shading in art work.

Loom: a frame used for weaving.

Mold: a shape for forming a solid object.

Oval: egg shaped.

Overlapping: one line or shape placed over another one.

Parallel: equal distance, never touching.

Portrait: a picture or sculpture of a face.

Print: pressing a paint covered object onto paper.

Profile: the side view of a head.

Relief: sculpture that is attached to a wall.

Rhythm: lines and shapes that happen over and over in the same or nearly the same way.

Shading: filling in spaces with pencil.

Symbol: a shape that tells about a thought or idea.

Weaving: a process where yarn is changed into cloth.

Yarn: thick thread.

Information (about art, about artists):

Television and movies are both art.

Television pictures always fill the whole screen.

Movie pictures always fill the whole screen.

Art is everywhere around us—shop-windows, buildings, printing, bridges, automobiles.

Getting to know different art helps people know what they like best.

Getting to know different art helps people make their own art better.

Artists mix their own ideas with those of other artists.

Artists and designers make inside as well as outside shapes interesting to look at.

Some artists try and imitate what they see.

Some artists make their feelings important and do not try to be realistic.

Some artists make only portraits of people.

Artists are always changing their art to try to improve it.

Architects often make models of buildings before the real building is put up.

Artists practice remembering by making drawings of things.

Parts of art works are made to contrast so they are noticed.

Artists erase parts of their work if they do not like them.

Clothes are made by weaving yarn.

Different rhythms in art give different feelings.

Shapes that overlap others look closer.

Media and techniques (about tools and materials):

The main idea in weaving is that the yarn goes over and under repeatedly.

Indians carved tree trunks to make totem poles.

Yellow and blue make green.

Shapes do not need outlines if they contrast with the surrounding shapes.

Art History:

None

CRITICISM:

1. MARY CASSATT, "THE BOATING PARTY," Figure I.

Literal Description:

A man, dressed in dark clothes is rowing a boat on a lake on a sunny day. The boat also has a sail.

The man's wife and baby are sitting enjoying the ride. They are dressed up in their best clothes.

The mother seems very calm and happy, while the baby is turning and twisting to look at different things.

Visual Analysis:

The curved shape of the boat seems to point to the figures of the mother and child. And so does the oar and the rope from the sail.

The light colors of the boat and the sail join together with the mother and her baby. The dark shape of the man balances the light parts of the picture.

Decorated surfaces are only used in the woman's and baby's clothes and this makes us notice them more easily. They contrast with the strong, dark shape of the father as he rows the boat.

Expressive Interpretation:

The picture tells about a family boat ride on a beautiful summer day. The mother and father are both happy and don't need to say anything.

2. ALBERT BIERSTADT, "IN THE MOUNTAINS," Figure D.

Literal Description:

A calm mountain lake fills most of the lower left side of the picture.

A level shore fills the lower right side. It has some trees on it.

Most of the shore line of the lake is a vertical cliff.

Cloud covered mountains rise up to fill the top part of the picture.

The sun is shining on the far end of the lake and on a waterfall.

Visual Analysis:

The main lines and shapes are vertical and give a feeling of great height. The reflections in the water add to this. So do the two waterfalls.

The shapes of the mountain peaks blend with the clouds to make the mountain seem to go on forever.

Expressive Interpretation:

The artist tried to show how the great mountains and lakes of Western America are often beautiful, peaceful places.

3. LOUISE NEVELSON, "SKY CATHEDRAL," Figure 85.

Literal Description:

This sculpture is made from fifty open wood boxes of different sizes that have been joined together to make a large rectangle.

Different shaped pieces of wood have been glued into arrangements inside each box.

The sculpture is painted black.

Formal Analysis:

The straight sides of the boxes contrast with mixtures of shapes in the arrangements of wooden pieces inside the boxes.

The shadows in the deep hollows of the boxes make a design of dark shapes all across the sculpture. This is balanced by another design made by the light as it is reflected by the pieces of wood attached to the fronts of the boxes.

Expressive Interpretation:

Cathedrals are large churches and in them are usually many different places where people can go and pray. The sculptor used the same idea when she created this mysterious black cathedral from fifty boxes, each of which is different.

C. DOING

Safety:

No new ones

Proficiency (care and use of materials):

Fold paper accurately.

Make different kinds of lines with pencil—pressing heavily/lightly, sharp/dull points, using the side of the point.

Cut a symmetrical shape by first folding paper and then cutting it.

Mold papier mâché over relief sculpture.

Mix different greens using yellow, blue, and black and white.

Mix paint to match the real colors of buildings.

Mix paint to match the real colors of faces.

Make a clear print.

Place prints next to each other for neat pattern making.

Scratch and press textures in clay.

Paint with thick dry paint of dry paper (and wet paper).

Paint with thin, watery paint on dry paper (and wet paper).

Art Production:

Flat Art:

Use pencil alone to make a picture.

Draw sketch ideas for a large picture.

Show your own art style in drawing or painting.

Print a repeating pattern.

Paint a design or picture that shows rhythm.

Weave a belt or headband.

Make a picture showing a center of interest.

Create a picture that is funny.

Use overlapping in a picture to show distance.

Draw a profile portrait with the parts in the correct places.

Draw a full-face portrait with the parts in the correct places.

Draw the textures that show on a face.

Draw a picture showing objects that have been remembered.

Finish off a picture that began as a blot.

Draw or paint people with curly, wavy, or straight hair.

Solid Art:

Model a portrait (including the neck) with all the parts in the correct places.

Model a relief with papier mâché.

Decorate clay sculpture with textures.

Build sculpture with small pieces of clay.

Mold objects using strip papier mâché.

Construct an interior space.

Construct a model building.

Make clay sketch ideas for a large piece of sculpture.

Show your own style in a piece of sculpture.

Model an egg-shape and decorate the surface.

Make a texture "feelie" box to include a range of textures.

GRADE FOUR

A. SEEING

Identify and Remember:

Designs and pictures made using rulers, compasses, and templates.

Five main shapes of trees. (Figure 111)

Concentric circles.

Objects that are near and far by colors.

Objects that are near and far by size.

FIGURE 111   The main shapes of trees

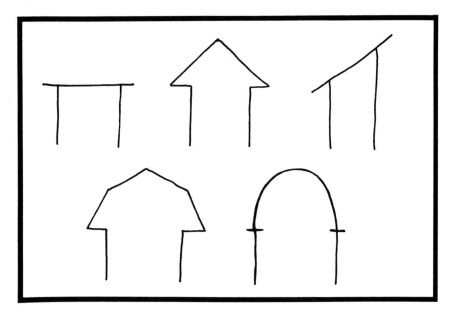

FIGURE 112   The different kinds of roofs on buildings

Objects that are near and far by overlapping.

Windows in buildings as dark-looking.

Television sets.

Kitchen appliances: cooking stoves, ovens, refrigerators.

Kinds of seating: dining room chairs, counter stools, lounge chairs, car seats, bus seats, church pews.

Tall buildings: churches, skyscrapers, castles, factories, power plants.

Kinds of roofs on buildings: flat, gabled, mansard (not by name), domed and shed. (Figure 112)

Different colors of people's skin.

Converging and diverging lines.

Situations where the wind is blowing strongly.

Compare/Distinguish between:

Sketches and finished pictures.

Transparent and opaque paint.

Art done quickly and art done slowly.

Visualize:

No new ones

Select:

Colors that will look best in a picture.

Shapes that will look best in a picture.

The kinds of masses that will look good in a piece of sculpture.

Parts of a picture for changing to improve it.

How art makes you feel (the works are to be selected either from artists' pictures in the color section or from similar works).

Which art works you like best (the works are to be selected either from artists' pictures in the color section or from similar works).

B. KNOWING

Definitions:

Asymmetry: balance where each side is different.

Balance: a good organization of all the parts of a design.

Color wheel: all the colors of the spectrum placed in a circle.

Complementary: Colors on opposite sides in the color wheel.

Concentric: circles inside each other, all with the same center.

Fantasy: dream-like art.

Foreground: parts of a picture that are close.

Free-hand: a drawing done without rulers, compasses or similar instruments.

Free-standing: sculpture that stands up by itself.

Gradation: a gradual change in color or shading.

Hard edges: sharp, clean edges.

Illustration: a picture that shows part of a story.

Landscape: a picture showing the outdoors.

Mass: a word used in art to describe all kinds of solidness.

Module: a simple, solid object that is used over and over in sculpture and architecture.

Opaque: not being able to see through.

Paint: a mixture of powdered color and glue.

Pottery: clay that has been baked in a special oven (a kiln).

Related colors: colors that are next to each other in the color wheel.

Right angles: square corners.

Sketch: a quickly drawn or modeled idea for a piece of art.

Slip: a creamy mixture of clay and water.

Soft-edges: blurred edges.

Stitchery: a picture or design made with thread and cloth.

Style: a personal way of making art.

Symmetry: balance where each side is the same.

Template: an object to draw around.

Three dimensions: solid: up and down; side to side; front to back.

Transparent: being able to see through.

Two dimensions: flat: up and down; side to side.

Unity: all parts of art look as though they belong together.

Information (about art, about artists):

Eyes tell stories by the way they look.

Mouths tell stories by the way they look.

Some artists paint mostly fantasies.

Artists often have to follow instructions.

Artists often have to do work that pleases other people.

Artists all try to be original in different ways.

Every country has its own kind of art.

Artists often use unusual colors.

Artists often use unusual textures.

Artists often use unusual shapes.

Artists often use unusual lines.

The position of light can make objects and shadows look more interesting.

Color symbols include Orange/Black (Halloween); Red/Green (Christmas).

Shape symbols include Hearts, Bells, Christmas trees, Pumpkins.

The height of a person measures seven times the head.

Pottery has been a form of art for thousands of years.

Media and techniques (about tools and materials):

Things shown in detail look closer.

Things that are brighter look closer.

Things that are bigger look closer.

Some artists paint quickly.

Some artists paint slowly.

Clay is kept moist in plastic sacks.

Clay can be stuck together with slip.

Upright lines always stay upright from every view.

Artists show light shapes against dark shapes to show distance.

Sculpture can be made by adding pieces or taking them away.

Tempera should always be used thickly.

Art History:

None

CRITICISM:

1. JACOB LAWRENCE, "THE POOL GAME," Figure E.

Literal Description:

Eight men are standing around a pool table watching one man make a shot at one of the other balls.

Visual Analysis:

All the details in the picture show in the faces and hands of the men. This makes us look there first.

The man who is playing pool is the only one who makes a horizontal shape. This contrasts with the others to make him the center of interest in the picture.

Expressive Interpretation:

The artist is telling us that pool players really concentrate when they are playing. Each one of the men is keeping his eyes fixed either on the player or the balls he is aiming at.

2. CHARLES BURCHFIELD, "NOONTIDE IN LATE MAY," Figure H.

Literal Description:

The picture is painted in transparent watercolors.

It shows small, medium, and large trees and plants growing in someone's backyard.

A fence seems to separate one piece of land from another, although the same flowering bushes are growing on both sides.

Formal Analysis:

The jagged edges of the light colored bush and the round flowers contrast with the dark parallel lines of the fence. But together, all these things make that part of the picture the most interesting to look at.

The swirling lines and shapes in the big tree at the back are linked with the bottom of the picture where the small plants have been painted with the same strong curving brush strokes.

Expressive Interpretation:

In this picture, Charles Burchfield helps us feel the glaring heat in this backyard at midday, where all the flowers, shrubs, and trees are bursting with new life.

To emphasize this feeling, he contrasts it with the stiff deadness of the straight lines in the house and the fence.

3. CONSTANTIN BRANCUSI, "THE KISS," Figure 53.

Literal Description:

A block of stone has been carved to show a man and a woman. They are facing each other and kissing.

Visual Analysis:

A block of stone has been carved away, so that the square edges of the block are as important as the shapes of the two people.

The most detailed carving is around the faces so that part attracts our attention most.

Expressive Interpretation:

Brancusi tried to solve the problem of showing the soft feeling of two people kissing without spoiling the hard feeling of the block of stone.

C. DOING

Safety:

Use a paper cutter safely.

Proficiency (care and use of materials):

Mix brown using red and green in different proportions.

Mix brown using red and black in different proportions.

Mix brown using yellow, red, and blue in different proportions.

Mix tempera to the consistency of cream.

Make blurred edges with paint.

Make blurred edges with crayons.

Make blurred edges with pencil.

Make smooth gradations with pencil.

Make smooth gradations with crayons.

Make smooth gradations with tempera paint, using white.

Make lines with crayons that are thin (sharpened point).

Mix paint to match the colors of given objects.

Use the side of a pencil to fill in spaces with an even grey.

Make a tracing using tracing paper.

Curl paper strips.

Stick clay together with slip.

Draw straight lines with a pencil and ruler.

Draw around shapes with a pencil.

Use a pencil compass accurately.

Draw concentric curves with a compass.

Make simple stitches with needle and thread (running, back, chain).

Apply small amounts of paste to the corners of paper and stick it down.

Thread a needle.

Paint up to lines accurately.

Make a cardboard loom.

Art Production:

Flat Art:

Make a balanced design or picture that is symmetrical.

Make a balanced design or picture that is asymmetrical.

Draw art by artists (to help remember what it looks like).

Paint art by artists (to help remember what it looks like).

Make quick sketch ideas for a picture.

Draw people in proper proportion.

Make pictures that show distance using size changes.

Make pictures that show overlapping.

Make pictures that show color brightness.

Make pictures that show detail.

Paint a picture slowly.

Paint a picture quickly.

Paint a picture using one color and black and white only.

Draw or paint a large finished picture from a sketch idea.

Make art using symbols.

Translate a color picture of a scene or group of objects into black, white and grey.

Draw or paint an artistic fantasy.

Change a picture to improve it.

Make a stitchery design or picture.

Draw art from other countries.

Solid Art:

Construct a piece of hanging sculpture.

Construct paper strip sculpture.

Build modular clay sculpture.

Place a light source to make sculpture look good.

Decorate parts of sculpture.

GRADE FIVE

A. SEEING

Identify and Remember:

Tints and tones of hues.

Diamond, octagon, and free-form shapes.

Familiar highway symbols: directions, food, fuel, no smoking.

Landscapes.

Portraits.

Realistic art.

Local examples of visual pollution.

Types of motor vehicles: farm tractors, sedans, station wagons, sports cars, vans, pick-ups, semi-trailers, school buses.

Types of buildings: homes, apartments, churches, supermarkets, service stations, factories, mines, docks, drive-in buildings (banks, movies, restaurants), schools, offices, stores.

Types of aircraft: passenger, private, bomber, fighter, transport, seaplane, glider, balloon.

Deciduous trees in winter.

Art of sub-Saharan Africa.

The centers of African art

Art of ancient Mexico.

The centers of ancient Mexican art.

Art of North American Indians.

The centers of North American Indian art: N.W. coast, S.W. desert, and Mexican sites.

The art of U.S. artists: Thomas Cole, Gilbert Stuart, Charles Caleb Bingham, Edward Hicks, Charles Wimar, Thomas Jefferson, John James Audubon, William Harnett, Frederick Remington, Louis Sullivan, Frank Lloyd Wright, Eero Saarinen, John Marin, Georgia O'Keeffe, Jackson Pollock,

Parts of scenes and pictures that are in shadow.

Light sources in scenes and pictures that are from above, below, front, back, side.

Concentric shapes in natural objects (tortoise shell, peacock feather, cut tree trunks, eyes, etc.).

Concentric shapes in man-made objects (wheel covers, pictures, etc.).

Artists who have made animals into designs – Celtic, African, New Guinea, Byzantine, Miro.

Compare/Distinguish between:

The way class art work was done with the way artists work.

Visualize:

Scenes from random arrangements (wood grain, stains, fire embers, etc.).

Select:

Art works that made you have a feeling you can describe (the works are to be selected from the color and black and white pictures by artists in the book).

Art works you liked best (the works are to be selected from color and black and white pictures by artists in the book).

B. KNOWING

Definitions:

Carve: to cut parts away in sculpture.

Creative: art that is different in a good way.

Dominance: the attention-getting part of a piece of art.

Horizontal: level.

Hue: the correct word for a color (blue is a hue).

Limner: early American travelling portrait artist.

Monoprint: a way of printing to make only a single print.

Plane: a flat surface.

Poster: a big sign using words and pictures.

Recombination: putting well known things together in new ways creatively.

Shade: a color (hue) mixed with black.

Shadow: where there is no light.

Stereotype: a shape that is used over and over without improvement.

Subordinate: parts of art works that are less important.

Tint: a color (hue) mixed with white.

Tone: black and white mixed to make grey.

Value: the lightness or darkness of colors (hues).

Vertical: straight up and down.

Wax resist: a way of picture making where watery paint will not cover parts that are waxy

Information (about art, about artists):

Artists often draw many sketch ideas before they begin their finished work.

Artists fill all the parts of their paper.

Designs can be horizontal, vertical, circular, or radiating.

Most objects can be shown as geometric shapes.

Artists get ideas from listening to music and reading words.

People get feelings from different lines, shapes, colors, and textures.

Asymmetrical balance is a kind of leverage where one part seems to pull another.

Symmetrical balance seems to be solid and still.

Many things we see look distorted to our eyes.

Art is always changing as young artists have new ideas.

Media and techniques (about tools and materials):

Plaster is made by adding powdered plaster to water. When the plaster sticks through the surface, it is all mixed together.

Objects can be made to look thinner with vertical lines.

Objects can be made to look fatter with horizontal lines.

Objects can be made to look stronger if they are vertical.

Objects can be made to look more peaceful if they are horizontal.

Objects can be made to look everlasting if they are pyramids.

Objects can be made to look more alive if they are rounded.

Objects can be made to look as if they are collapsing if they are diagonal.

Art History:

Early American artists painted landscapes and portraits. Their work tells us about how people lived and what places looked like.

Gilbert Stuart painted the portraits of famous people, such as George Washington. He learned to paint in London.

Thomas Jefferson was an architect as well as a great leader.

Edward Hicks painted scenes of things he imagined, also the way people lived just after the Revolution in Pennsylvania.

John James Audubon came from France in 1803 when he was 18 and painted the birds of America.

Thomas Cole came from England in 1818 when he was 17 and painted landscapes near the Hudson River in New York.

Charles Wimar came from Germany and painted pictures of Indians on the prairie.

Charles Caleb Bingham painted pictures about Missouri over a hundred years ago.

William Harnett was born in Ireland in 1848. He came to America when he was very young. His pictures are very realistic.

Frederick Remington painted cowboys and Indians on the prairie.

Louis Sullivan was the first great American architect. He invented the skyscraper.

Grant Wood lived in Iowa and painted the people and places he saw around him.

John Marin painted water color pictures in a very modern style. Most of his pictures show the coast of New England or buildings in New York City.

Georgia O'Keeffe lives in New Mexico and paints pictures of things she sees in the desert.

Eero Saarinen was born in Finland in 1910 and designed many important modern buildings in America.

Stuart Davis was one of the first American artists to paint abstract pictures.

Jackson Pollock painted abstract pictures by dripping paint instead of using brushes.

Two great Indian civilizations of North America were the Aztecs and the Mayas.

CRITICISM:

1. GEORGE BELLOWS, "STAG AT SHARKEYS," Figure C.

Literal Description:

Two boxers are fighting each other.

The referee is watching closely to see that the boxers fight fairly.

All the people are watching what the boxers are doing.

Visual Analysis:

The bodies of the boxers make a triangle shape.

The curves and angles of the boxer's bodies are full of action. They contrast with the roundness of the people's heads and the straight ropes of the boxing ring.

The boxers' bodies are the only big shapes in the picture that are painted with light colors.

Expressive Interpretation:

The artist is trying to make us feel the excitement of being at a boxing match, when the fighters and the audience are interested only in what is happening at that moment.

2. VARNETTE HONEYWOOD, "GOSSIP IN THE SANCTUARY," Plate 3.

Literal Description:

The shoulders and heads of two women fill most of the space in this picture. They are dressed in brightly colored clothes, with matching hats and jewelry.

The woman on the left is leaning forward, whispering into the other one's ear.

Behind the two women are other people at a church service.

A stained glass window can be seen at the top right of the picture.

Visual Analysis:

The golden hue of the dress and hat of the woman on the left matches the skin of the woman on the right to make a curved shape in the picture.

The white, pinks, and purples of gloves, beads, dress, and hat of the other woman add a top and a bottom to the golden curve to make a frame for the really important part of the picture.

The eyes of each woman seem connected because they are similar shapes.

Just as importantly, the shapes of the eyes are linked through one woman's mouth, and the white earring that marks the other woman's ear.

Expressive Interpretation:

The artist is trying to tell us about the importance of the church in the lives of Black people. It is a place where people can dream, and hope for better things, and also gossip with each other (an abbreviated explanation given by the artist).

3. JOSEPH STELLA, "BATTLE OF LIGHTS, CONEY ISLAND," Plate 2.

Literal Description:

The picture is full of small, brightly colored shapes.

If you look closely, the shapes at the bottom look like people.

In the middle, the shapes look like fairground swings, big wheels, and roller coasters.

The top looks like the night sky lit up with searchlights and fireworks.

Visual Analysis:

The very brightest colors are sandwiched between the top and bottom parts of the picture (a good way to see this is to squint your eyes).

Most of the curves are near the center of the picture. They are repeated over and over again to make a pattern that has a rhythm. All these parts of the picture seem to be spinning around so fast that you cannot see them clearly.

Expressive Interpretation:

Instead of painting a realistic picture of the giant fairground of Coney Island, New York, the artist made a design from what he saw. In this way he was able to tell about the flashing lights, the rushing fairground rides, and the jostling crowds of people in a much more exciting way.

4. ALEXANDER CALDER, "LOBSTER TRAP AND FISHTAIL," Figure 45.

Literal Description:

Lengths of steel wire are formed to make loops of different sizes and long curved lengths.

Nine pieces of metal shapes like fishes tails are attached to the ends of the long curved pieces of wire. This part of the sculpture looks like a shoal of fish swimming through the water.

At the top of the sculpture some flat pieces of metal make a shape either like a fish or a lobsterman's marker.

Opposite the fish shapes is a basket made of loops of thin wire that looks like a lobster trap.

Formal Analysis:

The large lengths of wire and the fishtail shapes repeat each other and seem to belong together.

The thin curved lines of the lobster trap contrast with the fishtail shapes. The basket seems lighter in weight and yet we know they balance exactly.

Expressive Interpretation:

The artist shows the freedom of fish as they swim together gracefully in the water. In contrast, the lobster trap hangs quite still and is not at all graceful. It is really very strong and can easily stop a careless lobster from escaping.

C. DOING

Safety:

No new ones

Proficiency (Care and use of materials):

Tear paper to make squares, circles and triangles.

Score cardboard and bend it.

Prepare plaster—powder to water—mix—pour—care over waste disposal.

Alter colored tissue by overlapping and gluing.

Mark the surface of paper with colored chalk that has been dipped in a mixture of water and sugar.

Tear paper in half cleanly after folding it.

Art Production:

Flat Art:

Make a design or picture showing rhythm.

Make a design or picture showing variety.

Make a design or picture showing dominance.

Make a design or picture showing symmetry.

Make a design or picture showing asymmetry.

Make a design or picture showing varied lines

Make a design or picture showing varied textures

Make a design or picture showing varied shapes.

Make a design or picture showing varied colors.

Make a design or picture showing varied light colors on dark paper.

Make a design or picture showing varied primary and secondary colors.

Make a design that has a vertical arrangement.

Make a design that has a horizontal arrangement.

Make a design that has a circular arrangement.

Make a design using familiar symbols, (Hearts, stars, crosses, etc.).

Decorate shapes and objects.

Make a monoprint.

Design a greeting card.

Make a poster.

Draw a local scene that looks ugly.

Draw an object realistically.

Draw a local scene that looks beautiful.

Draw familiar objects from memory.

Draw human figures involved in violent action.

Draw human figures in proportion—with/without a model.

Create a new form from known animals and/or objects.

Make a tissue paper collage with overlapping.

Solid Art:

Make plaster decorations.

Model with clay by feel only.

Model a human figure in proportion in clay—with/without a model.

Construct sculpture with empty boxes and cartons.

Make cardboard sculpture that shows planes and rhythm.

Make sculpture that has a special message.

Make sculpture that has a special feeling.

GRADE SIX

A. SEEING

Identify and Remember:

The grouping of objects in a design by sameness (similarity).

The grouping of objects in a design by closeness (proximity).

Objects in art where not all the parts are drawn in (closure).

Spirals in art and nature (shells, whirlpools, nebulae-outer space, Ionic capital).

Complementary colors in art/nature

Related colors in art/nature

Advancing and receding colors in art/nature

Hatching and cross hatching in drawing

A column that supports a roof.

The main shapes of arches (see Figure 113)

The main shapes of clouds and name the weather that goes with each (see Figure 114)

The main types of bridges (see Figure 115)

Household furniture and appliances: bedroom, bathroom, living room.

Household lights: table, floor, ceiling (area, spot).

Historic artistic styles: Egyptian, Greek and Roman, Oriental, Renaissance, Impressionist, Modern abstraction.

Sites of Egyptian art

Sites of Greek and Roman art

Sites of Oriental art

Sites of the Italian Renaissance

Sites of French Impressionist art

Sites of Modern Abstract Art

Individual artistic styles: Michelangelo, Leonardo, Van Eyck, Dürer, Tintoretto, El Greco, Rembrandt, Monet, Cézanne, Van Gogh, Picasso, Mondrian, Moore).

Foreshortening in art.

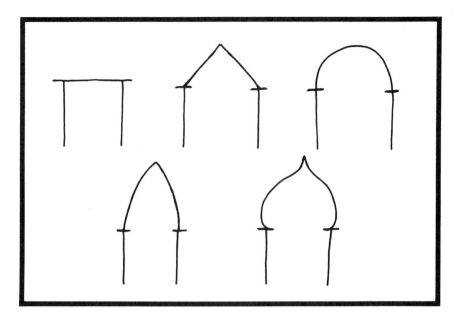

FIGURE 113   The main shapes of arches

FIGURE 114   Clouds

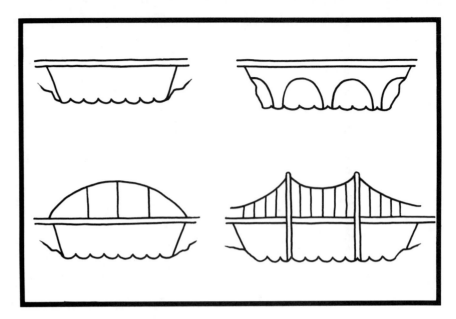

FIGURE 115 Bridges

Compare/Distinguish between:

No new ones

Visualize:

Geometric volumes in everyday objects (bodies, rocks, etc.)

Select:

Proportions of objects or people that are pleasing/displeasing

Art works by non-American artists that made you have a feeling you can describe (selected from throughout the book).

Art by non-American artists that you like/like best.

B. KNOWING

Definitions:

Abstract: not real looking.

Arch: an opening in a wall to let people through (often a window or door).

Bas relief: a very shallow sculpture carved in a wall.

Column: a post that helps support a roof.

Contour: the correct word for the edges of shapes.

Dome: a roof shaped like half a ball (half a sphere).

Decollage: a design where the main shapes are cut away to show what is underneath.

Engobe: a colored slip that is painted on to a pot to decorate it.

Eye level: the height of the eyes: the horizon line.

Flexibility: the ability to change ideas in the middle of a task.

Foreshortening: when shapes look shorter than they are

Fresco: a mural where the color is mixed with plaster.

Focus: parts of a picture that are sharp and clear.

Highlight: the parts of some pictures that show the brightest parts – often a shiny kind of reflection.

Illusion: unreal.

Monogram: a design made with a person's initials.

Motif: a unit to be repeated in a pattern.

Non-objective: things in art that do not look like anything.

Negative space: the spaces between the more important parts of an art work.

Perspective: showing distance on a piece of paper.

Positive space: the main shapes in an art work.

Proportion: a ratio of one measurement or area with another (e.g. length to breadth).

Representational: real-looking.

Sgraffito: lines scratched into a thin layer of clay to show an underneath color.

Spiral: a coil shape.

Still life: an arrangement of objects to be painted or drawn.

View finder: a small window for deciding what to put in a picture.

Information (about art, about artists):

Colors can be used symbolically so that red means danger and yellow means cowardly.

Objects often fit together in pictures because they are near each other. This is sometimes called proximity.

Objects often fit together in pictures because they look like each other. This is sometimes called similarity.

Artists often leave empty spaces in parts of their pictures to make people use their imaginations.

Stained glass is a kind of art.

Designing cities is a kind of art.

Halloween is a very old celebration when ghosts and spirits came out to harm people, and where cats had been evil people. Pumpkins are used because Halloween is also a harvest festival.

Drawing objects in proportion is done by finding out how many times a short measurement goes into a larger one.

Objects in a picture look closer when they are near the bottom.

Media and techniques (about tools and materials):

Half closing your eyes (squinting) makes it easier to see the design made by light and dark areas in a picture.

Art History:

Artists in ancient Greece and Egypt made pictures and designs with pieces of colored wax that were like crayons.

Egyptian art was about religion and life after death: the Pharoah was a god.

The Greeks and Romans planned their cities.

Most modern cities were never planned.

Greek buildings were held up by columns that supported flat beams.

The Romans invented arches, domes, and concrete.

Irish artists made brightly colored manuscripts that had lots of decoration in them.

Most Byzantine art was made in a country that today is Turkey.

Romanesque art imitates Roman art and began in Italy. It has round arches.

Gothic art began in Germany in the Middle Ages, and has pointed arches.

Stained glass windows were first made in the Middle Ages.

The most famous artists of the Italian Renaissance were Leonardo da Vinci and Michelangelo.

Two great artists of the Renaissance in Northern Europe were Jan Van Eyck in Belgium and Albrecht Dürer in Germany.

Baroque art shows swirling lines and shapes, flickering lights and darks.

Two important Baroque artists were Tintoretto in Italy and El Greco in Spain.

The greatest Dutch artist was Rembrandt Van Rijn. He lived 300 years ago and painted pictures that seem to be lit by spotlights.

Important European artists who worked in France a hundred years ago were Claude Monet, Paul Cézanne, Georges Suerat, and Vincent Van Gogh.

Modern sculptors, such as Henry Moore and Constantin Brancusi, made very simple-shaped work.

Two very important modern painters are Pablo Picasso and Piet Mondrian.

Modern architects, Pier Luigi Nervi and Le Corbusier in Europe and Frank Lloyd Wright and Buckminster Fuller in the United States, used concrete and thin steel skeletons in their buildings.

The greatest Oriental art was done in India, China and Japan.

African art is found everywhere in tribal life and tells about the importance of people: what they do; and where they are from.

Art symbols are also used in warfare and religion. African art is often made of carved wood, woven baskets, and cloth. Artists distort animals and human beings. Modern artists have found ideas in African art.

CRITICISM:

1. BEN SHAHN, "MINER'S WIVES," Figure F.

Literal Description:

A plain-looking woman fills most of the right side of the picture. Her eyes are sad and angry. She holds her hands tightly.

On the left, the woman's mother—another miner's wife—sits with her grandchild on her lap. They look sad, too.

Above the old woman hang some miner's work clothes that look as though they are not going to be used again.

Near the middle is a doorway in a brick wall. Two men are walking away in the direction of a mine building.

Visual Analysis:

The big, simple spaces of the ground, the woman's dress, and the brick wall contrast with the sharp-edged parts of the faces, the doorway, and the woman's hands.

The sharp-edged parts stand out because the pale colors contrast with the colors of the rest of the picture.

Expressive Interpretation:

Ben Shahn is telling us about a young family that has just been told that the father has been killed in a mine accident, and that the same thing happened to the grandmother when she was a young woman.

The artist tells about the horrible emptiness that people feel when a family loses its father. He is also telling us that the people who manage the mine don't really care about the miners and accidents happen all the time.

2. ABRAHAM RATTNER, "PLACE OF DARKNESS," Plate 5.

Literal Description:

Two large distorted heads fill much of the bottom of the picture. One is mainly red. The other is mainly green.

Above these heads is an angel lit by a candle. The angel, which has no face, is carrying a large helmet.

Facing the angel is a clothed skeleton, wearing a big hat, also a fierce-looking bird, and the heads of two horses.

On the right is a faceless figure wearing a cloak. There is a dagger in his belt.

On the top left is a mysterious head. In the distant moonlight there is a charging horseman carrying a lance.

Visual Analysis:

The picture has a circular design that focuses attention on the angel's body and helmet and on the skull of the skeleton.

The different kinds of green that make up most of the picture contrast in brilliance with the reds that are arranged around the center.

The sharpest contrast is between the yellow and cream of the area lit by the candle. This color is carried to the objects near the edges of the picture that have yellow and cream highlights.

Expressive Interpretation:

The artist's title, "Place of Darkness," and the things to be seen in the picture seems to tell us about a fearsome world. Not even the angel can be trusted, and it has a helmet to wear to disguise its faceless head.

3. FRANK STELLA, "SINGERLI VARIATION IV," Plate 4.

Literal Description:

The picture is circular.

It is filled with curved and straight parallel bands of color. Almost all of the colored bands are the same width.

The colors are all perfectly smooth and even.

Thin white lines separate the colored bands.

Visual Analysis:

The main curved lines seem to be held in place by pressing against the other edge of the circle and also against each other.

All the curves overlap each other in some way so none of them is more important than the others.

The horizontal bands of color contrast with the curves to make the composition seem stronger.

Expressive Interpretation:

The artist shows us that parallel bands of colors can make interesting non-objective pictures.

4. FRANK LLOYD WRIGHT, SOLOMON R. GUGGENHEIM MUSEUM, NEW YORK, Figure 116.

Literal Description:

A broad concrete tower rises in a spiral at one end. On the inside, people walk down a spiral ramp as they look at the art works.

Just above the street level is a wide concrete wall that goes all the way round the building.

FIGURE 116   The Solomon R. Guggenheim Museum, New York, Architect: Frank Lloyd Wright.

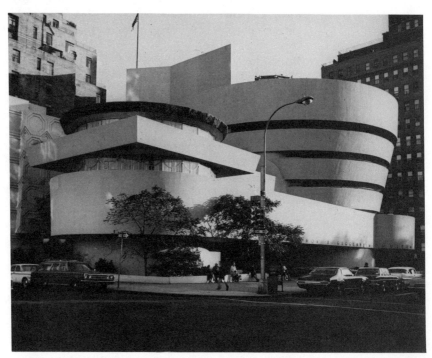

A smaller, circular tower rises at the other end from the broad tower.

It has a flat roof. This is the only part of the building that has any right angles.

Visual Analysis:

The simple spiral tower of the inside ramp is repeated in the outside design.

The horizontal wall above the street is broad and simple like the spiral of the tower and gives unity to the whole design.

The tower with the flat roof and right angle corners looks like a smaller version of the whole building and helps balance the main tower.

Expressive Interpretation:

The simple lines of the massive poured concrete walls focus attention on the spiral ramp where people walk as they look at the art works.

The artist is telling us that this museum is very unusual, because visitors take an elevator to the top and then walk down the spiral ramp to the bottom. He shows the ramp on the outside as well as on the inside, because he is proud of this idea and doesn't want to cover it up.

C. DOING

Safety:

No new ones

Proficiency (care and use of materials):

Mix small quantities of a color with its complementary to dull its brightness.

Mix related colors together to create another bright color.

Cast plaster in sand.

Draw an accurate grid for use in enlarging and reducing sizes of drawings.

Cover a heavily crayoned surface with india ink or black paint.

Apply engobe to pottery.

Scratch clean lines into engobe surfaced pottery.

Cut a spiral out of paper.

Art Production:

Flat Art:

Create art using an overhead projector.

Draw objects by feeling them.

Design a stained glass window.

Paint a picture in the style of one of the artists whose work has been used in class.

Enlarge a small area of a pictorial scene using a grid.

Draw a picture that gives the appearance of distance through shading.

Paint a picture that gives the appearance of distance through color changes.

Make pictures that show different kinds of weather, including appropriate cloud formations.

Make a design with spirals, like Celtic artists did.

Make a picture using the crayon etch method.

Draw your own monogram.

Draw a still life of rectangular objects in proportion.

Paint a landscape that shows the sky through the branches of trees.

Draw objects where foreshortening distorts their appearance.

Solid Art:

Construct and paint a mask that shows symbolism.

Model a piece of relief sculpture.

Construct sculpture with sticks (toothpicks, tongue depressors, etc.).

Make a model that solves an environmental problem.

Design and create a costume for a special event.

Design and create a hat for a special event.

Invent an animal by attaching scrap objects together.

Build and decorate a den from a large cardboard carton.

Decorate a slab or a pot using the sgraffito technique.

Make spiral designs with clay coils.

Construct a model for a building.

Carve a piece of sculpture to look like art from Africa.

Make a model of an animal or person using cloth that has been stiffened (with glue, plaster, etc.).

ART FORMS AND ART MATERIALS

Chapters 2 and 3 introduced a number of forms of art that were suitable for elementary school art programs together with the kinds of tools and materials that are typically found in schools. This section consists of a listing of all the art forms and art supplies from those chapters and from other parts of the book to help when you design your own lessons.

TWO-DIMENSIONAL ART

Drawing

Manila paper (40 to 50 lb. weight)

Newsprint paper

Tape or thumbtacks (to display work on the walls)

Pencils (fairly soft)

Erasers

Wax crayons

Oil pastels

Pen and ink (India ink)

Felt markers

Ball point pens

Colored chalks (sugar-water solution as a binder)

Rulers and compasses

Painting

Paper (see Drawing)

Colored construction paper

Transparent water color paint

Opaque tempera paint

Finger paint (glazed paper is necessary)

Soft brushes for watercolor

Stiffer brushes for tempera

Cans for water

Paint rags to clean brushes

Smocks or old shirts to protect clothing

Sponges and paper towels for clean up

A mop in the event of an accidental spill

A water supply (either running water or two buckets, one bucket full of clean water and an empty one for dirty water)

Collage

Paper (see Drawing)

Pictorial magazines

Various materials: corrugated paper, cloth, tissue paper, foil, cellophane, photographs

Scissors

Glue, paste, rubber cement

Stiff paste brushes (unless children use fingers)

Newspaper to prevent paste getting on furniture

Smocks to protect clothing

Print Making

Stamping: Paper (see Drawing)

Potato

Pen holder with reversed pen nib

Kitchen knife

Newspaper to protect furniture

Tempera paint brush, water, etc., or a paint saturated felt pad in a shallow dish

Paper towels

Pad of newsprint (to print on)

*Collograph
and
Linoleum:*   Newsprint paper (to print on)

Brayer

Printing ink (water based and oil based)

Glass sheet or metal cafeteria tray
Paste or glue
Cardboard
Linoleum and linoleum cutters
Black and white tempera
Brushes and water
Paper towels
Pad of newspaper

Textiles

Weaving: Construction paper
Cardboard
Wooden frame with nails at 1/4'' intervals
Scissors or sharp knife
Fairly thick yarn
Stitchery: Burlap, thick paper, or plastic foam meat trays
Large eyed needles
Variety of yarns and threads
Felt or cloth (for appliqué)
Macramé: Cord (textured or waxed)
A stick or length of dowel-rod

THREE-DIMENSIONAL ART

Modeling

Clay (oil or water based)
Water supply
Burlap (to work on)
Newspaper to protect furniture
Smocks to protect clothing
Rolling pin and two thin wood strips
Paper towels
Mop in the event of an accidental spill
Broom to sweep up clay scraps and dust
Kitchen knives

Papier-Mâché

Newspaper and other soft paper
Bucket and water
Paste (water soluble)
Newspaper to protect furniture
Smocks to protect clothing
Water supply

Construction

Stick materials (soda straws, toothpicks, popsicle sticks, dead twigs, etc.)
Cardboard
Construction paper
Glue
Newspaper to protect furniture
Scissors
Water supply
Stiff wire
Thread
Boxes, cans, bottles (discarded materials from home)
Masking tape
Aluminum spray paint
Paper sacks
Yarn or string

Carving

Clay
Plaster of Paris
Water supply
Bucket
Newspaper to protect furniture
Smocks to protect clothing
Kitchen knives
Old milk cartons (1/2 gallon and gallon)
Cardboard box
Sand
Plaster impregnated bandage
Broom to sweep up scraps

Environments

Cardboard boxes and cartons
Sheets of cardboard and paper
Glue or paste
Paints and brushes
Plaster of Paris
Plywood and wood strips

ORDERING SUPPLIES If your art program consists of specially selected lessons and sequences, then the art materials for that instruction must be available in sufficient quantities for the size of your class. When ordering consumable supplies, allow an additional 15% for wastage.

Most important is to be able to state as clearly as possible what tools and materials will be needed and when. A simple way of solving this problem is to make a chart and number across the top all the art lessons you plan on teaching during the year (see Figure 117). Down the left side you list alphabetically all the materials needed for the different lessons. In the last column you enter the total quantities of each material needed for a full year. Since class sizes vary from year to year, the quantities are best shown for groups of ten children. The requirements for an actual class enrollment of twenty-five or thirty are easy to compute based on what is needed for ten children.

Schools differ in the ways that supplies are ordered. Find out the procedure that is followed in the district where you teach and follow it exactly. Above all make your requests well in advance of the published deadline. If you have the opportunity, also get to know the people through whose hands supply orders must go. Your interest and initiative is likely to ensure the order receiving full attention.

The ideal time for ordering supplies is late spring. Orders are then filled

FIGURE 117 Art supplies chart

MATERIALS	1	2	3	4		60	QUANTITIES (for 10 students)
Brushes		*					10
Clay (water-base)				*			12 to 16 pounds
Crayons (oil pastels)			*				1 dozen boxes
Drawing paper	*	*	*			*	1 ream (500 sheets)
Paints (tempera preferred)		*					2 pints each: red, blue, yellow, green, orange, black, white
Erasers	*					*	1 dozen
Paste			*				1 large jar
Pencils (soft black)	*					*	1 dozen
Scissors			*				10
Water containers		*		*			10

LESSONS

during the early summer and arrive at the school in sufficient time to be distributed to teachers or placed in the school stockroom before the children return from their summer vacation. If a second order is required it is usually a relatively small one and is likely to be made before Christmas. Manufacturers and distributors of liquids such as paints and glues will often refuse to ship if the temperature is much below freezing, so you should try to avoid running out of such items during the cold winter months.

STORAGE AND CONSERVATION Art supplies are sometimes stored in a central stockroom and sometimes in classrooms. Where a single storage room exists, considerable cooperation is required among the teachers to make the fairest use of what is available. If some or all of your share of the available supplies are kept in your room, prepare yourself to control them. One of the secrets is to give every material its own labelled place in the room, where it can be checked quickly and easily. A few hours every month spent organizing the room in this way is a good investment for occasions when you will be preoccupied.

The tasks of distributing and collecting art materials are predictable. And if a lesson begins and ends well, the chances are that the instructional period will also be good. Several ways exist for distributing and collecting materials. One is by assigning children as monitors to be responsible for particular materials. Another is to distribute materials yourself. A third way is to put materials that are needed in a given lesson out for children to help themselves, cafeteria style, as they have need. No one way is best for all people; and you may find it necessary to move from one system to another. But decide in advance what is likely to be best for you and your situation, organize the task in detail, and practice it consistently. In this way, the least amount of time and energy will be consumed in non-instructional activities.

Smooth distribution rests in part on the efficiency of the collection at the end of the preceding lesson and thus binds the two tasks together. If, for example, all the brushes are collected and put away in the designated place in good condition, then the next painting lesson can begin without any shortages, delays, or complaints.

Art materials are most important for teaching art; but always remember that they are important only to the extent that they help a student learn something of value.

TOPICS FOR ART LESSONS

Art needs to be organized into effective lesson strategies if children are to learn the objectives. The following lists are intended as a reference guide to provide you with lesson ideas. Items are grouped into primary and intermediate levels as a further guide. Several topics may be combined in a single lesson. As you become more experienced, you will be adding ideas of your own to these suggestions.

Broad topics, in alphabetical order:

Adventure	Interesting looking people
Animals	Me, myself, I
Annual celebrations: Halloween, Thanksgiving, Hanukkah, Christmas, Valentine's Day, Easter, Memorial Day, Mother's Day	Meet the artist
	Movies and television
	Music and songs
	Neighborhood
Birthdays	Pets
Dancing	School
Dreams	Seasons of the Year: Summer, Fall, Winter, Spring
Games and sports	
Geography and environments	Showing action
Gifts and giving	Stories and poems
Historical people and events	Terrible happenings
Home and relatives	

ADVENTURE

Primary	Intermediate
Ship in a storm	The round-up
The brave fireman (visit)	Lost in the desert (or jungle)
Buried treasure	Space walk
The hold-up	St. George and the dragon
Fighting the great octopus	Riding the bucking bronco
The runaway horse (stroke a real one)	"Ready for lift-off" (sound track/ video)
The shipwrecked sailor—on a raft —on an island	Capturing the rustlers
	Cattle stampede
Rescued from drowning	Fire-engines race to the fire (movie)
Landing on the moon (see movie or video tape)	Frogmen to the rescue
	Escape from the red planet

ANIMALS

Primary	Intermediate
Clara the cow	Angry bull
Roly-poly pigs	Big gorilla
Chickens sitting on eggs	Big mosquito
Hens and chickens	Killer whale
The noisy cockerell	Hungry tiger
Friendly squirrels	Hungry sharks
Hungry Hippo	Patient crocodiles

The woodpecker
Elephant family
Butterflies and flowers
Bugs

Wild horses
Black stallion
Eagles flying high in the mountains
Camels in the desert
Giraffes eating trees
Rattlesnake

ANNUAL CELEBRATIONS

Primary	Intermediate
Halloween: Pumpkins Witches on broom- sticks Ghosts Wicked black cats Bats	Halloween: Fancy dress costume Mask
Thanksgiving: Thanksgiving at home A turkey farm	Thanksgiving: (as for primary)
	Hannukkah: 9-branch Menorah Feast of lights
	Christmas: Shopping for gifts Wrapping gifts ''T'was the Night Before Christmas'' (A Visit from St. Nicholas)
Valentine's Day: Cards Mailbox	Valentine's Day: Cards
St. Patrick's Day: Leprechauns Shamrock sym- bolism	St. Patrick's Day: The World is Green The Celtic Art of Ireland
Easter: Friendly bunnies Chocolate eggs	Easter: Decorating eggs Easter bonnets
Mother's Day: Card	Mother's Day: Card
Memorial Day: Parade	Memorial Day: Parade Picnic

BIRTHDAYS

Primary	Intermediate
My birthday cake	Party hats
Blowing out the candles	A fancy dress birthday party
My birthday party at home	Classroom birthday party
	Making wrapping paper
	Decorating a cake

DANCING

Primary

Ring around the roses
Like swaying flowers

Intermediate

Tribal war dance (rain dance, etc.)
Disco action
Square dance

DREAMS

Primary

Happy things
Nightmare
Fierce pirate with a gold tooth
My favorite wish come true

Intermediate

I was Superman (or Wonder-
  woman)
I had a robot for a friend
I found out what was going to hap-
  pen next year
I caught the biggest fish
My friend had a horse's head
I was Peter Pan
I was a dragon
I had a genie in a lamp
I can walk on the ceiling (on
  water, etc.)

GAMES AND SPORTS

Primary

Blindfold games (what it feels like;
  what it looks like)
Jumping rope
Jumping off the diving board
Tug-of-war
Hide and seek
Flying kites
Sledding
Guess what I can see

Intermediate

Surfing
Skiing
Football
Wrestling
Basketball
Ice hockey
Card games
Volleyball

GEOGRAPHY AND ENVIRONMENTS

Primary

Mountains and lakes
Big river
Farms and fields

Intermediate

Beautiful beach
High cliffs
Mountain waterfall
Hot desert

GIFTS AND GIVING

Primary	Intermediate
A picture	Necktie
A model	Necklace
	Bracelet
	Belt
	Flower vase
	Head scarf

HISTORICAL PEOPLE AND EVENTS

Primary	Intermediate
Christopher Columbus discovering America	Declaration of Independence
The first Thanksgiving	The ride of Paul Revere
Building the Statue of Liberty (or Golden Gate Bridge)	My favorite President or leader
	The Chicago fire (or San Francisco earthquake)

HOME AND RELATIVES

Primary	Intermediate
Mommy	A new baby
Daddy	My sister's wedding
Sister	Visiting Grandma's home
Brother	Helping cook dinner
Grandma	Cleaning house
Grandpa	Throwing out the garbage
Our kitchen	Slumber party
My bedroom	
Watching television	
Breakfast	

INTERESTING LOOKING PEOPLE

Primary	Intermediate
Clowns	Lion tamer
Bandits	King Arthur
	Robin Hood
	Muhammad Ali, the boxer
	Tightrope walker
	George Washington
	Abraham Lincoln

ME MYSELF, I

Primary	Intermediate
I am scared of the dark	I have a headache
I am very hungry	Me playing the piano (drums, violin, etc.)
Toothache	
I ate too much apple pie (popcorn, candy, etc.)	My mask shows a different me
	Laughing until it hurts
At the dentist	I am a Boy Scout/Girl Scout
I am a Cub Scout	What the taste of candy looks like

MOVIES AND TELEVISION

Primary	Intermediate
Saturday morning cartoons	"Take me to your leader"
Monster movie	Police adventure
Favorite program	Hospital story
	Outer space exploration

MEET THE ARTIST

Primary	Intermediate
The pictures in the book	The pictures in the book
An artist visits the classroom	Visit to an artist's studio

MUSIC AND SONG

Primary	Intermediate
Clapping rhythms	Musicians playing popular songs—top hits
"Rudolf the Red Nosed Reindeer"	
"Silent Night" (carols, etc.)	Art to match music (Mondrian's "Broadway Boogie-Woogie, etc.)
Singing at school	
	Rock concert

NEIGHBORHOOD

Primary	Intermediate
My friend, the policeman	At the laundromat
The happy mailman	The angry traffic cop
Ducks swimming in a pond	The back alley
A grassy park with trees	The fat truck driver
Play on the swings	Factories
Our church	Playing "Grey wolf"
A map showing how I get to school	Filling the car with gas
	At the shopping center

Animals on our farm
My secret hideout
Our gang
The apple orchard

PETS

Primary

Morris, the fussy cat
Bubbles, the goldfish
Ralph, the turtle
Bruno, the pet rabbit
Pretty Polly, the talking parrot

Intermediate

The yellow hunting dog ("Old Yaller")
The singing tom cat
Winston, the bulldog
Our cat with kittens

SCHOOL

Primary

My teacher is pleased with us
Our class singing
The school library
Our principal is a very important person
I like the school secretary
I like the school janitor
I like the school nurse
I like the school bus driver

Intermediate

Fire drill

SEASONS OF THE YEAR

Primary

Summer: Remembering what happened
    Hot lazy days
    Camp

Fall: Going back to school
   Trees lose their leaves

Winter: Building a snowman

Intermediate

Summer: Camping in the woods
    The tree house I built
    A visit to the zoo
    Rock climbing
    Fishing in the sea
    With my friends on the beach

Fall: Birds flying south for the winter
   Harvesting
   Foggy days
   Leaves falling from trees
   Frosty mornings
   Hurricane

Winter: Fishing through the ice

Snowball fight

Snowflakes

Icicles

Spring: Bright green leaves
grow on trees

The warm sun makes
flowers grow

Hibernating animals
(bear, groundhog,
chipmunk)

Spring: Baby animals (lambs,
calves, etc.)

The return of the birds

Farmers plant their
fields

STORIES AND POEMS

Primary

Nursery rhymes (Humpty-Dumpty,
etc.)

Robin Hood

Bible stories (Noah's ark, etc.)

"The Night Before Christmas"

Stories and poems from school
literature books

"The Frog Prince"

Intermediate

Paul Bunyan and his ox, and other
American myths

Punch and Judy

Stories and poems from school
literature books

My own cartoon comic strip

Science fiction (invasion of the
planet Earth, etc.)

TERRIBLE HAPPENINGS

Primary

Falling down stairs

Sick in hospital

My pet died

Factory smoke kills people

Intermediate

Automobile accident

Forest fire

The big tornado, volcano, etc.

An earthquake

The giant wave

The flood

Nuclear plant accident

index

Page numbers are in roman type. Page numbers that refer to figures are in *italic type*. Color plates are specifically marked.

299

Cardboard:
  for collograph printing, 40
  for sculpture, 66, 67
  for stencilling, 45
Carving, 75, 76, 77, 147, 180, 182, *183*,
  246, 255
Cassatt, Mary, *The Boating Party*, *208*, 263
Casting, 77, *179*
Chalks, 29, 43, *138, 208*, 224, *plate 10*
Children's art:
  intermediate, 143, *144, 145, 209, 210*,
    211, 212, 213, 234, 238, 247, 248,
    plates 11, 13, 14
  primary, 133, *135, 208, 210, 211, 213*,
    216, 222, 224, 231, plates 9, 10, 12
Children's text for lessons, 5, 216, 218,
  220, 222, 224, 235, 237, 240, 242
Clay, 137
  oil base, 56
  powdered, 56
  slip, 58, *59*
  substitutes, 57
  water base, 56, 75
Clay slabs, 58, *59*, 138
Cloud shapes, 279
Collage, 36, *38*, 211
Collograph, *see* Print making
Color:
  aerial perspective, 31
  complementary, 31
  cool, 31
  warm, 31
Constructed sculpture:
  box, 70, *71*
  sheet, 66, *67*
  stick, 64, *65, 74*
  wood scrap, 62, *64*
Contours, 24, *25*
Crayons, *see* Wax crayons
Creativity, 36, *37*, 72, *73*, 117, 124, 175,
  177
Cultural symbolism, 146, *147, 180, 183*
Curled paper strips, 66, *68*

D

Décollage, 39
Degas, Edgar, *Bronze statuette of a dancer*,
  179
Discursive and non-discursive thinking, 117
Doing, 4, 112, 159, 161, 170, 177
  art production, 170
  skills, 170
Drawing, 24, 31
  contours, 24
  gradations, 190, 191
  memory, 25
  people and pets, 96
  perspective, 26
Drymounting, 104, *105*

E

Educable mentally retarded, *see* Handicapped children
Education Policies Commission (NEA), 123-
  27
Emotionally disturbed, *see* Handicapped
  children
Environmental design, 82
Evaluation, *see* Measuring achievement
Exceptionality:
  gifted, 148, *149, 210*
  handicapped, 150

F

Feldman, Edmund B., 167, 169
Felt markers, 29, *136, 209*
Filing visuals:
  by lesson, 97
  by number, 99, *100*
  by topic, 98

G

Giacometti, Alberto, *Man Pointing, 65*
Gifted children, *see* Exceptionality
Glue, *see* Adhesives
Grids, *see* Pictures for teaching art
Grout, 72

H

Handicapped children:
  educable mentally retarded, 150
  emotionally disturbed, 151
  physically impaired, 152
Harnett, William Michael, *After the Hunt*,
  168, 169, *plate 6*
Homer, Winslow, *The Gulf Stream*, 195,
  204, 253
Honeywood, Varnette, *Gossip in the Sanctuary*, 6, 275, *plate 3*

I

Illustrations and diagrams:
  carbon paper, 101
  freehand, 92
  grids, 101, *103*
  photocopying, 92
  projections, 92, *93*, 102
  tracing, 101
Industrial design, 90
Inks:
  drawing, 28, *138, 165*
  printing, 39, 40

T

Tchelitchew, Pavel, *Tree into Hand and Foot, 163, 165*
Teacher rewards, 184
Teacher's text for lessons, 3, 214-48
Tempera paint, *see* Paints
Textbooks, 7, 17
Textiles:
  appliqué, 49, *213, plate 8*
  macramé, 49, *51, 52*
  printed, 48
  stitchery, 48, *50, 212*
  woven, 48, *49*, 87, *plate 14*
  yarn painting, 49, *213*
Three dimensional art, 55, 181, 288-89
Tracing:
  through plexiglas, 29, *30*
  with tracing paper, 101, *102*
Transparent, 32
Tree shapes, 266
Turpentine, 26, 27
Two dimensional art, 24, 55, 286-88

V

Visual memory, 119, 193
Vocations, 119

W

Warp, 48
Watercolor paints, *see* Paints
Wax crayons, 26, 29, *31, 135, 140, 216, 222, 238, 248, plates 9, 11*
Weaving, *see* Textiles
Wedging, 56
Weft, 48
Wright, Frank Lloyd, Solomon R. Guggenheim Museum, New York, 193, *284*
Wyeth, Andrew, *The Hunter, 207, 258*

X

X-acto knife, 66, *69*

Y

Yarn, 48
Yarn painting, *see* Textiles